GREATER SYRACUSE

CENTER OF AN EMPIRE

GREATER SYRACUSE

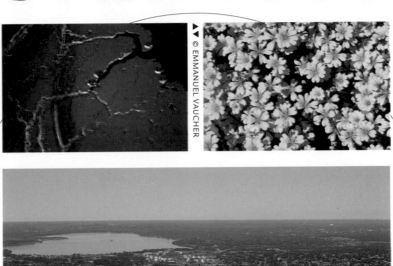

© EMMANUEL VAUCHER

© TOM WATSON

© EMMANUEL VAUCHER

CENTER OF AN EMPIRE

BY ROY A. BERNARDI
PHOTOGRAPHIC CONSULTING BY CHARLES F. WAINWRIGHT
PROFILES IN EXCELLENCE BY FRED WILSON AND KEVIN WILSON
CAPTIONS BY J. MICHAEL KELLY
ART DIRECTION BY GEOFFREY ELLIS

Greater Syracuse: Center of an Empire

"There's a pride to living in Syracuse. We have a hearty spirit, good for surviving long winters, and we take a sense of ownership in everything we do."

Profiles in Excellence

A look at the corporations, businesses, professional groups, and community service organizations that have made this book possible.

Photographers

Index of Profiles

LIBRARY OF CONGRESS CATALOGING-IN-PUBLICATION DATA

Bernardi, Roy A., 1942-
    Greater Syracuse : center of an empire / by Roy A. Bernardi and
photographic consulting by Charles F. Wainwright ; Profiles in
excellence by Fred Wilson and Kevin Wilson ; captions by J. Michael
Kelly ; art direction by Geoffrey Ellis
        p.   cm. — (Urban tapestry series)
    Includes index.
    ISBN 1-881096-64-5 (alk. paper)
    1. Syracuse Region (N.Y.)—Civilization.   2. Syracuse Region
(N.Y.)—Pictorial works.   3. Business enterprises—New York (State)-
-Syracuse Region (N.Y.)   I. Wainwright, Charles F., 1956-   .
II. Wilson, Fred, 1941-   . III. Wilson, Kevin, 1970-   .
IV. Title. V. Series.
F129.S8B47   1998
974.7'66—dc21   98-34565

Publisher: J. Robert Towery
Executive Publisher: Jenny McDowell
National Sales Manager: Stephen Hung
Marketing Director: Carol Culpepper
Project Directors: Henry Hintermeister, Paul Withington

Executive Editor: David B. Dawson
Managing Editor: Michael C. James
Senior Editors: Lynn Conlee, Carlisle Hacker
Editors/Project Managers: Mary Jane Adams, Lori Bond
Editors: Jana Files, Susan Hesson, Brian Johnston
Assistant Editor: Rebecca Green
Editorial Assistants: Allison Ring, Sunni Thompson
Editorial Contributors: George E. Mitchell, M.D., Patti Wilson

Creative Director: Brian Groppe
Photography Editor: Jonathan Postal
Profile Designers: Laurie Beck, Kelley Pratt, Ann Ward
Digital Color Supervisor: Brenda Pattat
Digital Color Technicians: Jack Griffith, Darin Ipema
Production Resources Manager: Dave Dunlap Jr.
Production Assistants: Enrique Espinosa, Robin McGehee
Print Coordinator: Tonda Thomas

URBAN
TAPESTRY
SERIES
TOWERY
PUBLISHING, INC.

By Roy A. Bernardi

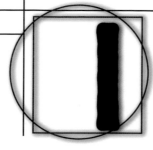

I AM OFTEN ASKED WHAT MAKES SYRACUSE SO SPECIAL. I THINK IT'S PRIMARILY THREE THINGS—THE AREA'S NATURAL RESOURCES, SO TO SPEAK. SYRACUSE IS SPECIAL BECAUSE OF ITS WEATHER, ITS PLACES, AND ITS PEOPLE. ■ YES, I DID SAY THE WEATHER. AND when you mention weather in Syracuse, the first thing that people think of is, of course, snow. In a typical year, Syracuse receives an average of 114 inches of snow, causing the city to be named the snowiest metropolitan area in the United States. Most of it can be attributed to lake-effect squalls off of Lake Ontario to the city's north.

© EMMANUEL VAUCHER

While Syracuse's snowfall totals are certainly striking, equally impressive is our region's ability to deal with it. Local municipalities maintain small arsenals of plows, salters, and sanders to move snow and keep traffic thoroughfares open.

© MICHAEL J. OKONIEWSKI

And for the most part, the people of Syracuse know how to handle the snow in another sense: We know how to enjoy winter's outdoor activities. Close to major downhill ski and snowboard areas, Syracuse is home to a variety of other winter pastimes, including everything from cross-country skiing to sledding to ice fishing to snowshoeing to snowmobiling. ☛

ANYONE WHO LIVES IN GREATER SYRA-CUSE MUST LEARN TO ROLL WITH MOTHER NATURE'S SNEAK PUNCHES, FROM LOATHSOME LAKE-EFFECT STORMS TO NASTY NOR'EASTERS. BUT THERE'S ALSO A BRIGHT SIDE TO LOCAL WINTERS— A TIME WHEN ANGLERS CAN LOOK FOR-WARD TO PULLING PERCH AND WALLEYES THROUGH THE ICE ON ONEIDA LAKE AND AREA SKI SLOPES HEAT UP WITH ACTIVITY.

THE CITY'S COLLEGIATE SPORTS SCENE WAS FOREVER CHANGED WHEN THE GLEAMING WHITE ROOF OF THE CARRIER DOME WAS INFLATED IN 1980. NOW, RAIN OR SHINE, SYRACUSE UNIVERSITY'S 50,000-SEAT INDOOR STADIUM FILLS WITH FOOTBALL FANATICS ON AUTUMN AFTERNOONS. THE MULTIPURPOSE VENUE ALSO HOSTS BASKETBALL, LACROSSE, AND SOCCER GAMES, AS WELL AS COUNTLESS MUSICAL ACTS.

But it's not just the abundant snow that makes Syracuse's weather special. Perhaps the most enjoyable part about weather in Syracuse is that it changes. In Syracuse, we experience the best that all four seasons have to offer. Besides picture-perfect winters, Syracuse has delightful springs, warm and sunny summers, and autumns full of spectacular color—perfect for picking apples in an orchard or cheering on the Syracuse University Orangemen football squad from a seat in the Dome.

SYRACUSE AND CENTRAL NEW YORK ARE IDEALLY LOCATED. WITHIN 750 MILES LIE MOST MAJOR NORTH AMERICAN MARKETS AND METROPOLITAN AREAS. AND LESS THAN TWO HOURS AWAY ARE FOUR MAJOR RESORT AND RECREATION AREAS—THE THOUSAND Islands, Finger Lakes, Adirondacks, and Catskills—making Syracuse a favorite location for many major companies and corporations looking to expand and relocate.

Syracuse is a livable city with affordable housing options, quality schools and institutions of higher learning, strong health care facilities, and a variety of recreational and cultural opportunities. Crouse-Hinds, Carrier Corporation, Mutual of New York, Welch Allyn, New Process Gear, Lockheed Martin, Bristol-Myers Squibb, and Anheuser-Busch (just to name a few) all have major operations in Central New York.

The list of today's industrial and corporate neighbors stems from a rich history of industrial giants once headquartered in Central New York, including the A.E. Nettleton Shoe Company, Porter-Cable, and the Franklin Automobile Company. In addition, Syracuse China, Marcellus Casket, Stickley Furniture, Cathedral Candle Company, and the Joseph J. Pietrafesa Clothing Co. still call the region home, continuing a rich manufacturing history that began decades ago. ☛

WHEN RESIDENTS NEED A RESPITE FROM CITY LIFE, THEY OFTEN MAKE THE TWO-HOUR DRIVE TO ADIRONDACK PARK, WHERE THE MYRIAD DIVERSIONS INCLUDE CANOEING, BIKING, FISHING, CAMPING, AND SKIING. FOR THE TRUE ADVENTURER, A CLIMB TO GIANT MOUNTAIN'S 4,627-FOOT CREST PROMISES A REWARDING PANORAMA.

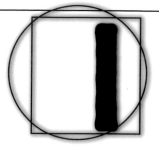'VE SAID THAT WHEN MANY THINK OF SYRACUSE, THEY THINK OF SNOW, BUT IT WAS ACTUALLY ANOTHER NATURAL WHITE SUBSTANCE THAT PUT SYRACUSE ON THE MAP—SALT. IN 1653, THE NATIVE IROQUOIS SENT WORD TO THE FRENCH IN QUEBEC, requesting that a "Black Robe"—as Jesuit missionaries were referred to at that time—travel to their country. In July of the following year, Father Simon LeMoyne made the multiday journey to the land that would become Syracuse and Onondaga County.

There, he lived among the native Onondaga— a part of the Iroquois Confederacy—for several months, and toured the entire region. It was Father LeMoyne who reached the salty shores of Onondaga Lake and realized its potential. At one time, Syracuse was known as the salt capital of the world.

SYRACUSE EARNED THE NICKNAME SALT CITY BECAUSE MANY OF ITS EARLY SETTLERS MADE A HANDSOME LIVING BY EXTRACTING SALT FROM SALINE SPRINGS ALONG THE SHORES OF ONONDAGA LAKE. TODAY, THE SALT MUSEUM IN ONONDAGA LAKE PARK RECOUNTS THE FASCINATING HISTORY OF THAT LOCAL INDUSTRY.

In 1784, a young man arrived in what was then known as the Land of Hiawatha to trade fur with the native Iroquois. Ephraim Webster, a Revolutionary War hero, became the first settler of European descent to make his home on the banks of Onondaga Creek just south of the lake's inlet. There, he built a crude camp that became known as Webster's Landing. Webster had a knack for dealing with Native American tribes at the time, as he spent much of his adult life traveling and trading across the Northeast. Often, the newly formed U.S. government would send Webster off into the wilds of Western New York on various diplomatic missions. It was natural that his journeys would bring him to Central New York, which was the primary location of the Iroquois. (The Onondagas, in fact, kept the Iroquois nation's central flame in the area.)

Webster eventually recruited new settlers, including Asa Danforth and Comfort Tyler, to join him in what is now known as Central New York. Most settlers chose not to build their homes in the swampy marsh at the foot of the lake, however, but looked further south to the impressive hills and rich soil of Onondaga Valley, Pompey, and Manlius. ☛

ONONDAGA COUNTY IS NAMED AFTER THE IROQUOIS INDIANS WHO LIVED IN THE AREA WHEN THE EUROPEANS FIRST ARRIVED. CENTURIES LATER, MEMBERS OF THE ONONDAGA NATION MAKE THEIR HOME SOUTH OF THE CITY, ALONG INTERSTATE 81 AND U.S. ROUTE 11. ACCORDING TO THE 1990 CENSUS, MORE THAN 3,200 OF THE COUNTY'S 468,000 RESIDENTS ARE NATIVE AMERICANS.

© BOB MAHONEY

**T**HESE EARLY SETTLERS, NEEDING TO REPLACE DWINDLING SUPPLIES OF SALT (THEN USED PRIMARILY AS A FOOD PRESERVATIVE), FOUND THE MARSHY BOG AT THE FOOT OF THE LAKE TO BE A SOURCE FOR QUALITY BRINE. BY BOILING THE surface brine in large kettles, the salt could be crystallized. The creation of this valuable commodity drew more and more settlers until 1795, when the State of New York took ownership of the salt brines surrounding the southern half of Onondaga Lake as part of an Indian land grant.

Shortly thereafter, in 1819, a young, successful lawyer from Onondaga Valley named Joshua Forman defied the common wisdom of the day and built his new home in the swampy clearing of present-day Syracuse. Forman realized the potential the area held; in 1822, as a member of the New York State Legislature, he sponsored legislation to lower the water level of Onondaga Lake by two feet, thus draining the swampy marshes and firming the land for future development. Through the following years, the growing settlement at the foot of the lake was

referred to by several names—Bogardus Corners, Milan, South Salina, and Cossitt's Corners. Other settlers followed, like Moses DeWitt, James Geddes, and John Wilkinson, who in 1819—as the area's first postmaster—suggested the swampy village on the banks of Onondaga Creek be renamed Syracuse after a lengthy poem describing the beauty of the similar city of Siracusa in Sicily.

Today, city parks and streets bear the names of these founding fathers. But it was Geddes who first expanded salt production into a large-scale operation. Besides the traditional boiling method, in which the forested hills of the surrounding county were stripped to fuel the large fires, Geddes introduced and expanded a solar evaporation process, whereby brine was pumped into large trays that were left exposed to the sun and wind. Overnight, the salt springs surrounding the lake were transformed into an area filled with salt-boiling blocks and solar salt vats. This area became so large that it spread from present-day Salina Street to Geddes Street, and an outgrowth of support industries opened across Syracuse's North End. ☛

USED TO PRESERVE MEAT AND CURE ANIMAL HIDES, SALT WAS LIKE WHITE GOLD TO THE EARLY RESIDENTS OF CENTRAL NEW YORK. UNTIL THE MID-1800S, SYRACUSE WAS THE ONLY LOCATION ON THE CONTINENT THAT EXTRACTED COMMERCIAL QUANTITIES OF THE SUBSTANCE, AND IN 1862, PRODUCTION PEAKED AT 9 MILLION BUSHELS. INITIALLY, BRINE SCOOPED FROM SPRINGS ALONG ONONDAGA LAKE WAS BOILED IN COPPER KETTLES. LATER, IT WAS ALLOWED TO EVAPORATE IN LARGE SOLAR VATS WITH SLIDING ROOFS.

As agricultural and industrial output across Upstate New York increased, the need for new, low-cost transportation sources grew. Geddes and other local businessmen joined the call for a waterway to be constructed across Upstate New York. In April 1820, the new canal's first boat—the *Montezuma*—arrived in Syracuse from the east, having followed the canal's course along what is present-day Erie Boulevard. Five years later, the canal was completed to Buffalo, linking the waters of Lake Erie to the Hudson River and the sea. The growing settlement at the foot of the lake eventually became the commerce and trading center of Central New York. ☛

FROM 1825 TO THE 1920S, WHEN THE ERIE CANAL WAS FILLED IN TO CREATE ERIE BOULEVARD, SYRACUSE WAS KNOWN FOR THE IMPRESSIVE CHANNEL THAT STRETCHED FOR FIVE MILES THROUGH THE HEART OF THE CITY. BUILT IN 1850 TO WEIGH CANAL-BOAT FREIGHT, THE WEIGHLOCK BUILDING, LISTED ON THE NATIONAL REGISTER OF HISTORIC PLACES, TODAY SERVES AS THE FOCAL POINT OF THE ERIE CANAL MUSEUM (ABOVE). AMONG ITS FEATURE ATTRACTIONS IS A REFURBISHED, 65-FOOT-LONG PASSENGER CANAL BOAT (OPPOSITE).

THROUGHOUT THE 19TH CENTURY, SYRACUSE GREW. IN FACT, BETWEEN 1820 AND 1830, SYRACUSE'S POPULATION GREW MORE THAN 200 PERCENT, ALTHOUGH IT DID NOT INCORPORATE AS A CITY UNTIL 1848. REASONS FOR SYRACUSE'S growth were increased salt production, support manufacturing, and agricultural growth, all of which were encouraged by the ease and low cost of transportation on the Erie Canal.

Among the many settlers who arrived year by year, many were immigrants from lands afar. The Irish mainly came to run the salt boilers and dig the canal, while the Germans came to farm and work the warehouses. As more and more immigrants entered the United States through the port of New York and traveled upstate in search of new

© JOHN G. HODGSON

employment opportunities, they brought with them new cultures, and a diverse Syracuse began to form. The Catholic faith began to take hold. Syracuse became a world leader in manufacturing, known for bicycles and typewriter production. Due to the German influence, major breweries sprang up with names like National, Zett's, Greenway, Bartels, Haberle, and Congress.

These immigrant influences can be seen in Syracuse today, and they contribute greatly to what we are as a community and who we are as a people. Irish, German, Ukrainian, Polish, Italian, Latino, African-American, and Southeast Asian—virtually all cultures are represented in modern Syracuse. ☛

YOU DON'T HAVE TO VENTURE FAR FROM SYRACUSE TO FIND PLEASANT REMINDERS OF A BYGONE ERA. VISITORS TO THE ERIE CANAL PARK IN SUBURBAN CAMILLUS CAN PEEK INTO THIS OLD BOATHOUSE, WHILE FARTHER SOUTH IN THE TULLY VALLEY, AGRARIAN ROOTS STILL RUN DEEP.

AVING GROWN UP IN SYRACUSE, I AM PRIVY TO UNDER-STANDING HOW SPECIAL OUR COMMUNITY TRULY IS. THERE IS A SPIRIT IN SYRACUSE UNMATCHED IN ANY OTHER COM-MUNITY. INDIVIDUALS OF MY GENERATION REMEMBER A downtown busy with excitement—Schrafft's for lunch, McCarthy's for fish, or White Castle for burgers. We shopped at D. McCarthy & Sons, Edward's, C.E. Chappell & Sons, Witherill's, and Dey Brothers. Our mothers enjoyed the Addis Company and Flah's, and we kids loved the Rocket Ship monorail at Edward's that took us all around the store. Ed Gouth's Hobby Shop was the place to go for toys and hobby goods, and a show was always playing at the grand downtown movie houses—the Paramount, RKO Keith's, Loew's, the Strand, and the Eckel.

City neighborhoods were filled with children and families. We swam at the salt pool at Onondaga Lake Parkway, and followed our mothers to the Regional Market to watch as live animals were purchased for supper and taken to the slaughterhouse. We played baseball in the streets and dreamed of someday playing on a true grass field alongside Mickey Mantle and Roger Maris. Those

TROLLEYS AND AUTOMOBILES SHARED CITY STREETS UNTIL 1931, WHEN THE CONVENIENCE OF PERSONAL TRANSPOR-TATION FINALLY PUT THE ELECTRIC RAIL-BUSES OUT OF BUSINESS. BEFORE CARS CAME ALONG, AREA TROLLEYS CARRIED UP TO 4 MILLION PASSENGERS ANNUALLY.

were the days when a good crack meant hitting the threads right out of a baseball. Street corners downtown had real live traffic cops stationed for service, and
every neighborhood had a watering hole and a landmark restaurant—places like
the Schnitzelbank and Cornerhouse on the north side; Wheeler's, Smorol's, and
Twin Trees to the west; Stampalia's to the east; and Campbell's in the valley.

While many of these traditions and places have gone, some still exist, even as
new establishments have sprung up alongside. Heid's still serves a great hot dog.
Columbus, Ragusa's, and DiLauro's still make great bread. You can still get a
good haircut at the Eastwood Barber Shop, eat a big bowl of pasta fagiole at
Sorrento's, and find a frosty beer awaiting your arrival at Coleman's or Nibsy's,
Syracuse's oldest operational tavern.

There's a pride to living in Syracuse. We have a hearty spirit, good for surviving
long winters, and we take a sense of ownership in everything we do. Syracusans always have an opinion, and we always know what's right. So, as much as Syracuse
has changed, it has stayed the same. And as a result, we have a terrific city that is
primed for tomorrow. ☞

A SYRACUSE CHIEFS OUTFIELDER LEAPS
HIGH TO SNAG A FLY BALL AT RUSTY
MACARTHUR STADIUM. IN 1997, WHEN
THE 63-YEAR-OLD BALLPARK WAS DEMOL-
ISHED TO MAKE WAY FOR P&C STADIUM,
THE CITY'S INTERNATIONAL LEAGUE TEAM
WAS RENAMED THE SKYCHIEFS. THE OLD
HEID'S OF LIVERPOOL SIGN MAY BE
GONE, BUT THE REGIONALLY FAMOUS
RESTAURANT, AN AREA LANDMARK FOR
MORE THAN 100 YEARS, IS STILL SELLING
ITS TASTY HOT DOGS.

ODAY'S SYRACUSE HOLDS MORE THAN 1,000 ACRES OF GREEN SPACE AND PARKS—AMONG THE HIGHEST IN THE UNITED STATES FOR A CITY OF ITS SIZE AND POPULATION. OUR CITY IS STILL ONE THAT CONTAINS MANY UNIQUE AND diverse neighborhoods. Syracuse University, LeMoyne College, and Onondaga Community College add a great deal as institutions of higher learning. A recreational day downtown can take you to a number of museums and attractions—the Museum of Science and Technology, the Erie Canal Museum, the Everson Museum of Art, the Onondaga Historical Association Museum, and Armory Square. ☛

ALTHOUGH NO LONGER THE RETAILING CENTER IT USED TO BE, DOWNTOWN SYRACUSE STILL PULSES WITH EXCITEMENT. P.J. DORSEY'S PUB & GRILL ON WALTON STREET IS ONE OF MANY SUCCESSFUL BUSINESSES THAT HAVE RECENTLY SPROUTED AROUND A REVITALIZED ARMORY SQUARE (OPPOSITE). A FEW BLOCKS AWAY ON EAST HARRISON AND SOUTH STATE STREETS, THE I.M. PEI-DESIGNED EVERSON MUSEUM HOUSES ONE OF THE NATION'S MOST INTRIGUING COLLECTIONS OF MODERN ART (ABOVE).

Syracuse boasts its own symphony orchestra, opera, and stage theater organizations. Major national attractions and entertainment venues find their way to Syracuse, often to the 50,000-seat Carrier Dome on the Syracuse University campus. Rusty MacArthur Stadium (originally the Syracuse Municipal Stadium),

built in 1934 for $255,000, was replaced in 1997 by the state-of-the-art, $32 million P&C Stadium, and the Syracuse SkyChiefs, an affiliate of the Toronto Blue Jays, now play baseball there. The American Hockey League's Syracuse Crunch brought professional hockey back home to the War Memorial, where one can also catch a Syracuse Smash lacrosse game.

In 1989, the 1.5 million square feet of gross leasable space at Carousel Center opened at the foot of Onondaga Lake, and a recently announced expansion to 3.2 million square feet will add 150 new stores and restaurants to make it one of the

largest shopping malls in America. One day soon, Syracuse's lakefront region will finish its renewal, complete with new office buildings, condominiums and patio homes, and retail shops and restaurants. ☛

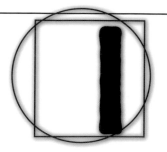I N 1998, SYRACUSE CELEBRATED THE 150TH ANNIVERSARY OF ITS INCORPORATION AS A CITY, WHEN THE VILLAGES OF SYRACUSE AND SALINA APPROVED A CHARTER AND MERGED INTO ONE. ON THE CUSP OF A NEW MILLENNIUM, SYRACUSE remains a special place to live, work, and raise a family. With the amenities of a big city and the friendliness of a small town, the city is poised to improve upon its reputation as an enjoyable and affordable place to call home for years to come. Its small size is conducive to creating many personal relationships, but its heritage, culture, and business structure enable it to compete with many of America's largest metropolitan areas.

Truly, Syracuse is a warm, inviting community with a welcoming appeal and a hometown environment. Because of that, I wouldn't think of living anywhere else. ■

COLORFUL VISTAS ON A BRIGHT SUNNY DAY: TULIPS RISE TOWARD THE VETER-AN'S MONUMENT IN CLINTON SQUARE, A POPULAR LUNCH-HOUR GATHERING SPOT FOR DOWNTOWN OFFICE WORKERS (BELOW), WHILE A CLEARING AT ONON-DAGA LAKE PARK IN NEARBY LIVERPOOL FRAMES A VIEW OF CAROUSEL CENTER, THE CARRIER DOME, AND OTHER LAND-MARKS OF THE CITY SKYLINE (OPPOSITE).

THE ECLECTIC MIX OF ARCHITEC-
tural styles in downtown
Syracuse reflects the enduring
strength of the local economy.

Located near the corner of South
Warren and East Genessee
streets, the circa 1870 SA&K
building and the 1927 State

Tower Building are next-door
neighbors with distinctly different looks (PAGES 28 AND 29).

Many of the commercial buildings in Syracuse are well-preserved examples of Victorian architecture. The renovated 1867 Gridley Building, at 101 South Salina Street, avoided the wrecking ball in the 1970s after citizen groups rallied to save its four-faced clock, which long served as the city's official timepiece (RIGHT). Another downtown landmark is the elegant SA&K office building, distinguished by its triangular shape and rounded roof corners (OPPOSITE).

▲ © RUSS McCONNELL

L IKE GHOSTS RELUCTANT TO LEAVE
home, faded signs of historic
Syracuse linger on the brick
walls of inner-city buildings
(PAGES 32 AND 33).

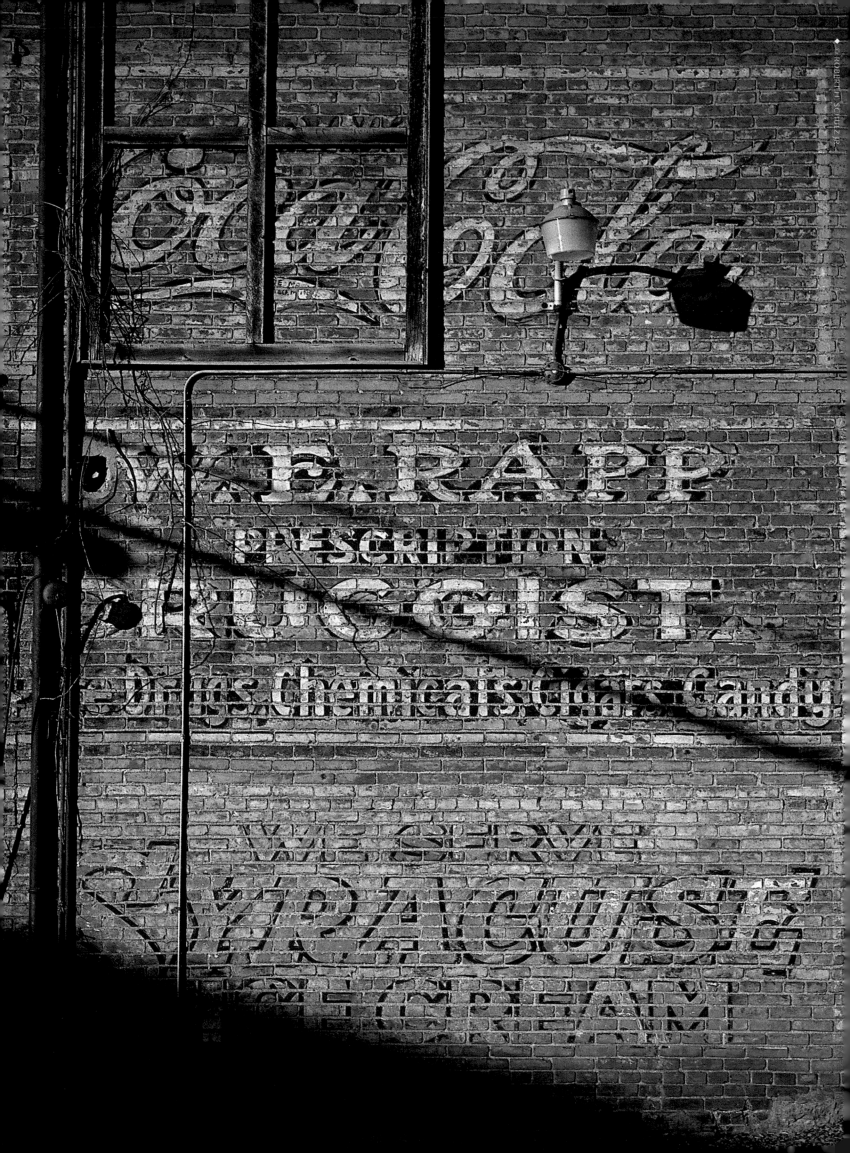

AGE-OLD ART FORMS CONVERGE in Columbus Circle, where local Italian-Americans erected a bronze statue of the continent's discoverer in 1932. Although several nearby buildings offer views of the stately columns and domed roof of the Onondaga County Courthouse, built in 1904, no one has a better vantage point than Chris himself.

SYRACUSE UNIVERSITY

WITH MORE THAN 12,000 undergraduate students, Syracuse University, founded in 1870, has earned a national reputation for its rigorous course offerings, including political science, journalism, and creative writing. Opened in 1873, the John Dustin Archbold Hall of Languages was the first permanent building on campus and is still used for classes (ABOVE). The landmark Hendricks Chapel, with its white dome and columned entrance, was completed 57 years later (OPPOSITE).

S TRANGE BEASTS TAKE SHAPE downtown in the reflective windows of a South Salina Street store (PAGE 38), while nearby, the twin towers of MONY Plaza appear ready to blot out the sun (PAGE 39).

MS•NY

THE ART DECO SCHOOL OF ARchitecture reached its local zenith in 1927, when Niagara Mohawk Power Corporation's headquarters building was completed (PAGES 40 AND 41). A standout even on today's skyline, the gleaming, 114-foot tower is garnished with a winged, stainless steel sculpture called the *Spirit of Light*.

DID YOU EVER WONDER WHAT happens to all those hubcaps that go rolling off the road on busy highways? A good many garnish the chain-link fence around Hiawatha Used Cars on North State Street (OPPOSITE). Yet, the Hiawatha hubcap haul pales in comparison to the yardful owned by Bill and Anna Soble of Lakeport (ABOVE). With a collection of 2,500 wheel covers, the Route 31 couple almost always has the one you're looking for.

FORMER RESIDENT JOHN WEDA poses happily in front of the smallest house in Syracuse, a 12-by-16-foot dwelling at 812 Danforth Street (OPPOSITE). By comparison, the city's largest birdhouse appears to be just the right size to make any fowl feel at home (LEFT).

46 GREATER SYRACUSE

THERE'S NO PLACE LIKE HOME, where a boy can take refuge from winter's wrath and a man can look back on a lifetime. The late Harry Mantor, a former street alcoholic who credited religion with breaking his dependence on the bottle, spent his last years surrounded by mementos in his Columbus Avenue apartment (ABOVE).

SYRACUSE IS ONE OF THE NA-
tion's snowiest cities, and
locals aren't reluctant to admit
it. If nothing else, the storms
that bury parked cars and chill
youngsters to the bone are character builders. For the record,
the city averages more than 114
inches of snow a year.

E VEN AS THE SEASONS CHANGE, Syracuse's neighborhoods endure as comfortable enclaves for the city's diverse residents.

© ROBERT H. SCHULZ JR.

© BUD LEE

ALTHOUGH A WELL-TENDED Victorian porch stands out as an architectural work of art (OPPOSITE LEFT), weathered facades in other parts of the city are striking in their own beauty.

WITH TURRETS AND TOWERS galore, restored Victorian houses make colorful statements amid the city's diverse historic architecture.

SYRACUSE MAY HAVE ITS SHARE of long, cold winters, but the promise of a colorful springtime is always worth the wait.

BECAUSE SYRACUSE IS LOCATED in the heart of Upstate New York's farm country, residents often have first pick of the season's mouthwatering, fresh produce. Every Tuesday from mid-June to mid-October, a farmer's market springs up in the parking lot at South Salina and East Jefferson streets downtown, while Park Street's Regional Market, the oldest and largest venue of its kind in the state, attracts thousands of patrons year-round.

Pass the . . . pumpkin? Although city streets will do for an impromptu pickup game, a father-and-son team play a little roundball of their own during harvesttime at a nearby farm.

I N A COMMUNITY THAT LOVES sports of every variety, the Orangemen of Syracuse University are the toast of the town.

For 11 straight winters, from 1984 to 1995, the team led the nation in attendance at its high-spirited home basketball games.

MINOR-LEAGUE BASEBALL HAS been a fixture of Syracuse summers since the 1920s, but with the 1997 opening of P&C Stadium, the game has reached a new level of excitement. Still, some things never change: Kids will always reach over the dugout roof for autographs and wait patiently behind the outfield fence for a home run souvenir.

WHILE MOST EVERYONE IN THE Salt City is a fan of Syracuse University sports, some supporters of the Orange are more enthusiastic than others.

A BIG WIN FOR THE SU Orangemen means cheers from
excited fans and a celebratory
bath for Coach Paul Pasqualoni
(PAGES 68 AND 69).

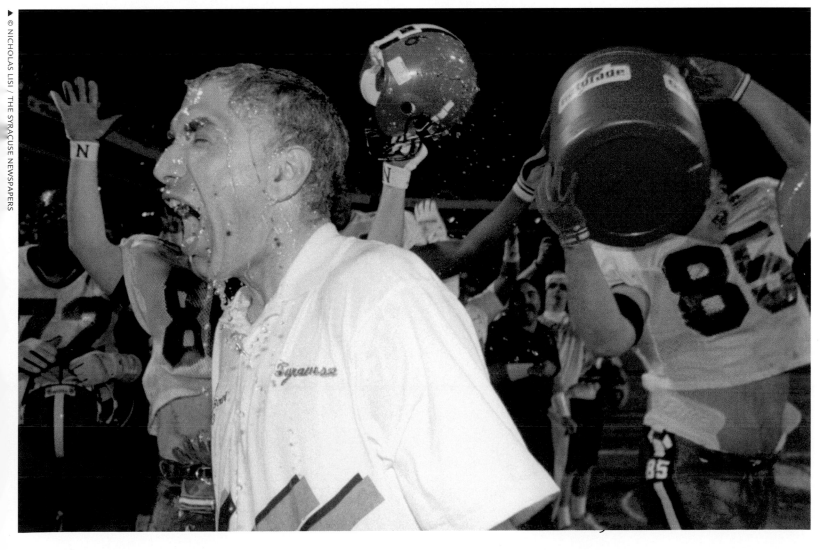

WHETHER IT'S A COLLEGIATE contest or a major-league match, the arena at the Onondaga County War Memorial comes alive during hockey season.

The venue fills to capacity with fans when the American Hockey League's Syracuse Crunch are at home (ABOVE), and also during the annual Syracuse Invitational

Tournament, a four-team contest that heats up the ice to benefit terminally ill children (OPPOSITE).

ASPIRING BOXERS START YOUNG in Syracuse, where fans and contestants alike have "flipped" for this high-spirited sport. The area's rich ring tradition played a big part in the development of the International Boxing Hall of Fame in nearby Canastota, home of former world champions Carmen Basilio and Billy Backus.

GREATER SYRACUSE

TAKING A CUE FROM THE TEETH of a corn-picking combine (OPPOSITE), ice-climbers don sharp spikes to get a grip on their sport (ABOVE).

GREATER SYRACUSE

WINTER USHERS IN ANOTHER season of sport in Greater Syracuse, where the right footwear is all you need for a trek up the ice or a stroll in the snow.

REST FOR THE WEARY: An exhausted equine tries to catch a few z's after doing his duty at Lorenzo, an early-19th- century estate in Cazenovia (OPPOSITE). The historic site, along with such getaways as Highland Forest in Fabius (ABOVE), has become a popular place for traditional, horse- drawn sleigh rides.

S ANTA'S HELPERS, NOT TO mention Old St. Nick himself, spread plenty of holiday cheer as their hay-heavy wagon makes its way around downtown Syracuse during the Christmas shopping season.

82

D INOSAUR BAR-B-QUE, LOCATED at 246 West Willow Street, is one of Syracuse's trendiest restaurants. Since the rib joint opened its doors in 1988, every- one from young urban profes- sionals to tattooed bikers has come to sample its savory blend of barbecue, beer, and blues.

GOOD FOOD, FRIENDLY FACES, and plenty of interesting conversation make everyone feel at home in Syracuse diners.

NOTHING SATISFIES A HEALTHY appetite like a heaping plate of mom-and-pop food at the local diner. Dozens of these all-American eateries pepper the area, including the 60-year-old Redwood Diner in East Syracuse and the Trolley Stop Diner, across East Water Street from City Hall. Grand Central Bakery, at the corner of Salina and Fayette streets, is a favorite breakfast spot for downtown workers, while the Liberty Diner reigns as the morning meeting place for residents of the city's Valley neighborhood.

ACTING AS BEACONS TO HUNGRY passersby, old-fashioned diners give patrons a real taste of the city. From Peter's Polar Parlor in Syracuse to Heid's hot dog stand in Liverpool to the Little Gem Diner near Onondaga Lake, local restaurants promise to leave your tummy—and your taste buds—satisfied.

C

SINCE 1982, DOUG CLARK HAS served up scads of fresh sea-food at his popular Skaneateles restaurant, Doug's Fish Fry. Throughout the year, but especially on summer-season Fridays, patrons line up for the restaurant's tasty fresh-fish sandwiches.

GREEN IS ALWAYS TOPS AT THE corner of Milton Avenue and Tompkins Street in Tipperary Hill. Former Mayor Tom Young salutes the neighborhood's Irish-American heritage as he tips his hat to the nation's only upside-down traffic light.

KNOWN FOR THEIR COLORFUL costumes, high-stepping antics, and all-around appreciation of a good time, the Mummers from Philadelphia strut down South Salina during Syracuse's St. Patrick's Day parade (PAGES 94 AND 95). With roots extending to the 17th-century European custom of masquerading and visiting with friends, Mummers clubs today perform all over the world.

WHO DOESN'T LOVE A PARADE? Syracuse salutes various cultures and ethnic groups with lively music, elaborate costumes, and plenty of fancy footwork.

G R E A T E R   S Y R A C U S E

THERE'S NO PLACE LIKE HOME: Among the area's unique celebrations is OzFest in nearby Chittenango, the birthplace of L. Frank Baum, who penned *The Wonderful Wizard of Oz*. Each year, dozens of Dorothys, a Tin Man or two, and a cadre of Cowardly Lions share the streets with a smattering of mild-mannered munchkins and more than a few not-so-wicked witches.

THE PATTERNS OF MAN-MADE design often mimic the delicate creations of Mother Nature. Here, balloonist David Longeill looks for his next passenger during the Coors Light Balloon Fest, held each summer at Jamesville Beach Park. The owner of Lighter Than Air Flights in Red Creek, Longeill has taken his colorful craft up, up, and away more than 1,300 times.

YOU NEVER KNOW WHAT CAR-toonish characters might show up for the annual St. Patrick's Day parade. Although Gumby may lead the pack in head-to-toe green, the guest list has also included Rocky the Flying Squirrel, the California Raisins, and the Cheerios honeybee.

PRIMITIVE MAN COULDN'T HAVE imagined how far the world would take that most basic of concepts: the wheel. Here, a Carrier Corporation technician tests a new air-conditioning fan (TOP), and the popular Big Wheel ride is assembled in time for the Great New York State Fair (BOTTOM).

D IFFERENT "SPOKES" FOR different folks: A kaleidoscope of colors is revealed as a giant hot-air balloon prepares for liftoff (TOP). Back on solid ground, a worker erects the framework for one of countless vendor tents at Harborfest in Oswego (BOTTOM).

SPIRITS SOAR AND STOMACHS flutter when fun-seekers climb aboard the midway rides at the Great New York State Fair. Once the spinning starts, brave souls can open their eyes to an exhilarating view of the festivities below.

A WORLD OF UNIQUE AMUSE-ments awaits curious visitors to the state fair, where the colorful midway beckons seduc-tively to those with an adventur-ous spirit and a pocketful of change.

GREATER SYRACUSE

WHEN AUGUST ROLLS AROUND, more than 800,000 people flock to the Great New York State Fair to vie for peculiar prizes, stuff their faces, and ride, ride, ride. First held in 1841, the event moved to its permanent site in suburban Solvay in 1890. The fairgrounds, also known as Empire Expo Center, now encompasses some 335 acres.

MORE THAN MERE FUN AND games, the state fair is a giant promotional venture for agriculture, industry, service or-ganizations, and even the military, where kids of all ages can find fun at every turn.

O RIGINALLY AN AGRICULTURAL exposition, the Great New York State Fair still features an impressive array of produce and livestock, including this shaggy-coifed Highland bull.

GOOD BREEDING IS NO YOKE to New York farmers, whose teams of oxen and other livestock often vie for the blue ribbon in state fair competition.

AT THE NEW YORK STATE FAIR-grounds, riders hold on tight to dreams of a rodeo victory. Although the venue's 45,000-seat coliseum is especially busy during fair season, it also plays host to rodeos, riding competitions, and other equestrian events throughout the year.

THE STATE FAIR'S WHIRLWIND of activity may wear you out, but one thing's certain: You'll soon be dreaming of next year's dose of fun.

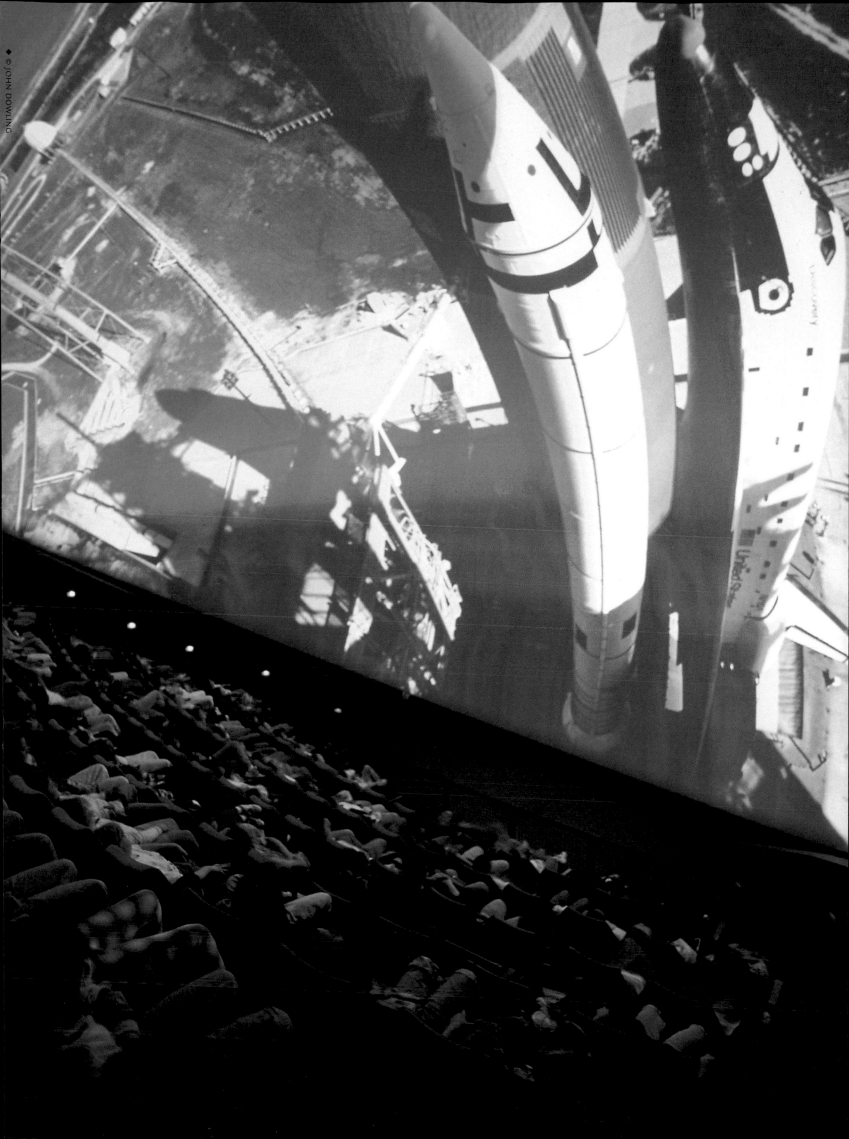

THREE, TWO, ONE . . . BLAST OFF!
A would-be rocket makes the
rounds on horseback during a
4-H costume competition at the
state fair (PAGE 120), while the
real thing generates heart-
pounding excitement on-screen
at the Museum of Science and
Technology's IMAX theater
(PAGE 121). If four wheels and
high speeds are more your style,
the theater can also put you in
the driver's seat for a larger-
than-life spin around the track
(LEFT).

T HE MUSEUM OF AUTOMOBILE History, at 321 North Clinton Street, chronicles the nation's automotive heritage—from Model Ts to modern-day Toyotas. In addition to an outstanding collection of classic cars, the museum's billboarded exterior is fast becoming one of the city's most-photographed tourist attractions.

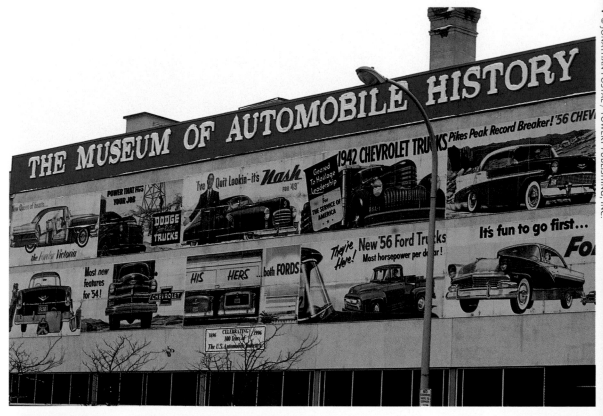

GREATER SYRACUSE

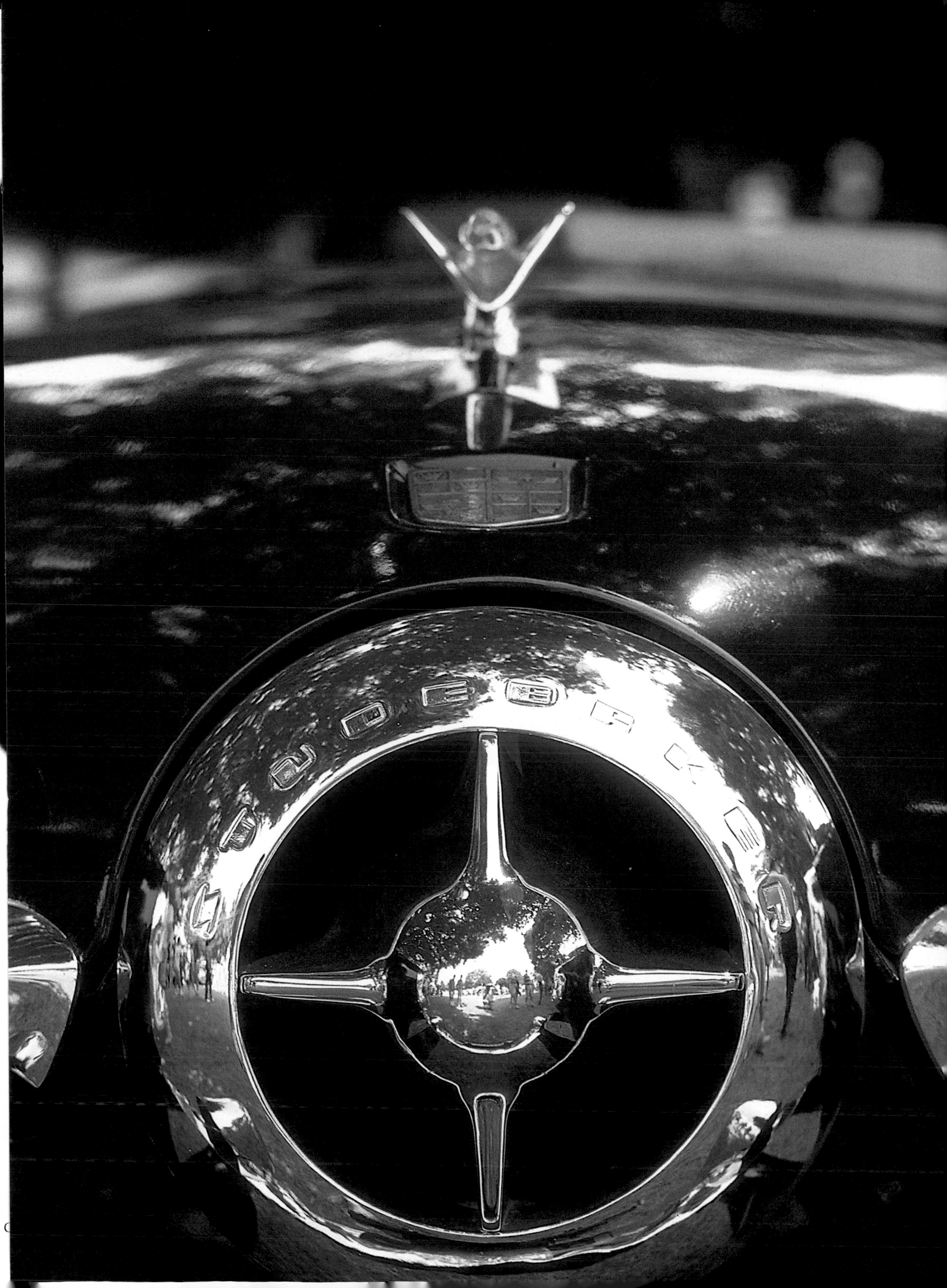
STUDEBAKER

NORMALLY, IT'S EASY TO GET around Syracuse, where Interstate 81 and the New York State Thruway intersect. The "olny" exception is when highway painting crews go awry.

S ITUATED IN THE GEOGRAPHIC center of New York, Syracuse is a hub for all modern modes of transportation. Planned for completion in fall 1998, the $19 million Intermodal Transportation Center, located near the Central New York Regional Market, will link the city's rail, bus, and taxi systems.

H AVING RECENTLY UNDERGONE a $50 million renovation and modernization, the Syracuse Hancock International Airport annually logs more than 1.1 million passengers and handles 26,000 tons of air cargo (PAGES 132 AND 133).

Surrounded by sparkling lakes, Syracuse residents can dive into a diversity of water sports when summer rolls around. Just east of the city in Fayetteville, a well-worn fleet of rental canoes stand ready for another busy season at Green Lakes State Park. On Onondaga Lake, a group of neatly stacked oars await their next call to action during an Intercollegiate Rowing Association regatta.

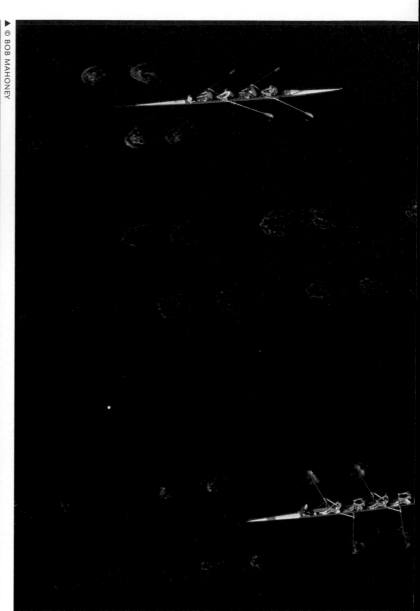

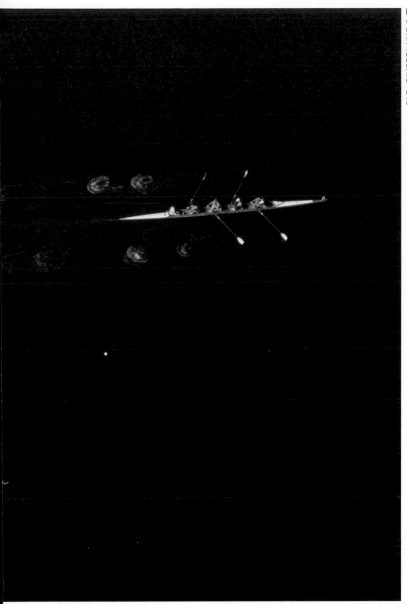

PRIOR TO 1995, THE INTERCOL-legiate Rowing Association held its annual regatta on Onondaga Lake for some 40 years. Since the race moved to Cherry Hill, New Jersey, the lake has been the site of several other major meets, including the U.S. Rowing Association's Club Nationals and Masters Nationals.

APOPULAR VENUE FOR SUMMER picnics in the early part of the 20th century, Chittenango Falls in nearby Madison County is today a breathtaking scenic landmark. Unfortunately, visitors are no longer permitted at the base of the 167-foot waterfall, because its rocky face is the last remaining habitat of the endangered ovate amber snail.

GREATER SYRACUSE

SYRACUSE MAY BE BEST KNOWN for its snowy winter weather, but when summer hits, youngsters take to the water in droves. While some carefree residents like to tumble and splash at Green Lakes State Park, more competitive souls put their strokes to the test in local high school swim meets.

Each April, thousands of competitors pound the pavement during the Mountain Goat Run, a 10-mile footrace that winds through downtown streets and traverses some of the city's steepest neighborhoods. Although participants start out elbow-to-elbow, speed and stamina quickly separate the pack.

LOOKING SNAPPY IN THEIR dress blues, police recruits march proudly through a graduation ceremony before it's time to hit the streets. Thanks to recent initiatives that have shored up the city's police force, Syracuse now boasts more than 540 men and women in blue—an all-time high.

SYRACUSE IS JUSTIFIABLY PROUD of the valiant contributions its sons and daughters have made in times of war. Showing their esteem for the area's heroic veterans, spectators salute a Battle of the Bulge survivor during a Memorial Day parade in Baldwinsville (OPPOSITE), and history buffs at Sainte Marie among the Iroquois, a restored colonial French fort in Liverpool, reenact the sights and sounds of combat (ABOVE).

REMINDERS OF RESIDENTS' patriotic spirit greet you at every turn in and around Syracuse, where the stars and stripes are a colorful part of everyday scenes in almost any season. Each Memorial Day at the state fairgrounds, war veterans participate in a traditional watch fire, during which old or damaged flags are burned as a symbolic homing beacon for the nation's missing in action and prisoners of war (OPPOSITE).

HOME TO THE SOLDIERS AND Sailors Monument, Clinton Square provides the perfect backdrop for a moving Veterans Day ceremony—a time for soldiers to remember their fallen comrades and civilians to face the glory and horror of combat.

INSPIRATIONAL STATUARY ABOUNDS in and around Syracuse. Framed by monuments to past residents, a robed woman greets visitors to Walnut Grove Cemetery in Jamesville (OPPOSITE), while a snow-covered Virgin Mary bows her head in reverential prayer outside downtown's Cathedral of the Immaculate Conception (LEFT).

FOLKLORE HOLDS THAT A SPEC-tral figure named Claire haunts the balcony of the Syracuse Area Landmark Theatre on South Salina Street. Although witnesses have described her wavy, blonde hair and long, white gown, skeptics wonder if she is truly the ghost of a former stagehand's wife, as the legend states, or just a clever promotional scheme to boost box-office receipts.

OPENED IN 1928 AS THE LOEW'S State Movie Theatre, the ornate Syracuse Area Landmark Theatre was slated for the wrecking ball in 1977, but was saved by a community fund-raising effort that earned it a place on the National Register of Historic Places. Today, the restored hall is a showplace for concerts, plays, and classic motion pictures.

THE PICTURE OF REVERENCE, members of the children's choir at St. James Episcopal Church in Skaneateles lift up their voices during the recessional at a Sunday service.

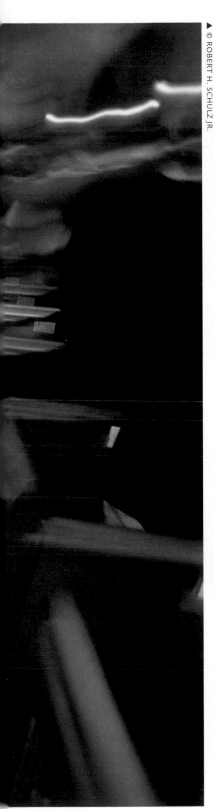

THE ANNUAL CHRISTMAS CAROL Sing at Syracuse University's Hendricks Chapel always comes to a moving close with a candle-light rendition of "Silent Night."

AN ORGANIST TUNES UP FOR Sunday afternoon mass at downtown's Cathedral of the Immaculate Conception, spiritual headquarters for the Roman Catholic Diocese of Syracuse.

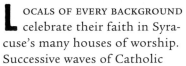OCALS OF EVERY BACKGROUND celebrate their faith in Syracuse's many houses of worship. Successive waves of Catholic immigrants—including Germans, Italians, and, most recently, Vietnamese—have found a home at the Assumption Roman Catholic Church, with its twin spires that stand tall amid near north side homes (LEFT). And in rural Fabius, the distinctive red doors of the First Baptist Church draw attention to an otherwise simple, well-kept facade (RIGHT).

T HE CONGREGATION AT ST. Mary's Russian Orthodox Church in nearby Jamesville finds inspiration in its richly decorated cathedral, where religious art and iconography abound.

F ROM CEREMONIAL DANCES AT the Great New York State Fair (TOP) to a silhouette sculpture at the Sainte Marie among the Iroquois museum (OPPOSITE TOP), Central New York's Native Americans strive to perpetuate an ancient culture in a rapidly changing world.

SEVERAL LOCAL NATIVE AMERI-can leaders have done their part to keep their heritage alive, including Leon Shenandoah, the Tadadaho—chief of chiefs—of the Iroquois Confederacy until his death in July 1996 (BOTTOM), and Keller George, a member of the ruling council of the Oneida Nation (OPPOSITE BOTTOM).

LEGALIZED GAMBLING HAS brought both prosperity and controversy to the Oneida Nation. Although profits from the Turning Stone Casino have spun off more than 3,000 jobs at Oneida-owned businesses—85 percent of them filled by non-Indians—many tradition-minded Iroquois have scorned the venture, citing the moral implications of easy money.

A N OLD-FASHIONED BARBER-
shop is one of the few
places where a guy can still let
his hair down. Vito Peluso is the
man with scissors and a sympa-
thetic ear at Loew's Professional
Barber & Unisex Shop on South
Clinton Street (OPPOSITE), while
the folks at the State Tower Barber & Stylist Shop on East Water Street are sure to give you a
trim you can live with (ABOVE).

GREATER SYRACUSE

© BUD LEE

NOTHING MAKES YOU FEEL MORE at ease than a smile from Mom to welcome you home. Coming in a close second is the friendly service at Sha-Ling's Chinese Takeout on North Clinton Street, which often includes a Mom-like good-bye and Godspeed to send you on your way (LEFT).

NO SMOKING

99¢
SPECIAL
FRIEDRICE
SOUP
PIZZA

MOTOR OIL ISN'T USUALLY served with much style these days, but at Syracuse's Museum of Automobile History, a vintage pitch-person presents her products with panache. Nearby, in the bustling Armory Square district, a cardboard window-shopper, paused outside the Artifice Gallery on Walton Street, is a playful example of art imitating life.

ONCE DOMINATED BY MAJOR department stores, Syracuse's central business district has evolved into a melting pot of commerce and culture. Thousands of office workers patronize restaurants, boutiques, and other small businesses located on South Salina Street, Warren Street, and other downtown thoroughfares.

TAKIN' IT TO THE STREETS: In Syracuse, it's not uncommon to see artists practicing their craft along local sidewalks. Here, musician Chris James strums a tune outside the Blue Tusk restaurant, while artist John Kramer puts the scene to paper.

ELIJAH HARRIS—WHO CALLS HIMself the Voice of M Street, for the University neighborhood's Marshall Street—often takes his act on the road, singing for patrons of the Crown Bar & Grill on Fayette Street.

LOCAL FOLK MUSICIAN AND songwriter Libba Cotten became a legend, not only for the music she made but for how she made it. A lefty, she taught herself to play a right-handed guitar upside down. Before she died in 1987, at the age of 92, Cotten's songs were performed by such folk greats as Pete Seeger and Peter, Paul & Mary.

A MUSICAL STYLE THAT TRULY overflows with emotion, gospel is the genre of choice for Charles Cannon and the Bells of Harmony, whose performances draw their share of faithful listeners.

WHATEVER YOUR MUSICAL appetite, Syracuse is well equipped to satisfy it. While punk rocker Jon Case pumps up the crowd during Nothing to Do Night at North Syracuse Junior High School (BOTTOM), David "The Boogie Man" Corcoran deftly handles his squeeze box at the Hotel Syracuse (OPPOSITE TOP). Even the wall murals seem to have fun at Styleen's Rhythm Palace, one of the hippest clubs in town (TOP AND OPPOSITE BOTTOM).

CENTRAL NEW YORK'S MUSICAL offerings run the gamut, from the classical chords of the Syracuse Symphony Orchestra (OPPOSITE) to the frenzied riffs of local band Earth Crisis during a performance at the Lost Horizon nightclub (ABOVE).

NOTHING COULD BE COOLER on a sultry June day than grooving to the sounds of saxophonist Sonny Rollins (TOP) during Jazz Fest in Clinton Square. Some 50,000 people flock to Syracuse each year for the event, which is now distinguished as the Northeast's largest free jazz festival.

IF IT TAKES THE BLUES TO PUT you in a dancin' mood, don't miss the New York State Blues Festival, held downtown in July. The fun-filled, three-day celebration attracts inventive performers like James Peterson (TOP), not to mention throngs of enthusiastic fans.

L ATINO DANCERS STRUT THEIR stuff during a colorful World in the Square show. Every weekday during the summer, Hanover Square treats downtown workers and shoppers to noontime entertainment, ranging from big bands to Elvis impersonators.

Members of the Cut-Ups square dance group step lively during a Rotary Club benefit at the Blackrock Campgrounds in nearby King Ferry.

OES TAP AND HANDS CLAP when local belly dancer extraordinaire Zoe Antemis shifts into high gear. Elsewhere, more refined types are content with a traditional waltz or two.

STARS IN THE MAKING: Tap dancers wait for the curtain during a recital at Skaneateles' Waterman Elementary School (TOP), where country swingers and Texas two-steppers take their own turn on stage at the annual Spring Sing (BOTTOM).

GREATER SYRACUSE

NO MATTER YOUR AGE, BICYCLES
are a safe and popular mode
of transportation in the Syracuse area. Luckily, the fuel you'll
need to continue your trek is
usually right around the corner.

GREATER SYRACUSE

THE SCENIC LAKES AND RIVERS that dot Greater Syracuse are ideal for wetting your line, taking a dip, or strolling among nature's landmarks. The stone bridge in Onondaga Park is also a popular spot for wedding-party photos (PAGES 194 AND 195).

THE GOLDEN HUES OF EARLY morning and late afternoon remind locals how fortunate they are to live in the center of an empire, where natural beauty and a rich history provide the ideal backdrop for a promising future.

PROFILES IN EXCELLENCE

A LOOK AT THE CORPORATIONS, BUSINESSES, PROFESSIONAL GROUPS, AND COMMUNITY SERVICE ORGANIZATIONS THAT HAVE MADE THIS BOOK POSSIBLE. THEIR STORIES—OFFERING AN INFORMAL CHRONICLE OF THE LOCAL BUSINESS COMMUNITY—ARE ARRANGED ACCORDING TO THE DATE THEY WERE ESTABLISHED IN GREATER SYRACUSE.

A.G. Edwards & Sons, Inc. ■ A.J.M. Management Services, Inc. ■ Anheuser-Busch, Inc. ■ Bell Atlantic ■ Benjamin Rush Center ■ Blue Cross and Blue Shield of Central New York ■ Bristol-Myers Squibb Company ■ The Business Journal ■ Byrne Dairy ■ C&S Companies ■ Central New York Regional Transportation Authority ■ Chase Manhattan Bank ■ Coyne Textile Services ■ Crouse Radiology Associates ■ Crucible Materials Corporation ■ Crucible Service Centers Division ■ Crucible Specialty Metals Division ■ Devorsetz Stinziano Gilberti Heintz & Smith, P.C. ■ Dumac Business Systems, Inc. ■ Eagle Comtronics, Inc. ■ Empire Medical Management, Ltd. ■ General Super Plating Co., Inc. ■ Genesee Inn: A Golden Tulip Hotel ■ Götz Puppenfabrik and Götz Dolls Inc. ■ Hancock & Estabrook, LLP ■ Harden Furniture ■ Haylor, Freyer & Coon, Inc. ■ Higbee, Inc. ■ Internist Associates of Central New York, P.C. ■ Jaquith Industries Inc. ■ KeyBank N.A. ■ Le Moyne College ■ Lockheed Martin Ocean, Radar & Sensor Systems ■ Loretto ■ M&T Bank ■ Muench-Kreuzer Candle Company ■ New Venture Gear, Inc.'s New Process Gear Division ■ Niagara Mohawk ■ O'Brien & Gere Limited ■ Panthus Corporation ■ Philips Broadband Networks Inc. ■ Pyramid Brokerage Company, Inc. ■ Radisson Plaza, Hotel Syracuse ■ Residence Inn by Marriott ■ Royal & SunAlliance ■ The Scotsman Press, Inc. ■ Stickley Furniture ■ Syracuse Hematology/Oncology, P.C. ■ Syracuse Hospitals ■ The Syracuse Newspapers ■ Syracuse University ■ Syroco, Inc. ■ Time Warner Cable ■ TWG Construction Company, Inc. ■ United HealthCare of Upstate New York ■ University Orthopedics & Sports Medicine, P.C. ■ Upstate Administrative Services, Inc. ■ V.I.P. Structures ■ The Widewaters Group ■ WSYR-570 AM Cox Radio, Inc. ■WTVH-5

The Syracuse Newspapers	1829
KeyBank N.A.	1832
Harden Furniture	1844
Syracuse Hospitals	1869
Syracuse University	1870
Crucible Materials Corporation	1876
Crucible Service Centers Division	1876
Crucible Specialty Metals Division	1876
Panthus Corporation	1884
New Venture Gear, Inc.'s New Process Gear Division	1888
Hancock & Estabrook, LLP	1889
Syroco, Inc.	1890
Royal & SunAlliance	1895
Stickley Furniture	1900
Jaquith Industries Inc.	1919
WSYR-570 AM Cox Radio, Inc.	1922
Radisson Plaza, Hotel Syracuse	1924
Muench-Kreuzer Candle Company	1925
Loretto	1926
Haylor, Freyer & Coon, Inc.	1928
Benjamin Rush Center	1929
Coyne Textile Services	1929

SINCE BEFORE THE CIVIL WAR, HARDEN FURNITURE has been committed to producing fine, heirloom-quality furniture in a family tradition that has spanned five generations. It is the oldest family-owned furniture manufacturer in the nation and one of the few

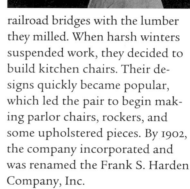

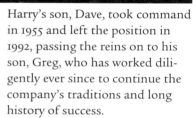

CLOCKWISE FROM TOP: HARDEN FURNITURE BEGAN IN 1844, WHEN CHARLES S. HARDEN SR. SETTLED IN MCCONNELLSVILLE AND PURCHASED A SAWMILL ON FISH CREEK, WHERE HE AND HIS SON, FRANK, BUILT RAILROAD BRIDGES AND FURNITURE WITH THE LUMBER THEY MILLED.

MOST OF THE WORK THAT GOES INTO PRODUCING EACH FINISHED PIECE OF HARDEN FURNITURE IS STILL DONE BY HAND, AS IT WAS IN THE COMPANY'S EARLIEST DAYS.

HARDEN MANAGES ITS OWN FOREST PRESERVES—FROM WHICH IT HARVESTS MUCH OF THE WOOD USED IN ITS PRODUCTS.

SINCE HARDEN'S BEGINNING, COMPANY FORESTERS HAVE ENSURED PROPER AND RESPONSIBLE MANAGEMENT OF HARDEN'S FOREST LAND, WHICH PRODUCES A HARVESTABLE MATURE CHERRY TREE IN APPROXIMATELY 90 YEARS.

still privately held. Founded in 1844 as C. Harden & Son, the company is known today as Harden Furniture, and occupies more than 500,000 square feet of manufacturing facilities in McConnellsville and has a staff of more than 560 employees, many of whom are expert craftspeople in the art of furniture making. Harden manages its own forest preserve—from which it harvests much of the wood used in its products—and owns its own saw- mill, allowing the greatest possible quality control of materials used to make the company's products. Although mechanization is essential to the manufacturing process, most of the work that goes into producing each finished piece is still done by hand, as it was in Harden's earliest days.

From Bridges to Chairs

Charles S. Harden Sr., after several years of working on the Illinois Central Railroad and then searching for gold at Pikes Peak, settled in McConnellsville in 1844. Purchasing a sawmill on Fish Creek, he and his son, Frank, seized an opportunity to build

railroad bridges with the lumber they milled. When harsh winters suspended work, they decided to build kitchen chairs. Their designs quickly became popular, which led the pair to begin making parlor chairs, rockers, and some upholstered pieces. By 1902, the company incorporated and was renamed the Frank S. Harden Company, Inc.

Frank's sons—Harry, Charles, and Clarence—later joined the growing family business. Harry became company president in the late 1930s, and Charles—who also served as president of Camden Wire—was elected president of Harden following Harry's death.

Harry's son, Dave, took command in 1955 and left the position in 1992, passing the reins on to his son, Greg, who has worked diligently ever since to continue the company's traditions and long history of success.

Harden Furniture survived the depression, World War II—during which the company manufactured rifle stocks for the war effort—and the recessions of more recent memory. Thanks to its visionary leadership, Harden has fostered a current period of growth unprecedented in its 154-year history. The late 1990s have seen the introduction of several new lines of furniture, as well as an increase

in the company's exports—more than 15 percent of its products are sold to international customers.

Furniture for Any Home

Harden produces furniture in a broad range of styles—traditional and transitional—to suit needs in every room of the home. Some of these include 18th-century, European, and Shaker-inspired designs; wall systems and entertainment centers; and a line of modular pieces that can be configured for any home office environment. In addition to residential furniture, Harden also performs work for large and small commercial organizations, generally producing items such as conference tables, desks, and seating.

A hallmark of Harden furniture is the care and craftsmanship that go into each creation. Through its highly trained and dedicated craftspeople, the company pays strict attention to the details that separate Harden Furniture from its competitors in the minds of customers.

The wood—primarily solid black cherry—is carefully selected by on-site mill specialists with the aid of computerized equipment. As the construction process begins, hand-carved details, dovetail joinery, and floating-panel construction are added to make each piece unique and characteristic of Harden's high standards in craftsmanship. All furniture is sanded by hand during Harden's 21-step finishing process, which includes hand-rubbed finishing and waxing. The same quality standards are achieved for Harden's upholstered furniture, which features kiln-dried hardwood frames, double-doweled and glued joints, eight-way hand-tied springs, and more than 1,000 different choices in upholstery styles and patterns.

The beauty and quality of Harden furniture is regularly noted in home decorating magazines, such as *Colonial Homes*, *House Beautiful*, *Interiors*, and *Country Living*. The White House, the U.S. Senate, and several foreign embassies have furnishings produced by Harden's commercial division.

The Harden "Family"

As a testament of Harden's commitment to its employees, the company treats everyone on its staff like family. In fact, many local families can be credited for having several generations in the company's employment. In addition, Harden remains committed to the McConnellsville community by helping to maintain and advance local institutions. Harden has been responsible for the construction of churches, a community house, a fire department, a post office, and an elementary school in the hamlet.

Harden cares about the environment as well—its forest reserves (now in excess of 10,000 acres) yield approximately 3.5 times more wood than would be produced naturally. Company foresters ensure proper and responsible management of the land, which produces a harvestable mature cherry tree in approximately 90 years—a process that usually takes more than 120 years without intervention. In addition to forest preservation, Harden uses ozone-friendly upholstery materials and conducts research into developing nonhazardous finishing substances.

Founded on family tradition and community pride, the future of Harden Furniture can best be described in the company motto: "Fine furniture from generation to generation." In response to the competitive and ever changing market, Harden product lines are regularly reviewed and analyzed, with customer and dealer commentary guiding the company's decisions. By following this course, Harden Furniture will continue to be a mainstay in homes and businesses for generations to come.

CLOCKWISE FROM TOP:
HARDEN PRODUCES FURNITURE IN A BROAD RANGE OF STYLES—TRADITIONAL AND TRANSITIONAL—TO SUIT NEEDS IN EVERY ROOM OF THE HOME.

THE BEAUTY AND QUALITY OF HARDEN FURNITURE IS REGULARLY NOTED IN HOME DECORATING MAGAZINES.

A HALLMARK OF HARDEN FURNITURE IS THE CARE AND CRAFTSMANSHIP THAT GO INTO EACH CREATION.

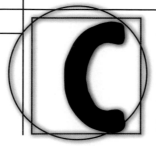

CENTRAL NEW YORK RESIDENTS ARE SERVED BY FOUR Syracuse-based acute care hospitals: Community General Hospital, Crouse Hospital, St. Joseph's Hospital Health Center, and University Hospital of the State University of New York (SUNY) Health Science Center at Syracuse.

During the past 20 years, through the Hospital Executive Council, the Syracuse Hospitals have worked together to develop ambulatory care programs, a new nursing home, programs to reduce acute care stays, and a combined laboratory program.

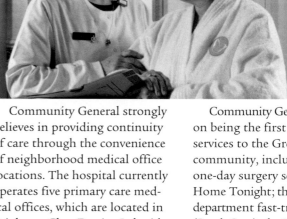

Community General Hospital

Located on Onondaga Hill, Community General Hospital is a 356-bed, acute care facility that has been offering health care services for more than 35 years. Accredited by the Joint Commission for the Accreditation of Healthcare Organizations, Community General Hospital continually updates its many services, which include emergency, medical, surgical, maternity, and intensive care, as well as rehabilitation and inpatient psychiatric care. In addition, the hospital provides numerous outpatient testing and community health education services.

Community General strongly believes in providing continuity of care through the convenience of neighborhood medical office locations. The hospital currently operates five primary care medical offices, which are located in Brighton, Clay, Dewitt, Lakeside, and Mattydale. The hospital also provides outpatient rehabilitation, including outpatient physical therapy, industrial rehabilitation, and certified hand therapy services.

Community General prides itself on being the first to provide many services to the Greater Syracuse community, including the first one-day surgery service, called Home Tonight; the first emergency department fast-track program (ReadyCare); the Wound Care Center, designed to treat nonhealing wounds; industrial rehabilitation; and the Comprehensive Women's Service, including the Wellspring Breast Care Center. Community General Hospital also operates an on-site, 50-bed skilled nursing unit.

Crouse Hospital

Crouse Hospital has been caring for generations of families for more than a century. The hospital has grown to provide a complete range of primary and specialty inpatient and outpatient services, as well as community health education programs.

Crouse is Central New York's largest provider of maternity care services—delivering more than 4,000 babies annually—and is the designated regional referral center for high-risk neonatal intensive care services. In mid-1999, the new, state-of-the-art Kienzle Family Maternity Center at Crouse Hospital is scheduled to open, providing expectant mothers and their families with the best of all worlds: compassionate, personalized care and

COMMUNITY GENERAL HOSPITAL'S WELLSPRING—A COMPREHENSIVE BREAST CARE TREATMENT CENTER—OFFERS ACCESS TO A FULL SPECTRUM OF BREAST CARE, INCLUDING SCREENING, DIAGNOSTIC, THERAPEUTIC, EDUCATIONAL, AND SUPPORT SERVICES, ALL UNDER ONE ROOF.

CROUSE HOSPITAL PROVIDES 24-HOUR URGENT CARE SERVICES THROUGH CROUSE PROMPTCARE.

the availability of the latest medical technology. Other areas of specialty include cardiac care, including the area's only pediatric cardiac catheterization lab; pediatrics; oncology; outpatient ambulatory surgery; 24-hour urgent care services through Crouse PromptCare; and Partnership for Health, an innovative, community-based approach to diabetes management offered in collaboration with Wegmans Food Markets.

Crouse nurtures partnerships with its physicians through the Crouse Physician Hospital Organization. With a firm belief that quality and caring go hand in hand, the organization and its physicians, nurses, and support staff work together to redefine the process of how care is delivered, putting in place patient-focused programs not only to maintain and enhance quality, but also to reduce the cost of providing care.

St. Joseph's Hospital Health Center

St. Joseph's Hospital Health Center is a 431-bed, not-for-profit, comprehensive medical facility offering a network of health care services, founded and operated by the Sisters of St. Francis. Specialty services include cardiac care, which encompasses catheterization, surgery, electrophysiology, and rehabilitation. In 1997, for the second consecutive year, St. Joseph's Hospital was cited by the New York State Department of Health for having the lowest risk-adjusted mortality rate among all 32 hospitals in the state that perform coronary artery bypass surgery.

Other services offered by St. Joseph's Hospital include orthopedic care; maternal/child health, including the Birth Place and a newly renovated Level III neonatal intensive care unit; pulmonary care and thoracic surgery; inpatient/outpatient mental health services, including the Comprehensive Psychiatric Emergency Program; primary care; hemodialysis; ambulatory surgery; emergency care, including Fast Track; sleep laboratory; and Syracuse's only hospital-based certified home health care agency.

St. Joseph's Hospital has satellite facilities in Syracuse's north-ern, eastern, and western suburbs. Services include outpatient surgery, dialysis, pain management, behavioral medicine, and family medicine. The hospital offers wellness programs, including the Worksite Wellness Program and the Wellness Place, which is located at the Great Northern Mall in Clay. A teaching hospital with medical residencies, St. Joseph's Hospital also has its own school of nursing that offers a two-year associate's degree.

University Hospital of the SUNY Health Science Center

University Hospital is situated on the campus of the SUNY Health Science Center (HSC), adjacent to Syracuse University, and is the teaching hospital for the HSC's College of Medicine. More than 700 medical students, 300 allied professionals, and 100 advanced-nursing students receive the majority of their training at this facility.

In addition to academic medicine, University Hospital offers a wide range of primary and specialized medical services through a variety of sites, including the University Health Care Center in downtown Syracuse and University Health Care Manlius. University Hospital includes a regional trauma center, burn center, AIDS care center, and poison control center, as well as the site of the Joslin Center for Diabetes, one of only 11 Joslin Centers nationwide.

University Hospital's emergency department is responsible for the coordination of all ambulance care in the Syracuse region. Additionally, the hospital is the site of the region's only dedicated pediatric emergency department. It is well known for its orthopedic surgery department and its Physical Medicine and Rehabilitation Center.

Tertiary care is offered through University Hospital's specialized inpatient services and state-of-the-art medical equipment. The hospital features a regional kidney and pancreas transplant center, a bone marrow transplant unit, an epilepsy center, adult and pediatric oncology services, and adult and pediatric open-heart surgery. University Hospital also operates a renal lithotripsy unit and is the only upstate New York site of a Leksell Gamma Knife, a radiosurgery device that enables neurosurgeons to treat brain tumors without open-skull surgery.

TOP: UNIVERSITY HOSPITAL IS SITUATED ON THE CAMPUS OF THE SUNY HEALTH SCIENCE CENTER (HSC), ADJACENT TO SYRACUSE UNIVERSITY, AND IS THE TEACHING HOSPITAL FOR THE HSC'S COLLEGE OF MEDICINE (INSET).

BOTTOM: FAMILY-CENTERED CARE IS THE HALLMARK OF THE BIRTH PLACE AT ST. JOSEPH'S HOSPITAL HEALTH CENTER. KIND AND ATTENTIVE NURSING CARE IS COUPLED WITH MODERN, SPACIOUS BIRTHING ROOMS AND NEWLY RENOVATED MATERNITY ROOMS.

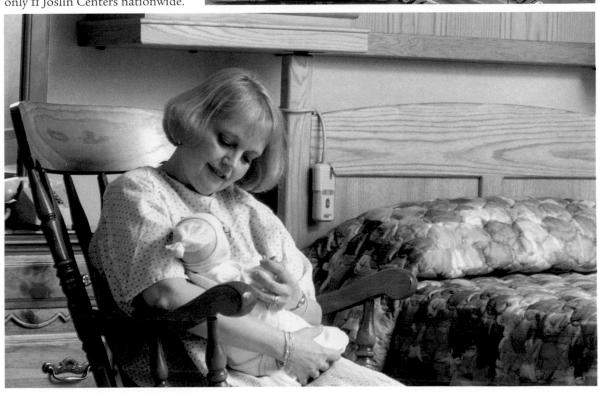

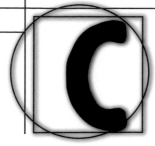

CHARTERED IN 1870 BY METHODIST EPISCOPAL ministers, Syracuse University (SU) began its long history of educational excellence with a class of 34 men, seven women, and one building, the Hall of Languages. Students followed a strict curriculum consisting of algebra, elocution, geometry, history, Greek, Latin, physiology, and rhetoric. In 1874, SU offered the nation's first bachelor of fine arts degree.

Today, SU is a major national research university, with 18,000 full- and part-time undergraduate and graduate students. Spread across a total of 963 acres, the university now maintains 266 buildings, several of which, like the Hall of Languages, have been declared state historical landmarks. SU's 13 schools and colleges offer more than 200 undergraduate majors in both liberal arts and professional studies, as well as numerous master's and doctoral degree programs.

Promoting Excellence

Syracuse University is striving to become the nation's leading student-centered research university by its efforts to promote learning through teaching, research, scholarship, creative accomplishment, and service. Along the way, the university has earned critical acclaim in the form of the 1996 Theodore M. Hesburgh Award for Faculty Development to Enhance Undergraduate Learning and several favorable critiques from *U.S. News &*

World Report, including number one rankings nationally for SU's graduate programs in public affairs and broadcast journalism.

SU has 807 full-time, 95 part-time, and 475 adjunct professors, and boasts a student-faculty ratio of 12 to one. Eighty-seven percent of the faculty hold doctorate or professional degrees. The student body is diverse, hailing from all 50 states and more than 90 countries. Students not only attend classes on campus, but also have the opportunity to study abroad at SU centers in England, France, Italy, Spain, Zimbabwe, and Hong Kong. Through the Internet, many students across the United States and in other countries are taking advantage of SU's innovative distance-learning programs.

Serving the Community

SU offers many community-oriented programs to students. The Soling Program brings together students from various disciplines to learn problem-solving skills while working as a team on various projects for organizations on campus and in the community. The Center for Public and Community Service coordinates the volunteer efforts of hundreds of

SU students at more than 400 public service organizations in the Syracuse area.

A vital part of the Central New York economy, SU is the third-largest employer in Onondaga County. In the 1996-1997 fiscal year, the university paid out more than $175 million in salaries and wages to its faculty, staff, and student employees. In that same period, SU paid more than $56 million in taxes and fees to city, state, and federal governments, and purchased more than $60 million in goods from businesses within the county. Several more million dollars poured into the local economy as the result of the March 1997 NCAA Eastern Regional Men's Basketball Tournament and other sporting events, and a handful of major concerts held at the Carrier Dome.

SU is also a centerpiece of culture, with several university-operated or -affiliated art galleries, diverse music offerings from the College of Visual and Performing Arts, theater performances from Syracuse Stage and the SU Drama Department, and music and information programming from two FM radio stations (WAER and WJPZ).

SYRACUSE UNIVERSITY'S STUDENT-CENTERED FOCUS, STELLAR FACULTY, STATE-OF-THE-ART TECHNOLOGICAL CAPABILITIES, AND HISTORIC, STATELY SETTING MAKE FOR AN IDEAL LEARNING ENVIRONMENT.

EW VENTURE GEAR, INC.'S NEW PROCESS GEAR Division, the world's largest single producer of four-wheel-drive transfer cases for the automotive industry, began in Syracuse as the New Process Rawhide Company in 1888. Originally builders of rawhide

boats and other products, the company found that its patented process for producing exceptionally hard and durable rawhide could be adapted to make gears.

These gears were employed in electric trolleys, and led to the organization's transition to the design and manufacture of metal gears for the burgeoning automotive industry in the early 1900s. No longer producing rawhide products, the company was renamed the New Process Gear Corporation (NPG) in 1912.

The Chrysler Connection

NPG was nursed through the depression by Chrysler Corporation founder Walter P. Chrysler, who acquired New Process Gear in 1934, and Anthony A. Henninger, who was president of NPG from the mid-1930s through the mid-1950s and who later became the mayor of Syracuse.

NPG became a division of the Chrysler Corporation in 1957 and remained so until 1987, when it was purchased by Acustar, Incorporated. In 1990, NPG combined with General Motors' Hydramatic Plant in Muncie, Indiana, forming New Venture Gear, Inc. (NVG)—the first joint venture between two of the Big Three auto manufacturers in the United States. Focused on the manufacture of four-wheel-drive transfer cases, compounders, and transaxles for front-wheel-drive manual transmissions, NVG is headquartered in Troy, Michigan.

Originally constructed in 1960, the NPG plant on New Venture Gear Drive in East Syracuse has undergone several additions and modernizations since that time. The facility boasts more than 1.5 million square feet of building space on 130 acres of land and employs 3,400 individuals. NPG's customers—which include Chrysler, General Motors, and Ford—represent 70 percent of the North American market share, and this figure grows each year. The company is also a global leader in drivetrain products and is currently looking at future expansion in the overseas market.

A Company Noted for Quality

NVG's high product quality has made it a Certified Supplier to the Chrysler Corporation. It has also been awarded Ford Q1 and GM Mark of Excellence designations. And quality improvements have reduced warranty conditions by more than 80 percent, earning NVG the drivetrain industry's first QS 9000 and ISO 9000 certifications from the International Organization for Standardization.

NVG takes a proactive approach to meeting the needs of its customers. According to Erwin Browne, labor relations supervisor at NVG, rapid growth of the company in recent years is attributed to the popularity of vehicles that employ its products: front-wheel-drive and four-wheel-drive cars, trucks, and sport utility vehicles. In anticipation of continued demand for new products, a $5.2 million design and development facility was erected in 1995. As a result, the company can design, test, and introduce new drivetrain products in record time. "We can't afford to wait for the auto industry to come to us," says Browne. "We lead them in new directions with our products."

ORIGINALLY CONSTRUCTED IN 1960, THE PLANT FOR NEW VENTURE GEAR, INC.'S NEW PROCESS GEAR DIVISION IS LOCATED ON NEW VENTURE GEAR DRIVE IN EAST SYRACUSE. THE FACILITY HAS MORE THAN 1.5 MILLION SQUARE FEET OF BUILDING SPACE ON 130 ACRES OF LAND AND EMPLOYS 3,400 INDIVIDUALS.

PHOTOS BY FINE-MANLIUS, NY

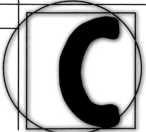

RUCIBLE HAS BEEN MAKING SPECIALTY STEEL IN Syracuse continuously since 1876. Known today as Crucible Materials Corporation, the company is a cornerstone of the local industrial community. Founded on a tradition of metallurgical expertise and tech-

KLINEBERG INC.

nological innovation, the corporation has been granted more than 1,000 patents throughout its history. With a reputation for the highest-quality products, Crucible has maintained its position as a market leader, even in today's competitive business climate.

As one of the largest private revenue generators in Central New York, Crucible pours $56 million into the area each year in the form of salaries, wages, and benefits, as well as $41 million in local goods and services. Employee owned since 1985, Crucible Materials Corporation consists of five U.S.-based divisions and one wholly owned U.K. subsidiary.

The Syracuse area is home to Crucible's corporate headquarters, as well as two of its divisions: Crucible Specialty Metals Division, a specialty steel mill, located in Geddes, and Crucible Service Centers Division, a steel sales and distribution company headquartered in Camillus, with a network of 27 warehouses throughout North America. The corporation's three other domestic companies are Crucible Compaction Metals Division, a powder metallurgy production facility in Oakdale, Pennsylvania; Crucible Research Center, located in Pittsburgh; and Trent Tube Division, a manufacturer of specialty pipe and tubing, head-

quartered in East Troy, Wisconsin, with additional facilities in Carrollton, Georgia, and Chicago. Crusteel, Ltd., based in Sheffield, England, distributes Crucible products throughout the United Kingdom and continental Europe.

Sheffield Origins

Crucible's roots can be traced to 1776, when Naylor and Sanderson Steel Mill was established in Sheffield, England, to produce fine-quality tool steel using the crucible method. During the 1800s, the company—then known as Sanderson Brothers—exported increasing quantities of tool steel to America, and decided to establish a steelmaking plant in Syracuse because of the city's proximity to major U.S. transportation lines, including the Erie Canal and the New York Central Railroad. In 1876, Sanderson purchased Sweet Iron Works and established Sanderson Brothers Steel Company.

The Crucible Method of Steelmaking

In 1883, Sanderson Brothers Steel Company built a new gas-fired crucible melting furnace. This high-temperature furnace

held up to 30 graphite pots, called crucibles, each charged with 60 to 100 pounds of iron plus selected alloy additions. Once the metal charge became molten at 3,000°F, each crucible was then lifted from the furnace with long-handled tongs, and the liquid steel was poured, or "teemed," into individual ingot molds. The crucible method, though labor intensive, produced the highest-quality tool steels available at the time.

Working in the melt shop was tough, hot work. The pourer, or "teemer," often wrapped his legs in wool and burlap and thoroughly soaked them with cold water as protection from the intense heat. A representation of the teemer, which was used as Crucible's company logo for many years, is still used by the Specialty Metals Division, and the *Teemer* is the title of its quarterly newsletter.

Merging into the 20th Century

As the United States entered the 20th century, the demand for special-purpose tool steels increased rapidly. Although the crucible process ensured high quality, its output was relatively low compared to other steelmaking methods of the day. To meet increased

demand, 13 steelmaking firms using the crucible method—including Sanderson Brothers—merged in 1900 to form the Crucible Steel Company of America. By joining forces, these companies could more efficiently use their skilled craftsmen and specialized facilities to produce a wider range of high-quality products.

C.H. Halcomb Jr. became the first president and general manager of the new corporation, but he resigned two years later and established his own Halcomb Steel mill in Geddes. In 1911, Crucible acquired Halcomb Steel and combined it with a new Sanderson plant, which was erected adjacent to the Halcomb plant. The Sanderson-Halcomb Works became today's Crucible Specialty Metals Division, the entrance of which still bears the inscription Halcomb Steel Company in stone.

Pioneering Research and Technology

At the technological forefront throughout its history, Crucible can lay claim to many metallurgical firsts. In 1906, the first electric-arc melting furnace in the United States was installed at the Halcomb plant. This "Old No. 1" Heroult electric-arc furnace now stands as a designated ASM (American Society for Materials) historical monument at Station Square in Pittsburgh.

Crucible Rex AA steel, patented in 1907, was the first tool steel to include vanadium, and it is still recognized today as a standard high-speed steel. In fact, Crucible owns more than 70 percent of all patents issued in the entire history of tool steel production, in addition to numerous patents for stainless steels, automotive valve steels, titanium alloys, superalloys, and even rare-earth magnetic materials. Crucible was the first company to commercially produce vacuum-arc remelted steels; the first to develop P/M (powder metallurgy) tool steels, produced by the patented CPM (Crucible Particle Metallurgy) process; and the first to develop and patent a titanium gas atomizer.

With a corporate focus on metals technology and customer service, Crucible continues its tradition of developing new materials to withstand the most demanding applications.

Consolidation and Incorporation

To improve efficiency in production, Crucible's Syracuse plants were consolidated in 1947 to form the Sanderson-Halcomb Works, which was renamed Syracuse Works of Crucible Steel in 1966. Colt Industries bought Crucible Steel Corporation of America in 1968, and the Syracuse Works became Colt's Crucible Specialty Metals Division. In 1983, Colt Industries consolidated its basic materials group as Crucible Materials Corporation, headquartered in New York City. In 1985, Crucible's salaried employees purchased all of the corporation's stock through a leveraged buyout and relocated Crucible Materials Corporation's headquarters to Syracuse. As owners of the company, Crucible's employees all have a direct stake in the ongoing success of the corporation. Profit-sharing programs at every level enable Crucible to attract and retain some of the finest, most motivated people in the industry.

Good Neighbors

Approximately 850 of the corporation's 1,700 employees live and work in Central New York. Crucible is a major contributor to the United Way, and was recognized in 1998 by the United Way of Central New York as having made the highest per capita donations of any industrial business in the area. Additionally, Crucible supports WCNY public radio and television, Syracuse Symphony, and the Rescue Mission, and actively participates in Junior Achievement, the Boy Scouts, and various high school career opportunity programs. Throughout all divisions of the corporation, Crucible employees can always be found willingly donating their time and efforts to assist the Central New York area.

The Future

Crucible Materials Corporation CEO John Vensel believes the company's future lies in its advanced P/M alloys and in its service centers. "In 10 years, we will be known more for our innovative CPM alloys and our growing customer-service capability than for our conventional steel production." According to Dave Yates, member of the board of directors and president of both Crucible Specialty Metals and Crucible Compaction Metals divisions, "Just about everyone in the Syracuse area knows someone who works or has worked at Crucible. We all take pride in the impressive heritage of our company, and we feel a civic responsibility to the Syracuse community, which we call home."

THE MAIN OFFICE BUILDING AT CRUCIBLE SPECIALTY METALS DIVISION BEARS THE INSCRIPTION "HALCOMB STEEL COMPANY," REFLECTING ITS HISTORIC ORIGINS.

▶ KLINEBERG INC.

KNOWN AS THE TOOL STEEL PROS®, CRUCIBLE SERVICE Centers Division is the market leader for sales and service of tool steel in North America. From its divisional headquarters on West Genesee Street in Camillus, Crucible Service Centers operates a distribution network of 27

KLINEBERG INC.

steel service centers, strategically located in major metalworking areas. Dedicated to customer service, each of its warehouses carries a wide selection of steel stock designed to service the cutting tool, injection mold, die casting, and metal forming markets. Taking a proactive approach to individual market needs, Crucible offers leading-edge technology, along with tailored inventories and value-added processing. With an extensive sales force, staff metallurgists, in-house Management Information System (MIS) expertise, and skilled warehouse employees; comprehensive steel processing capabilities; a trucking fleet; and the technological support of Crucible Specialty Metals, Crucible Research, and Crucible Compaction Metals, it's no wonder this young company is a success.

Spun off from the Specialty Metals Division in 1989, Crucible Service Centers was designed to be a customer-responsive, independent sales organization servicing the tool steel market. Since its inception, the division has grown from 300 to 400 employees and from 14 district locations to 27, including service centers in Canada and

HEADQUARTERED ON WEST GENESEE STREET IN CAMILLUS, CRUCIBLE SERVICE CENTERS PROVIDES A WIDE VARIETY OF TOOL STEELS IN THE EXACT SIZE, SHAPE, AND FINISH REQUESTED BY THE CUSTOMER.

SPUN OFF FROM THE CRUCIBLE SPECIALTY METALS DIVISION IN 1989, CRUCIBLE SERVICE CENTERS OPERATES A DISTRIBUTION NETWORK OF 27 STEEL SERVICE CENTERS, STRATEGICALLY LOCATED IN MAJOR NORTH AMERICAN METALWORKING AREAS.

Mexico. Crucible Service Centers has become the global market leader in sales of high-performance tool steels, with worldwide sales of its CPM (Crucible Particle Metallurgy) products carried out through international partners.

A decentralized organization, each service center is run by a local district manager with the particular selection of tool steels and value-added services determined by the needs of the local industry. Initially handling only the steel products manufactured by Crucible, the service centers soon began to broaden the scope of their inventories in order to offer one-stop shopping to their tool steel customers. By relying on its corporate background in steelmaking and maintaining the corporation's unrelenting commitment to quality, Crucible Service Centers strives to ensure that all steel products are carefully selected and meet stringent specifications. As a testament to these efforts, Crucible Service Centers received its first ISO 9002 certification in 1997 for its Cleveland warehouse and Camillus headquarters operations. Programs and audits are under way for the certification of the other locations.

With 45 of its 400 employees living and working in the Syracuse area, the heart of the company is

certainly located in Central New York. In fact, many of the employees in the regional service centers began their careers in Syracuse. Technical sales training seminars and management meetings frequently bring groups of Crucible Service Centers employees to the area. In addition, customers, suppliers, and trading partners from all over the world are regular visitors to the Camillus headquarters.

Harry O'Brien, president of Crucible Service Centers, comments, "Our focus today is on maintaining outstanding customer service in order to grow our market share. Currently, we have a particular emphasis on the global sales and marketing of our CPM products. People buy from Crucible because of our customer service, our reputation for quality, and our technical expertise. We offer the broadest selection of tool steels available, but also work with customers to develop new, innovative, problem-solving materials for special applications. With the help of Crucible Specialty Metals, Crucible Research, and Crucible Compaction Metals, we offer our customers unparalleled technical support, and can provide truly comprehensive customer service. That is what really sets us apart from the competition."

EVERY DAY, THE STEELWORKERS AT THE CRUCIBLE Specialty Metals Division turn raw materials into the most sophisticated engineered steels known to man. The specialty steel mill, located on State Fair Boulevard in Geddes, produces a wide variety of steels found in applications ranging

from aerospace to subterranean wells. Crucible's products are high-value, high-performance alloys, sold by the pound rather than by the ton. A world leader in the production of automotive valve steels, Crucible Specialty Metals is a certified supplier to the demanding automotive market. Not only does the company's steel meet the most stringent specifications, but its documented quality systems, process control methods, and cost-effective manufacturing processes also surpass critical customer requirements.

The mill covers more than 60 acres and comprises 20 different departments. Modern melting facilities include a unique induction-melt gas atomizer with a HIP (hot isostatic pressing) vessel for the production of the patented, high-performance CPM (Crucible Particle Metallurgy) steels, as well as a 40-ton, electric-arc furnace with an AOD (argon oxygen decarburization) refining vessel. Hot finishing mills include a 2,000-ton forge press, a 26-inch cogging mill, an automated rod-and-bar mill, and special-purpose hand-rolling mills. Heat-treating and annealing facilities, as well as a comprehensive bar-finishing department, enable shipment of a wide variety of products.

The premier products of the Specialty Metals Division are high-performance CPM tool steels. Developed in collaboration with Crucible Research Center, the CPM process involves gas atomization of prealloyed molten steel to form powder. The powder is consolidated through the HIP process into 100 percent dense compacts, which are processed through the mill alongside conventional ingot product. The resultant properties of the CPM bars are far superior to conventionally melted steels. In most applica-

tions, CPM tool steels offer improved wear resistance, toughness, and grindability. Moreover, the CPM process enables the production of alloys with unique or enhanced properties that cannot be made by conventional steelmaking methods.

As a long-standing corporate citizen, Crucible strives to improve air and water quality for its Syracuse neighbors. Millions of dollars have been spent and more than 100,000 man-hours have been devoted to controlling air and water pollution. Each day, Crucible's own wastewater treatment plant purifies about 3 million gallons of process cooling water recycled from the various rolling mills and furnaces. The melting facilities and grinding facilities are equipped with air pollution control systems, and in 1997, a computer-controlled shot blaster was added to Crucible's state-of-the-art conditioning department, replacing all caustic pickling. In keeping with today's environmental emphasis on conversion and recycling, as opposed to disposal, many of the mill's solid metal wastes and collected grinding dusts are kept carefully segregated and are remelted in subsequent heats of steel. Other particulate wastes are commercially recycled to retrieve alloy, which is then reused. Even the slag is recycled to recover the metal content, and the remaining product is crushed and used as a substrate for road beds and parking lots.

In addition to its technological and environmental accomplishments, Crucible Specialty Metals Division is proud of its safety record. Crucible received the 1998 Donald G. Schell Award for Excellence in Occupational Safety and Health from the Safety Council of Central New York. Safety is serious business at Crucible

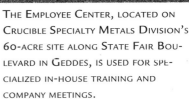

Specialty Metals Division, and of 650 union members, 67 are safety leaders and two are safety chairmen. Crucible's 15-member management-union Safety Action Steering Committee includes the company's executive vice president.

A steel mill, by its nature, is a tough and potentially hazardous place to work. With the broadest product line of all specialty steel companies, the daily work at Crucible is far from routine. Many generations of Central New York families have proudly sent sons and daughters through Crucible's gates, which proclaim, "Through these doors pass the best steelmakers in the world."

THE EMPLOYEE CENTER, LOCATED ON CRUCIBLE SPECIALTY METALS DIVISION'S 60-ACRE SITE ALONG STATE FAIR BOULEVARD IN GEDDES, IS USED FOR SPECIALIZED IN-HOUSE TRAINING AND COMPANY MEETINGS.

IN THE MODERN, EFFICIENT MELT SHOP AT CRUCIBLE SPECIALTY METALS DIVISION, THE MOLTEN STEEL IS TEEMED FROM THE 40-TON LADLE INTO A REFRACTORY RUNNER SYSTEM, WHICH FILLS SEVERAL INGOT MOLDS SIMULTANEOUSLY FROM THE BOTTOM, ENSURING GOOD SURFACE QUALITY.

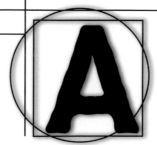

A

S YOU MIGHT EXPECT OF AN ORGANIZATION THAT supplies and supports some of today's most advanced computer, manufacturing, and construction technology, Panthus Corporation is in many ways a new company. Yet, the firm that was known as Syracuse Supply has been

a cornerstone of the Syracuse business community since 1884. Today, the organization that was once exclusively a local supplier provides a variety of equipment and technology-based services to clients across the nation and internationally through an integrated network of companies.

Panthus' Equipment Distribution group consists of Syracuse Supply Construction Equipment (SSCE), which serves customers in New York State; 2SQ (2S for Syracuse Supply, Q for quality), which serves machine tool customers throughout New York and into Pennsylvania; and Syracuse Supply Leasing, which provides leasing options to customers of both organizations. SSCE distributes and repairs a variety of construction and contracting equipment lines, primarily Caterpillar, while 2SQ supplies machine tools, parts, accessories, and engineering services for the most advanced manufacturing technologies.

Panthus' Technology Services companies—New York Systems

Exchange, New Creative Systems, Universal Computer Leasing, and Lighthouse Capital—lease computers, perform system upgrades, and remarket equipment to domestic and international clients. Panthus computer system clients include major national and multinational corporations.

"Because we aren't tied to any one brand of computer equipment, we can be more objective and flexible in recommending the best solutions to meet a client's needs," notes Panthus President Stephen J. Suhowatsky.

In sum, the Panthus companies comprise what Suhowatsky describes as the Panthus Galaxy—a group of organizations that, though diverse, thrive on the same management principles, draw on the same human resources, and leverage corporation synergies to gain competitive advantage.

A History of Changing with the Market

The roots of Panthus Corporation can be traced to the development of precision manufacturing in Central New York during the late 19th century. Company founder Fred Scott saw that the region's growing technological sophistication would support a company

supplying the best tools and materials required by growing industries. Scott named his company Syracuse Supply (SYSU). Soon, its customer base included leading manufacturers of typewriters, fine china, and luxury automobiles. SYSU was also serving the needs of regional contractors. Sales grew steadily until 1930, when the Great Depression resulted in a loss of 60 percent of the company's revenue.

SYSU bounced back by responding to the needs of the federal government's massive road-building program of the 1930s. The company became a major distributor for several large-equipment manufacturers, including the Caterpillar Tractor Company. By the late 1930s, Syracuse Supply was once again prosperous, and it continued to grow during World War II. Through the 1950s and 1960s, company management emphasized an increased range of customer services, as SYSU guided expansion through much of New York State and into Pennsylvania, Vermont, and Minnesota.

Modern Times

When Suhowatsky became SYSU president in 1983, he found that inventory turnover was slowing and sales were declining—problems inflation had masked.

PANTHUS CORPORATION'S RESPONSE TO JOB SITE NEEDS IS CRITICAL TO CUSTOMERS' SUCCESS.

THE PANTHUS GALAXY IS A COLLECTION OF AUTONOMOUS BUSINESS UNITS (STAR CLUSTERS) WHERE NEW BUSINESSES ARE BORN AND EMERGE IN RESPONSE TO CHANGES IN THE MARKETPLACE, AND EXISTING BUSINESSES (STARS) GROW AND MERGE INTO BIGGER BUSINESSES (STAR CLUSTERS).

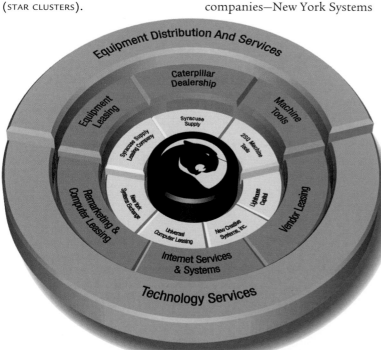

He acted quickly to strengthen the company's understanding of its markets and to get it out of businesses that weren't performing satisfactorily.

In the mid-1980s, Suhowatsky led the acquisitions of New York Systems Exchange (NYSE) and Primacare Health Resources, bringing Syracuse Supply into two new business areas. NYSE had an established presence in mainframe and peripheral computer equipment leasing to Fortune 200 companies, and Primacare was a major regional home health care company in 13 states, providing respiratory and infusion therapy and available medical equipment. The strength of these businesses helped offset the cyclical nature of the other Syracuse Supply business areas.

Suhowatsky decentralized SYSU management, empowering employees as the company divided into separate business units in a program named the New Spirit Campaign. Suhowatsky says giving employees stock in the company tied to company performance and making employees more directly responsible for company operation paved the way for diversified growth and expansion.

In 1990, after defending against two takeover attempts, the company was taken private by a management team headed by 20-year New York State Senator and Board Member H. Douglas Barclay and Suhowatsky. "Our employees and our future were both major beneficiaries," Suhowatsky notes.

In 1995, it became evident that continued success in home health care would require Syracuse Supply to become a national player—something that would require

massive investment. Management chose instead to sell the business and use the capital to purchase Universal Computer Leasing (UCL), one of Germany's five largest independent computer leasing companies for mainframe systems. This acquisition was SYSU's entry into the international market, bringing the company the advantage of an international exchange of best practices.

Also in 1995, Syracuse Supply founded New Creative Systems, Inc., to test, certify, reconfigure, and resell/release pre-owned computer equipment. Headquartered in Texas, the new company serves customers across the nation. SYSU also established Lighthouse Capital, Inc., in Syracuse to lease personal computers and telephone equipment to small businesses. Lighthouse goes to market through a nationwide network of vendors.

In 1998, in reflection of the greatly broadened nature of its integrated businesses, the company chose a new name, Panthus Corporation. "It's a name that suggests strength and agility: attributes essential to success in today's competitive environment," says Suhowatsky.

Today, Panthus is continuing its rapid evolution. In addition to expanding its equipment distribution and technology service businesses, it has opened a new business, Panther Rentals, to rent construction equipment to small contractors. In response to trends in computer needs, Panthus' leasing services are adding client/servers and services aimed to assist clients in developing their own communication networks and systems.

As Syracuse Supply, the company has been listed regularly among the Syracuse Chamber of Commerce's top 100 companies. Suhowatsky says that, thanks to the quality of the company's employees, he expects Panthus will be a strong presence in the Syracuse 100 for years to come.

"We attract the best employees because we offer opportunities to grow with the company as well as incentives to top performers. I consider our people our intellectual capital. We'll do everything possible to see that they are better trained, more innovative, and more skilled, all of which gives a competitive advantage. When markets change, we respond by challenging and reinvesting in our people, says Suhowatsky.

Continuing and building on a tradition of success that goes back well over a century, Panthus promises to continue a rich and unique Syracuse success story well into the next century.

CLOCKWISE FROM TOP LEFT: 2SQ MACHINE TOOLS OFFER CUSTOMER PRODUCTIVITY AND QUALITY ENHANCEMENTS WITH STATE-OF-THE-ART EQUIPMENT AND SERVICE.

THE COMPUTER-TESTING FACILITY AT NEW CREATIVE SYSTEMS, INC. IS LOCATED IN HOUSTON.

THREE OUT OF FOUR EMPLOYEES AT SYRACUSE SUPPLY ARE INVOLVED IN CUSTOMER SERVICE.

PANTHER RENTALS SERVICES A BROAD RANGE OF CUSTOMERS WITH SHORT-TERM EQUIPMENT RENTALS.

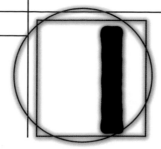

N 1889, THEODORE E. HANCOCK ORGANIZED THE firm of Hancock, Beach, Peck, and Devine in Syracuse with offices in the White Memorial Building. In doing so, he laid the groundwork for the law firm known more than 100 years later as Hancock & Estabrook, LLP.

Yesterday

The history of today's Hancock & Estabrook law firm is tied inextricably to the lives of the Hancocks: Theodore E. Hancock; his son Stewart F. Hancock, who succeeded him and guided the law firm into the modern age; and Stewart F. Hancock Jr., who rejoined the firm recently after a distinguished career serving on New York State's highest tribunal, the Court of Appeals. The Hancock name is similarly interwoven into the fabric of the Syracuse community and its history and development.

Whether in private industry, public service, or the arts, the Hancock & Estabrook law firm has played and continues to play a major role in Central New York. From the moment Syracuse visitors arrive at Hancock International Airport—named after Clarence E. Hancock, the

founder's son and a former partner—the impact of the firm's founding family is readily apparent.

Today

Hancock & Estabrook currently employs 70 lawyers, 14 paralegals, and 80 support personnel. The firm occupies three floors of MONY (Mutual of New York) Tower I, one of the major landmarks in the heart of downtown Syracuse.

In addition, the firm stays in touch with the seat of state government through its satellite office in Albany.

Since its founding, Hancock & Estabrook has been Central New York's leader in the area of corporate law. The firm's clients range from corporations traded on national stock exchanges to small local businesses, from emerging companies to long-standing enterprises. Hancock & Estabrook's reputation for excellence in handling complex mergers and acquisitions, financing transactions, and business continuity planning is unsurpassed. This reputation is undoubtedly complemented and enhanced by the firm's unrivaled expertise in sophisticated business and individual tax planning and advice. Hancock & Estabrook is often retained to assist other significant law firms in the role of special tax counsel.

CLOCKWISE FROM TOP:
STEWART F. HANCOCK SR. FOUNDED THE MODERN-DAY FIRM OF HANCOCK & ESTABROOK, LLP.

JOHN L. MURAD JR., ESQ., IS CHAIR OF THE FIRM'S LITIGATION DEPARTMENT.

RICHARD W. COOK, ESQ., SERVES AS CHAIR OF THE BUSINESS DEPARTMENT.

Hancock & Estabrook is the only Central New York general practice law firm with a full-service in-house intellectual property practice. The firm has the ability to assist clients with patent prosecution, copyright and trademark registration, and all forms of licensing arrangements. In addition, the firm's patent attorneys are supported by several federal court trial lawyers experienced in defending and enforcing all forms of intellectual property rights.

The trial and appellate department of Hancock & Estabrook is recognized and highly respected throughout the Northeast. With an emphasis on contract and commercial litigation, product liability, medical malpractice defense, and personal injury litigation, the firm has developed a deep stable of bright, aggressive litigators. These trial attorneys are supported by a talented appellate group comprised of former judicial clerks. This unique group offers extensive experience in appellate procedure, brief writing, and oral advocacy leading to an extraordinary rate of success on appeals.

Hancock & Estabrook's environmental attorneys have a well-deserved reputation for success and expertise in representing clients in all civil and criminal environmental matters, including hazardous

waste spills, air and water pollution, OSHA compliance, environmental impact reviews, and toxic torts. The firm also offers an extremely broad-based and active labor and employment practice; expertise in health-care-related issues for physicians, hospitals, and nursing homes; estate and financial planning expertise in the preparation and administration of wills, trusts,

and foundations; real estate services that include handling complex commercial matters, zoning, eminent domain, foreclosures, real property tax assessment matters, and all varieties of conveyances; and extensive experience and expertise in representing creditors and debtors in bankruptcy matters.

Tomorrow

Hancock & Estabrook will enter the next millennium with an energetic and aggressive pool of attorneys committed to following its founding philosophy: to provide quality legal services in a timely and cost-effective manner. The firm's continued growth despite difficult economic times in Central New York can be attributed to youthful competitiveness and a proactive approach to client service. "We listen carefully to each client's unique circumstances and then we deliver responsive service," says Donald A. Denton, the firm's managing partner. Hancock & Estabrook's strategic plan calls for continued growth, excellence of service, and commitment to clients and community. The firm's strategic plan reflects a philosophy that has served Hancock & Estabrook for more than 100 years and will guide it well into the next century.

DOREEN A. SIMMONS, ESQ., IS CHAIR OF HANCOCK & ESTABROOK'S ENVIRONMENTAL DEPARTMENT.

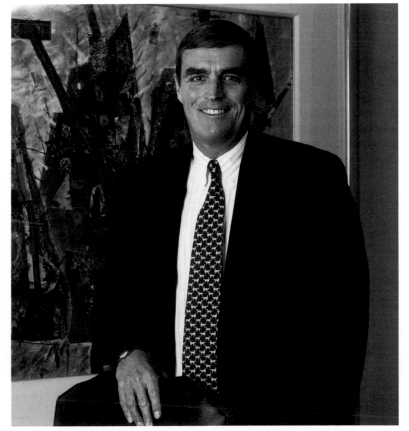

"WE LISTEN CAREFULLY TO EACH CLIENT'S UNIQUE CIRCUMSTANCES AND THEN WE DELIVER RESPONSIVE SERVICE," SAYS DONALD A. DENTON, THE FIRM'S MANAGING PARTNER.

SYROCO, INC.

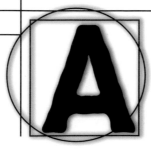

ARMED WITH A NEW, STRATEGIC FOCUS RESULTING from its new Initiative 2000, Syroco, Inc. plans to dramatically enhance its market leadership position on both its Home Décor and Outdoor Resin Casual Furniture businesses. "Given the new Syroco Initiative

2000," John Fravel, president and CEO, says, "the senior management team is focusing on new product development and putting new technology in place as we move into the new millennium."

Founded in 1890 as Syracuse Ornamental Company by Adolph Holstein, a European immigrant and master wood-carver, Syroco, Inc. is now owned by Marley, plc of England. Syroco has grown over the past 108 years through innovative adaptation to changing markets and dedication to its customers. Employing an average of 800 people, Syroco is the nation's largest producer of outdoor resin furniture and wall decor items, such as ornately framed mirrors and clocks.

The Early Years

Holstein, in his East Water Street shop in Syracuse, produced exquisitely handcrafted carvings for many of the fashionable homes and institutions in New York State, including the Governor's Mansion in Albany. By the early 1900s, Syracuse Ornamental Com-

▼ PHOTOS BY FINE-MANLIUS, NY

pany developed a compression molding technique using Syroco Wood—a mixture of wood flour and resins—to produce almost perfect replicas of the original carvings. As the furniture industry caught wind of this new and inexpensive process, demand increased steadily until the Great Depression. Although Syracuse Ornamental Company suffered somewhat during this era, the company survived because its processes were useful to a growing, new market: radio manufacturing. Syracuse Ornamental produced ornate speaker grills and tuning knobs for companies like RCA, Atwater Kent, Emerson, and Philco.

During the 1930s, the company began producing decorative novelty items—such as ashtrays, pipe

racks, and bottle openers—that soon became its main focus of production throughout the 1940s. New proprietary products were developed in the early 1950s, as the company began to produce decorative wall accessories, such as mirrors, sconces, and wall clocks.

In 1958, the company moved to its present site in the nearby village of Baldwinsville, and the company name was changed to Syroco. When its production facilities were moved to this location in 1960, Syroco began shifting from compression molding to injection molding, a process that produced a more stable and cost-effective product. Today, the company's two primary product lines are Home Décor and Outdoor Resin Casual Furniture.

CLOCKWISE FROM TOP:
EMPLOYING AN AVERAGE OF 800 PEOPLE, SYROCO IS THE NATION'S LARGEST PRODUCER OF OUTDOOR RESIN FURNITURE AND WALL DECOR ITEMS, SUCH AS ORNATELY FRAMED MIRRORS AND CLOCKS.

AGGRESSIVE SALES AND MARKETING, AND IMPROVED LOGISTICS ALLOW SYROCO TO CONTINUE GROWING AND EXPANDING ITS CUSTOMER BASE.

AT SYROCO, A RICH TRADITION CONTINUES TO FIND EXPRESSION IN A MODERN, 500,000-SQUARE-FOOT MANUFACTURING FACILITY, WHERE HANDCRAFTED EXCELLENCE MERGES WITH STATE-OF-THE-ART MOLDING AND FINISHING TECHNOLOGIES.

Syroco Home Décor

Home Décor products reflect innovation, creativity, and value. A rich tradition continues to find expression in a modern, 500,000-square-foot manufacturing facility, where handcrafted excellence merges with state-of-the-art molding and finishing technologies. In addition to a 200,000-square-foot warehousing and shipping area, the facilities contain a full tool and die shop, complete engineering department, and fabrication and product assembly areas.

Syroco products differentiate themselves in a variety of important ways. Each new product project begins with extensive market research, which allows the company to anticipate and react to market opportunities. Designs are initially brought to life by extremely talented wood-carvers, representing a rich heritage from Italy, Germany, Poland, and the United States. "Computers can't emulate what the master carver brings to the operation," says Frank D'Eramo, senior vice president of eastern operations at Syroco. "Our wall decor items offer the beauty of old-world craftsmanship at a price anyone can afford."

The company's ability to express intricate detail and fine nuance truly sets its products apart. Special techniques allow the creation of molds that retain the integrity and emotion of each unique wood carving.

Final finishing is done by a dedicated team of experts utilizing a variety of superior techniques, which include painting, staining, glazing, crackle veiling, and processing to simulate bright or antique gold finishes.

Syroco Outdoor Furniture

By leveraging its unique product design capabilities and its plastic injection-molding technology, Syroco created a second major business in the 1980s: Outdoor Resin Casual Furniture. Offering a full range of casual seating, dining, and lounging products, Syroco thrust itself into industry leadership in the 1990s.

The company markets its products nationally to such major retailers as Wal-Mart, Kmart, Target, Service Merchandise, Home Depot, Lowe's, and Sam's Club, as well as numerous regional discount, supermarket, and drugstore chains. New focus is being placed on growing the Canadian and international markets, as well as the commercial/contract market, in which hotel and restaurant chains constantly repurchase outdoor seating, dining, and lounging products.

Aggressive sales and marketing, and improved logistics allow Syroco to continue growing and expanding its business base. The company's additional regional manufacturing and warehousing in Northwest Arkansas and Southern California has improved order processing and has allowed Syroco to exceed customer expectations for service.

The continuous flow of new products, merchandising elements, and new programs has positioned the company as the leading marketer of outdoor resin casual furniture—a position which Syroco plans to maintain as it goes forth into the new millennium.

CLOCKWISE FROM TOP:
SPECIAL TECHNIQUES ALLOW THE CREATION OF MOLDS THAT RETAIN THE INTEGRITY AND EMOTION OF EACH UNIQUE WOOD CARVING.

BY LEVERAGING ITS UNIQUE PRODUCT DESIGN CAPABILITIES AND ITS PLASTIC INJECTION-MOLDING TECHNOLOGY, SYROCO CREATED OUTDOOR RESIN CASUAL FURNITURE IN THE 1980S, WHICH OFFERS A FULL RANGE OF CASUAL SEATING, DINING, AND LOUNGING PRODUCTS.

SYROCO'S ABILITY TO EXPRESS INTRICATE DETAIL AND FINE NUANCE TRULY SETS ITS PRODUCTS APART.

KNOWN FOR THE FINANCIAL STABILITY OF ITS international parent, the Syracuse offices of Royal & SunAlliance (RSA)—formerly Royal Insurance—have provided individual and commercial clients with reliable protection for more than 100 years. Through its

worldwide network of offices, the London-based company serves customers in 120 countries and works through independent agents and brokers throughout the United States. Although headquartered in North Carolina, the U.S. operation of RSA regards New York as its flagship state because of the critical mass and the outstanding performance of its network of offices.

RSA opened its Syracuse business in 1895. Initially housed in the 25,000-square-foot Kemper Building on Salina Street, the company moved to 716 James Street in 1955 and to its present, 50,000-square-foot 1045 James Street office in 1973. The company added a commercial lines branch at Division Street during 1993, and together, the two facilities employ more than 300 people.

Personal and Commercial Lines

The James Street facility serves as RSA's personal lines center, providing centralized underwriting and processing for all RSA clients in the United States. In addition, the company markets a variety of personal lines products, including home owners', automo-

bile, VIP personal umbrella, and boat insurance. Assigned risk business is handled from a satellite office in South Dakota.

As one of 30 branches nationwide, the commercial lines division offers general liability, auto, property, workers' compensation, and umbrella products. Additionally, the office processes claims and provides risk management, loss prevention, and other support services to retail, service, manufacturing, and contracting businesses in Central New York, the Southern Tier, and as far east as Albany.

A Great Place to Work

RSA operates on the belief that a successful business must be a good employer. To achieve top employee performance, the company offers competitive pay, profit sharing, clearly stated expectations, fair and honest treatment, and performance feedback. RSA's concern for the quality of life of each employee is shown by its family-related programs, flexible hours, holiday parties, and celebrations when employees achieve

their goals. The company's involvement with the American Red Cross, American Heart Association, local charities, and educational institutions testifies to its outstanding corporate citizenship. RSA employees also participate in local charitable activities.

As a global company, RSA has achieved financial stability by its diversity of risk exposure—made even greater by the recent merger of Royal Insurance and the 200-year-old SunAlliance. "A hurricane in Florida won't wipe us out because we have so many clients in other regions of the world," says Commercial Lines Branch General Manager and Resident Vice President Dave Macintosh.

According to RSA Personal Lines Field Executive John Gruninger, an insurance company's reputation depends on how fairly, promptly, and equitably it handles claims. "This is the moment of truth," says Gruninger. "We compete with many good companies for an agent's business, and our well-documented claims performance has won the trust of the most reputable agents in Central New York."

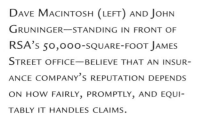

DAVE MACINTOSH (LEFT) AND JOHN GRUNINGER—STANDING IN FRONT OF RSA'S 50,000-SQUARE-FOOT JAMES STREET OFFICE—BELIEVE THAT AN INSURANCE COMPANY'S REPUTATION DEPENDS ON HOW FAIRLY, PROMPTLY, AND EQUITABLY IT HANDLES CLAIMS.

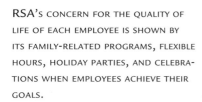

RSA'S CONCERN FOR THE QUALITY OF LIFE OF EACH EMPLOYEE IS SHOWN BY ITS FAMILY-RELATED PROGRAMS, FLEXIBLE HOURS, HOLIDAY PARTIES, AND CELEBRATIONS WHEN EMPLOYEES ACHIEVE THEIR GOALS.

DAVE FEILING PHOTOGRAPHY

HEADQUARTERED IN SYRACUSE, JAQUITH INDUSTRIES manufactures a variety of specialized, useful, high-quality metal products for the airport lighting, construction, and commercial laundry industries. Jaquith Industries enjoys worldwide recognition for its innovative Vega®

Airport Equipment, which includes in-ground light bases, junction boxes, and transformer housings; aluminum and fiberglass frangible approach lighting masts; and other vital illumination and monitoring equipment support components. Installed at all major U.S. civilian and military airports, as well as airports around the world, Vega® Airport Equipment products are manufactured to Federal Aviation Administration, military, and International Civil Aviation Organization specifications.

BMF® metal forms are used to contain concrete and shape sidewalks, curbs, roads, median barriers, gutters, runways, bridge parapets for cast-in-place and pre cast construction, and many other customized flatwork applications.

Jaquith's Custom Contract Fabrication area produces outer shells and stainless steel cylinders for its commercial laundry equipment manufacturing neighbor, G.A. Braun, Inc.

A Long History

Incorporated in 1919 as the Chemical Toilet Company by Willard E. Jaquith and Charles L. Carpenter, the company initially produced commodes and chemical toilet systems. It later became a leading manufacturer of metal septic tanks and fuel-oil storage tanks. In 1927, the company moved into the plant on East Brighton Avenue, and during the 1930s, it developed and patented a heat-circulating fireplace known as the Healilator. Following Carpenter's death in 1929, Jaquith assumed the company's presidency and soon changed its name to San-Equip Inc. During the 1930s, the East Brighton Avenue facility was expanded to accommodate the addition of large gasoline and fuel storage tanks, which were added

to the company's product line. Willard Jaquith died in 1938 and Kenneth Jaquith became president. Continued growth through acquisition and expanding markets during the 1940s and 1950s led to the company's being renamed Vega Industries Inc. in 1955. In 1960, as part of the Construction Products Division, the company saw both the start of the Airport Product Line and the beginning of the relationship with G.A. Braun. Binghamton Metal Forms (BMF) was purchased in 1961 and moved to the current location. In 1969, the company split into three divisions with the Construction Products Division eventually taking over the Syracuse facility.

In 1976, Donald S. Jaquith—son of Kenneth Jaquith and grandson of the founder—purchased the Construction Products Division from Vega and in 1977, Jaquith Industries was born. Jaquith's airport lighting inpavement supports; edge-marker light bases; transformer housings, covers, adapters, and base plates; and aluminum and fiberglass approach lighting masts have been installed at major airports on six continents. Airports in New York, Paris, Rome, Warsaw, Beirut, Bogotá, Hong Kong, Mandalay, and Toronto are just a few that have installed Vega® Airport Equipment.

For more then 75 years, BMF® has been expanding to meet the changing demands of the construction industry. The Custom Contract Fabrication area continues to produce outer shells and stainless steel cylinders for G.A. Braun Inc.'s industrial laundry and dyeing equipment, as well as specialized weldments and fabrications for other local industries.

Twenty years ago, Donald Jaquith's belief that the Syracuse operation could be a viable enter-

prise was based on the skill and ability of its people. Their ability to integrate both standard production and customized products is a credit to their ingenuity and creativity. Jaquith Industries remains competitive in today's global market by heeding suggestions, taking responsibility (especially regarding safety), making equipment improvements, and cross training its employees. The loyalty and trust of its customers has helped to make Jaquith Industries a thriving and progressive manufacturing company. By maintaining its dedication to producing quality products, the company is sure to continue its long history of success well into the 21st century.

JAQUITH INDUSTRIES ENJOYS WORLDWIDE RECOGNITION FOR ITS INNOVATIVE VEGA® AIRPORT EQUIPMENT, WHICH INCLUDES IN-GROUND LIGHT BASES AND OTHER VITAL ILLUMINATION AND MONITORING EQUIPMENT SUPPORT COMPONENTS FOR AIRPORTS AROUND THE WORLD.

STICKLEY FURNITURE

FOUNDED IN 1900 BY LEOPOLD AND JOHN GEORGE Stickley in Fayetteville, New York, Stickley Furniture earned a reputation of producing high-quality solid wood furniture during its first six decades in business. In 1956, a year before his death, Leopold Stickley was named

Revered Dean of Cabinet Makers, whose art and craftsmanship have contributed mightily to American home life.

By the early 1970s, Stickley was on the verge of bankruptcy. When Alfred and Aminy Audi bought Stickley in 1974, the ailing company had 24 employees and $235,000 in annual sales. As president of New York City-based E.J. Audi, Inc., a family business with roots dating back to 1928, and Stickley's largest dealer, Alfred had long been acquainted with Stickley furniture. "For Alfred, saving Stickley was preserving a uniquely American tradition," says Aminy, who is now company executive vice president. "The first few years were tough. The odds were one in 10 that we would make it. It took a lot of faith and hard work to stay afloat."

At first Stickley struggled just to meet the payroll each week, but now the company has 950 employees, sells its furniture worldwide, and boasts more than $90 million in annual sales. Stickley

In 1974, Alfred and Aminy Audi bought Stickley, which was on the verge of bankruptcy (top).

Stickley moved to its present location in Manlius, New York, in 1985. Since then, the factory and showroom have grown from 136,000 to 365,000 square feet (bottom).

moved to its present location in Manlius, New York, in 1985. Since then, the factory and showroom have grown from 136,000 to 365,000 square feet.

According to Alfred and Aminy, Stickley's success comes from the incomparable quality and value of its furniture, and uncompromising integrity in dealing with customers and employees. The company has further enhanced its reputation by setting high standards

throughout the organization and creating a caring and nurturing family atmosphere. The Audis are committed to running a very profitable company, but they are more concerned with the legacy they will leave to those who follow in their footsteps. Two of their three children are already actively involved in Stickley.

Unparalleled Quality

Stickley is perhaps most widely recognized for its mission furniture, a style made popular in this country at the turn of the century by Gustav and Leopold Stickley. By 1917, interest in mission—or Arts and Crafts—had dwindled and it gradually went out of vogue. In 1989, Stickley helped revive the interest in mission by reissuing 33 original mission designs, and the company has since introduced many newly designed mission pieces. Today, mission furniture is among the most popular and sought after furniture categories.

Other Stickley design collections include Traditional 18th Century, made of solid mahogany or solid cherry, and Early American, made of native New York State solid cherry. In 1995, the company purchased an upholstery plant and, more recently, it launched the 21st Century and Metropolitan collections. The Stickley product is available through company-owned showrooms throughout New York State, as well as authorized Stickley dealers and interior design showrooms around the United States, Europe, and the Far East.

Because of its unique design, unparalleled construction, and fine finish, Stickley furniture is the standard by which others are measured. In addition to its beauty, Stickley furniture is made to last for generations, and its value appreciates with age. Says Aminy,

"People are pleasantly surprised by the price of Stickley Furniture. It is by no means inexpensive, but it is a great value, given its quality, inherent beauty, and longevity."

A Stickley piece of furniture starts with the highest-quality wood—usually solid cherry, solid mahogany, or quartersawn white oak. Stickley uses leading-edge technology to detect flaws in wood before cutting.

Next, using the finest construction methods known to cabinet-making, individual parts are precision cut by machines and fitted by experts, who initial, date, and number each piece. Then, every piece is thoroughly hand sanded, thus opening the pores of the wood. When the sanding is completed, the piece is hand finished and hand rubbed—a process that takes an average of four days. The finish is mixed on-site. "You can see your reflection in the finish of a Stickley table," says Aminy. "Age only enhances the beauty of each piece."

Quality control standards at Stickley are very high and well defined. Although the company has people specifically assigned to quality control, its goal is to instill in every employee an uncompromising sense of quality. "Quality construction ensures endurance. Our furniture is meant to be passed on from generation to generation." says Alfred.

Even Hollywood has taken notice of the company's quality pieces, which "differ from antiques in time only," according to Aminy. Stickley has been featured in such films as *A River Runs Through It,*

Dead Again, She's the One, Faithful, and *Another Stakeout.*

Unique Family Atmosphere

The Audis take pride in the family atmosphere they have fostered throughout Stickley's growth. Monthly meetings and monetary rewards for good ideas and new employee referral encourage employee participation. In addition, Stickley sponsors many social events for its staff members and their families, including an annual summer picnic, a Christmas party, and a Thanksgiving dinner, where the owners and management serve the workforce.

Employees at Stickley enjoy a wellness-oriented benefits package, which includes medical and dental coverage, a weight-loss clinic paid for by the company, stress management courses, a smoking cessation program (with monetary incentives for those who succeed), and counseling services.

Stickley is also committed to providing the healthiest, safest work environment possible. The company employs one full-time and one part-time nurse on-site,

and provides the services of a physician. The company was an early supporter of drug testing for its employees to promote safety. A state-of-the-art dust collection system ensures the highest-possible air quality.

The company is also highly devoted to supporting the Syracuse community. Stickley employees participate in dozens of local organizations, including the Junior League, Syracuse Symphony, Crouse Irving Memorial Foundation, Hospice of Central New York, AmVets, Syracuse Stage, Children's Miracle Network, Literacy Volunteers, and Vera House.

Stickley's success and dedication to its hometown community—and its vast community of employees—have not gone unnoticed. The company has won the Greater Syracuse Chamber of Commerce Business of the Year Award for 1995, and the 1997 Entrepreneur of the Year Award for upstate New York. Although the company has had its ups and downs over the years, Stickley Furniture seems well positioned to outfit the nation's furniture needs well into the 21st century.

CLOCKWISE FROM TOP LEFT: STICKLEY DESIGN COLLECTIONS INCLUDE THE RECENTLY LAUNCHED 21ST CENTURY COLLECTION.

A CRAFTSMAN AT STICKLEY FURNITURE HAND RUBS A HEPPLEWHITE SIDEBOARD.

EVERY PIECE OF STICKLEY FURNITURE IS THOROUGHLY HAND SANDED, THUS OPENING THE PORES OF THE WOOD. WHEN THE SANDING IS COMPLETED, THE PIECE IS HAND FINISHED AND HAND RUBBED—A PROCESS THAT TAKES AN AVERAGE OF FOUR DAYS.

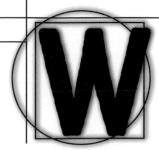

SYR-570AM—THE SYRACUSE AREA'S SOURCE FOR news, talk radio, and weather—began humbly as WBXW in 1922 in the home of Clive Meredith, a ham radio operator. Broadcast from a single room with a staff of five, the station adopted the call letters WMAC in 1923.

There have been many changes in the years since. In 1929, Meredith moved the operation to new studios—converted rooms in the Hotel Syracuse, with the sinks still in them—and changed the station's call letters to WSYR. The facility was moved to the Syracuse University (SU) gymnasium in 1931. Colonel Harry C. Wilder purchased WSYR in 1932, increasing the staff to 39 and moving it to larger facilities in the Syracuse-Kemper building. That same year, the station became affiliated with the Red and Blue Network, which would later become NBC.

Some of the great orchestras of the 1930s—including those of Carmen Cavallero and Tommy and Jimmy Dorsey—became popular through WSYR, which broadcast across the nation on the NBC Network. WSYR was there as the *Hindenburg* exploded May 6, 1937. During World War II, WSYR was broadcasting 24 hours a day, and at the close of the war, Program

BRIDGEWATER PLACE AT 500 PLUM STREET IS THE HOME OF COX RADIO IN SYRACUSE. IN ADDITION TO WSYR-570 AM, THE COX UMBRELLA OF LOCAL RADIO STATIONS INCLUDES WHEN (AM 620), WBBS (104.7 FM), WYYY (Y94), AND WWHT (107.9 FM).

Director Fred Hillegas launched the crusade to build the Onondaga County War Memorial, which was dedicated in 1951.

Growing with the Times

WSYR was the first to bring FM radio to Central New York in 1946, at a frequency of 93.5 and later 94.5 megahertz. In 1947, the station made the initial gift to implement a television training program at SU, the first of its kind nationally. Samuel I. Newhouse, who also owned the Syracuse *Post-Standard*, purchased the company later that year, and in 1950, WSYR Television was founded.

A new site was constructed for WSYR on James Street in 1957. One of the first in the nation to introduce FM stereo in 1961, WSYR was also the first in the area to equip itself for civil defense emergency broadcasts in 1965. WSYR again moved in 1980 to the Syracuse Mall on Clinton Square.

When the federal government ruled in 1983 that a single organization could not own radio, tele-

vision, and newspapers, WSYR radio was sold to Katz Broadcasting. In 1986, Park City Communications (a subsidiary of Katz) and employees at WSYR purchased the station from Katz, forming a new company: New City Communications. WSYR and other local New City stations entered the current facility at Plum Street in 1990.

Award-Winning Broadcasting

The station was one of six in the nation to receive the National Association of Broadcasters' Crystal Award for community service in 1996. In 1997, WSYR's 75th anniversary, the station was awarded the prestigious Edward R. Murrow Award by the Radio and Television News Directors Association. It was also given two awards by the New York State Broadcasters Association for Best Public Affairs Program and Best Newscast.

Also in 1997, Cox Radio, Inc. acquired New City Communications and all the stations under

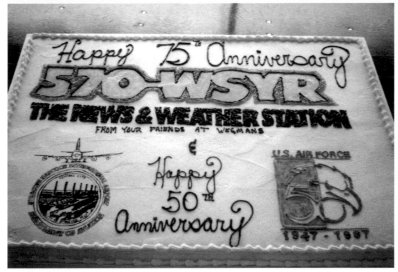

its umbrella. In addition to WSYR, these include WHEN (AM 620, sports radio), WBBS (104.7 FM, country), WYYY (Y94 FM, adult contemporary), and WWHT (Hot 107.9, Top 40).

"Our audience wants to know what's going on nationally," says Joel Delmonico, vice president and general manager of WSYR, WBBS, and WHEN in Syracuse, "but what they really care about is what's going on locally." More than 100,000 listeners weekly turn to WSYR for news, talk radio, traffic information, and weather. The station is affiliated with CNN and recently created an alliance with ABC.

Besides having the largest local radio news team, WSYR hosts the area's only local talk show, a forum for global as well as local issues. As the flagship of the New York State Radio Network, WSYR feeds SU basketball and football broadcasts to almost 20 stations statewide. SU games are also broadcast live over the Internet, reaching a growing international audience.

Employing approximately 150, WSYR emphasizes growth and advancement opportunities for the people who make its success a reality. "We focus on a person's strengths, then put them in a situation to develop them," says Delmonico. "Success is just a by-product of a happy person enjoying their work." This attitude has attracted talent from across the nation.

WSYR's results-driven advertising department helps businesses set and achieve their goals—not just through radio, but all media. The department develops strong relationships with clients in order to facilitate the kind of communication vital to providing the best service. Providing businesses with consultation much like that of an ad agency, WSYR creates promotional spots with state-of-the-art digital audio production facilities. Allowing seamless editing as well as the ability to manipulate sounds and words, this technology also makes distribution quicker, easier, and cleaner.

Serving Syracuse

Public service is a cornerstone of the WSYR mission. The station works closely with local nonprofit organizations in pro-

motion and fund-raising. During the snowstorm that hit the North Country at the beginning of 1998, WSYR and its sister stations interrupted its usual format in order to hold a daylong radiothon that raised more than $200,000 for the relief effort.

WSYR's commitment to the community reaches beyond its involvement in fund-raising and other community service activities. "We want to be a part of the economic resurgence of the area," says Delmonico. The station is involved in the Metropolitan Development Association, as well as the DaVinci Project to bring new technical talent to the area.

With deep roots in a growing community and rising top-line revenues, "The next few years look really exciting," says Delmonico. "We're proud to be a part of it all."

CLOCKWISE FROM TOP LEFT: THE OFFICES OF COX RADIO OFFER A SPECTACULAR SKYWARD VIEW THROUGH THE ATRIUM.

COX RADIO EXPANDED ITS FACILITIES TO INCLUDE THE FOURTH FLOOR OF BRIDGEWATER PLACE, WHERE THE OFFICES FOR WBBS-104.7 FM AND COX INTERACTIVE MEDIA ARE LOCATED.

FROM WSYR'S CONTROL ROOM, THE STATION BROADCASTS A VARIETY OF PROGRAMMING, INCLUDING THE AREA'S ONLY LOCAL TALK RADIO SHOW AND NEWS FROM THE LARGEST LOCAL RADIO NEWS TEAM.

IN 1997, WSYR CELEBRATED ITS 75TH ANNIVERSARY, AS THE U.S. AIR FORCE CELEBRATED ITS 50TH ANNIVERSARY.

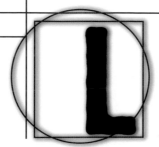

LOCATED IN THE HEART OF THE BUSINESS AND entertainment districts of downtown Syracuse, the Radisson Plaza, Hotel Syracuse has built a reputation as the premier hotel in Central New York. Since actor Jackie Coogan registered as its first guest in 1924, the

Hotel Syracuse has been dedicated to providing its guests with the highest-quality service the city has to offer.

Easily accessible from Interstate 81 and the New York State Thruway, the Hotel Syracuse is also within walking distance of many key downtown locations, such as the Onondaga County War Memorial, Civic Center, Landmark Theatre, Armory Square, MONY building, and OnCenter. Syracuse University and the Carrier Dome are within one mile of the hotel, and the Carousel Mall and Hancock Airport are within a 10-minute drive. "This is the hub of Syracuse," says Fred Grabosky, general manager of the hotel. "When conventions come to

the area, they support downtown business."

Charming and Unique

With 420 rooms and 30 deluxe suites, more than 35,000 square feet of banquet space, and 22 meeting rooms of varying sizes, the Hotel Syracuse is well equipped to handle the thousands of guests and hundreds of conventions, charity and social events, and parties it hosts each year.

The Hotel Syracuse also has three extravagantly furnished ballrooms. The Grand Ballroom is every bride's dream reception site, boasting crystal chandeliers hanging from its 60-foot-high, concave ceiling, and a balcony overlooking its beautiful hardwood dance floor.

The Grand Ballroom accommodates up to 500 people and is the only one of its kind in upstate New York. The Persian Terrace has elegance and charm, accommodating up to 400 and featuring a built-in stage. The Imperial Ballroom, with its handsome burgundy, russet, brass, and crystal decor, is the largest of the three ballrooms with a capacity of 1,000 people.

The Hotel Syracuse features three themed restaurants. A sports bar and grill, where customers can watch their favorite sports teams on one of 25 television sets, is open seven days a week for lunch, dinner, and drinks. The Maine Lobster Company, nominated as one of Syracuse's

MORE THAN $6 MILLION WAS SPENT BY THE RADISSON PLAZA, HOTEL SYRACUSE IN 1993 TO RETURN THE PUBLIC AREAS, MAIN LOBBY, 100 OF ITS HISTORIC BEDROOMS, AND THE GRAND BALLROOM TO THEIR ORIGINAL 1920S SPLENDOR.

best seafood restaurants, serves Maine lobster and fresh seafood for lunch and dinner. Bernardi's Bistro, a politically themed restaurant, is named after the mayor of Syracuse and features some of the area's best steaks and pastas.

The Hotel Syracuse also has more than 75,000 square feet of retail and office space for its guests' convenience, including a florist, gift shop, dry cleaners, bingo hall, realtor, law offices, and USAirways ticket office. The facility provides free, enclosed parking space and a business center, with office and secretarial services for business guests.

Elegantly Modern

The Hotel Syracuse offers the charm and elegance of yesteryear, beautifully restored to the way it was 74 years ago," says Grabosky. The Radisson Plaza, Hotel Syracuse is a featured member of the National Historical Hotels of America Group. The current facility is approximately twice the size of the original hotel. More than $6 million was spent in 1993 to return the public areas, main lobby, 100 of its historic bed-

rooms, and the Grand Ballroom to their original 1920's splendor. In 1994, a complete fitness center was added, lavishly decorated with tropical plants, palm trees, and a 50-foot-high, running waterfall by the hotel's indoor pool. The fitness center includes fully equipped weight and aerobic training facilities.

Future Growth

Poised for growth, the Radisson Plaza, Hotel Syracuse plans more renovations to usher in the 21st century. By the end of 1998, restoration on a tunnel from the hotel to the Convention Center and War Memorial will be complete. In early 1999, 134 rooms will be added for a total of 554 rooms. All 554 rooms will be outfitted with coffeemakers, hair dryers, and irons. As Syracuse grows, so will the Hotel Syracuse, maintaining its tradition of nearly three-quarters of a century of providing high-quality service in surroundings that combine yesterday's charm with the conveniences of today.

AS SYRACUSE GROWS, SO WILL THE HOTEL SYRACUSE, MAINTAINING ITS TRADITION OF NEARLY THREE-QUARTERS OF A CENTURY OF PROVIDING HIGH-QUALITY SERVICE IN SURROUNDINGS THAT COMBINE YESTERDAY'S CHARM WITH THE CONVENIENCES OF TODAY.

WITH 420 ROOMS AND 30 DELUXE SUITES, MORE THAN 35,000 SQUARE FEET OF BANQUET SPACE, AND 22 MEETING ROOMS OF VARYING SIZES, THE HOTEL SYRACUSE IS WELL EQUIPPED TO HANDLE THE THOUSANDS OF GUESTS AND HUNDREDS OF CONVENTIONS, CHARITY AND SOCIAL EVENTS, AND PARTIES IT HOSTS EACH YEAR.

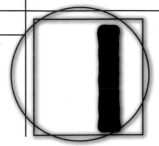

MUENCH-KREUZER CANDLE COMPANY

N 1925, BROTHERS ALEXIS AND NORBERT MUENCH and their cousin Frederick Kreuzer founded the Muench-Kreuzer Candle Company—also popularly known today as Emkay—in Syracuse. Destined to become the largest manufacturer of church candles in the United States,

the young company acquired a reputation for high quality and consistency in its church candles made from blended waxes.

Still in its original location on Hiawatha Boulevard, the privately held company employs 100 people in its 140,000-square-foot, three-building facility used for manufacturing, warehousing, and shipping products. Muench-Kreuzer also owns a distribution center in Los Angeles and a Chicago-based dealership. Although primarily serving clients in the United States, the company ships products to Canada, the Caribbean, and Africa.

Today, Muench-Kreuzer is comanaged by Executive Vice President and COO Fred C. Kiesinger and Executive Vice President of Sales and Marketing Carol Egle. Kiesinger says, "Since we complement each other, the arrangement works well."

According to Kiesinger, Muench-Kreuzer directs 80 percent of its business to the religious market, 10 percent to contract work, and 10 percent to commercial stores. The company sells to the clergy through distributors that rep-

resent various denominations: the 130-member National Church Goods Association and the 4,000-member Christian Booksellers Association.

Cornerstone in Syracuse

As a long-standing Syracuse-based company, Muench-Kreuzer employed 400 people during the 1960s to make and sell church candles and decorative gift candles. "As offshore competitors came to dominate the gift market, American candle makers cut back," says Kiesinger. "Although we still make commercial candles, we restructured our company to specialize in traditional church candles, vestments, oil-based candles, and specialized wax products."

As the first candle company to diversify in this way, Muench-Kreuzer purchased the Pennsylvania-based Abbey Brands, a business with 50 years' experience in producing high-quality albs, or vestments for Catholic priests. After researching the market for other denominations, Muench-Kreuzer introduced a successful line of women's albs, an abbey shirt,

and an upscale vestment line called Royal Abbey, a product previously produced only in Belgium.

In addition to the traditional paraffin and beeswax candles, Muench-Kreuzer entered the expanding oil candle market by purchasing a manufacturer of these products. Muench-Kreuzer also worked closely with European countries to develop a way to mass-produce fire-retardant, reclaimable devotional lights made of plastic to replace the cumbersome glass products used by the Catholic Church.

With its high-production equipment, Muench-Kreuzer produces a standard line of candles for the church industry, and recently added nearly $400,000 worth of annual inventory to honor its on-time delivery commitment. The company also makes specialized decorated candles for churches.

As part of its contract work, Muench-Kreuzer makes specialty products for the craft market. "If a client asks us to make specific colored and fragranced granulated wax, we prepare trial samples and show them to the customer, who

WITH ITS DEDICATED WORKFORCE AND ATTENTION TO SERVICE AND QUALITY, MUENCH-KREUZER CANDLE COMPANY IS POISED TO CONTINUE ITS LONG HISTORY OF SUCCESS WELL INTO THE NEXT CENTURY.

then selects a sample. Then, we produce, bag, and label it," says Kiesinger. "The craft kit eventually appears in large retail stores."

A noteworthy example of Muench-Kreuzer's ingenuity in candle making is its specially formulated candle that burns well in an environment of 5,000 other burning candles. This unique product was devised for Our Lady of San Juan in Texas, the largest shrine in the United States.

Muench-Kreuzer recently revamped its inventory control and manufacturing systems to allow its church distribution centers to serve both small and large dealers. By its willingness to fill the orders that small dealers can afford to place, the company has gained a large share of the small-store market. Muench-Kreuzer services both $25-per-year and $250,000-per-year customers.

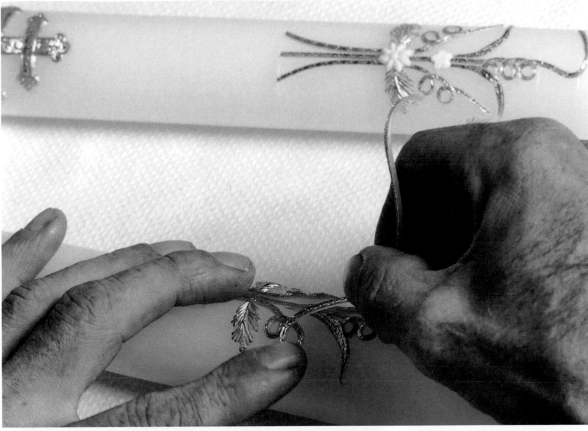

A Dedicated, Safety-Conscious Workforce

In addition to offering an excellent benefits package, Muench-Kreuzer is highly attentive to the personal needs of its employees, many of whom have worked for the company for 16 to 40 years. "Candle making is a craft," says Kiesinger, "and it's hard to find quality-conscious people. Our team-oriented employees know that they must make a high-quality product for us to remain competitive."

As a joint management-employee concern, safety is addressed at Muench-Kreuzer through regular monthly safety meetings and building tours. The company uses New York's OSHA regulations inspection service annually, and addresses whatever problems are discovered. "OSHA respects this group and the people who take advantage of their services," says Kiesinger.

Continuous Improvement

Muench-Kreuzer takes great pride in its improved service to customers over the last six years. "Our previous turnaround time was up to 10 days from receipt of order to shipping," says Kiesinger. "With our upgraded

equipment and production scheduling system, we've reduced it to two to three days or, for our most common items, only 24 hours."

Since 1992, Muench-Kreuzer has invested $1.5 million in new equipment and upgrades of current candle-producing systems, in order to better serve the clergy market. According to Kiesinger, Muench-Kreuzer's core business of religious products has remained stable, even during economic downturns. The company plans to continue improving its products and manufacturing processes, as

well as acquiring companies that enhance its service to the religious market.

"Our customers are the same, whether they need candles, vestments, or other products," says Egle. "And rather than try to learn the needs of a new customer, we use our knowledge of the customers we already serve, which include all denominations."

With its dedicated workforce and attention to service and quality, Muench-Kreuzer is poised to continue its long history of success well into the next century.

MUENCH-KREUZER MAKES SPECIALIZED DECORATED CANDLES FOR CHURCHES AS WELL AS A RANGE OF OTHER PRODUCTS (TOP).

WITH ITS HIGH-PRODUCTION EQUIPMENT, MUENCH-KREUZER PRODUCES A STANDARD LINE OF CANDLES FOR THE CHURCH INDUSTRY, AND RECENTLY ADDED NEARLY $400,000 WORTH OF ANNUAL INVENTORY TO HONOR ITS ON-TIME DELIVERY COMMITMENT (BOTTOM LEFT AND RIGHT).

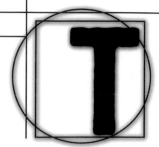

HANKS LARGELY TO LORETTO, A VOLUNTARY, NOT-for-profit organization that has grown to be the premier geriatric caregiver in Central New York, Syracuse is truly a great place to grow old. Originally founded in 1926 by the Syracuse Roman Catholic Diocese as the Loretto Rest Home for the Aged, the facility was given to the community in 1975 and rededicated as Cunningham Hall. The Cunningham Skilled Nursing Program has boasted an occupancy rate of more than 95 percent ever since. Additionally, with an annual budget exceeding $55 million, Loretto has a visible impact on the local economy.

With more than 15 local facilities and programs, plus one in Utica and another in Oswego, Loretto improves the quality of life for its clients and their families by offering diversity in long-term adult care services under one umbrella. Loretto's integrated delivery system offers seamless transitions between types and levels of service, from independent living to full-time skilled nursing care.

Many Levels of Service

Loretto provides many levels of service to its more than 5,000 clients, whether they are living in its facilities or in their own homes. Independent Living programs offer housing to healthy and active adults who no longer feel safe or comfortable as home owners. Older adults who cannot live independently but don't require skilled nursing care may choose Supportive Living programs. These programs offer medication monitoring, bathing supervision, dressing assistance, and laundry services as needed. Finally, Residential Health Care programs are available to those needing intensive, 24-hour skilled nursing care.

For older adults who wish to remain in their homes, Home and Community Based Care provides medical, transportation, and support services of varying degrees, depending on the needs of the individual. In addition, consultants are available to assist individuals with choosing appropriate programs. Other services include Lifeline, a personal emergency response system, and Loretto's Ambassador Program, providing temporary stays in a supportive or skilled setting.

Loretto's Home Health program provides health and social services to older adults in the privacy of their own homes. The coordinated care and support begins with a care plan. The Home Health team bases the care plan on the person's nursing, social, and environmental needs, and makes appropriate recommendations. This program allows older adults to receive the services they need while maintaining a safe and independent lifestyle in their own home or apartment.

Independent Living Services (ILS) is a Program for All-Inclusive Care for the Elderly (PACE). ILS

SEEKING TO ANTICIPATE AND INFLUENCE THE NEW DIRECTIONS ADULT CARE WILL TAKE ON ALL FRONTS, LORETTO OFFERS PROGRAMS STILL IN THEIR INFANCY ON THE NATIONAL LEVEL (LEFT).

LORETTO PROVIDES MANY LEVELS OF SERVICE TO ITS MORE THAN 5,000 CLIENTS, WHETHER THEY ARE LIVING IN ITS FACILITIES OR IN THEIR OWN HOMES (RIGHT TOP AND BOTTOM).

is designed to serve older adults who are frail and need skilled nursing care, yet wish to remain living independently. The ILS interdisciplinary team of health care professionals provides all medical, social, rehabilitative, and supportive services to participants.

Enriched Housing and the Assisted Living Program (ALP) offer alternatives to those who fall in between the levels of care offered by Loretto. These programs provide services much like those of home- and community-based care within a residential setting.

Dedicated to Excellence

L oretto's compassionate, self-motivated team of more than 1,200 health care professionals includes doctors, nurses, social workers, and support staff dedicated to excellence in the field of gerontology. Loretto is extremely selective about whom it employs, and offers excellent educational opportunities for career advancement.

Loretto recognizes excellence, which occurs on a daily basis, according to Senior Vice President Steve Volza. "When it comes to motivation, we do a lot," he says, "but it doesn't come close to what our people do for themselves and each other." The organization involves employees when decisions are made.

Loretto is organized in matrix fashion, where individuals at different levels of the organization are involved in the decision-making process, without a rigid chain of command. Everyone has access to a wide variety of people within the organization, from high-ranking administrators to those with specialized expertise. "We are much like a democracy," says Volza. "Things may take more time in that regard, but a better decision is reached."

With nearly 75 years of professional geriatric expertise and experience, Loretto has gained a deep understanding and insight into the needs of the elderly and their families. The organization is at the cutting edge of geriatric service delivery through involvement in local public arenas

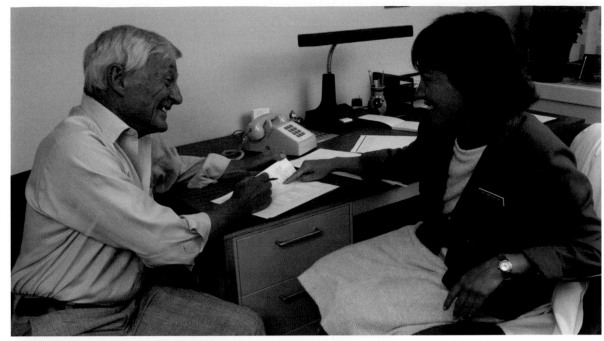

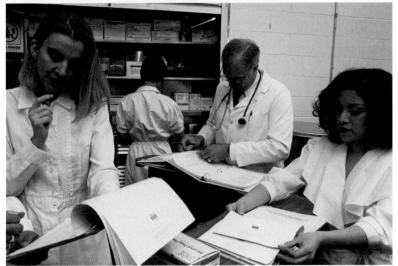

and professional associations. Seeking to anticipate and influence the new directions adult care will take on all fronts, the company offers programs still in their infancy on the national level. Many of Loretto's key executives sit on several state and federal political action committees to keep the company on the forefront of political change and new program development.

For most of its history, Loretto has been able to financially support itself, but with rising costs, economic fluctuation, and insurance reimbursement cutbacks, maintaining the organization's array and depth of services has been increasingly difficult. As a result, in 1993, the Loretto Foundation was established to solicit alternative funding sources for the organization.

Through the changing times of the past seven decades, Loretto

has never lost its focus on Central New York's older adults and their families. Laying the foundation for future endeavors, Loretto will integrate new software into its systems over the next two years. This software will provide more accurate information about customer needs and the services being delivered, in an effort to provide quality services in an integrated manner. As Loretto continues to introduce innovative and cost-effective programs to the community, quality care and compassion will always come first.

Loretto is distinguished among long-term-care organizations by its commitment to service coordination and continuing care management for all its clients. Loretto believes it is not enough to provide excellent service. Services need to be carefully coordinated so that the individual gets what is needed when it is needed.

T

HE HIGHEST-QUALITY INSURANCE PRODUCTS AND
services reflect Haylor, Freyer & Coon's (HF&C) commitment to its most valuable asset: its customers. For 70
years, the agency has upheld this commitment by providing
its clients with state-of-the-art, customized insurance pro-

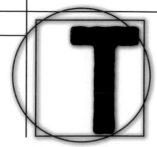

HAYLOR, FREYER & COON, INC. IS
THE LARGEST INDEPENDENT INSURANCE
AGENCY IN CENTRAL NEW YORK AND
IS RANKED AMONG THE TOP 100 INDE-
PENDENT AGENCIES IN THE NATION.

grams maintained and enhanced
by annual coverage reviews, loss
control engineering, and in-house
claims handling. Today, with annual billings exceeding $110 mil-
lion, HF&C remains dedicated
to this formula and, as the 21st
century approaches, will continue
to explore product and service
options to provide the most comprehensive insurance protection
available.

Staffing from the Beginning

HF&C began as McClusky &
Haylor in 1928. Its founders,
Burnet Haylor and James McClusky,
opened their doors with three
employees and a desire to make
a difference in the Syracuse community. They began as personal
insurance providers, but soon
expanded their operation to include small-business insurance.
Throughout the Great Depression
and World War II, McClusky &
Haylor stood behind their clients
and took steps to ensure the needs
of the community were met.

One such step was taken in 1952
with the introduction of MHD,
Inc., or the Mobile Home Division.
MHD, Inc. provided commercial
and personal coverages to mobile

home owners and dealers, and
later grew to include specialized
programs for manufacturers,
haulers, and installers of manufactured homes. This division is
now known as the Manufactured
Housing Division and is the largest manufactured housing insurance provider in New York State.
Its inception not only proved profitable for HF&C, but also laid
the groundwork for a young concept known as niche marketing.
In this environment of targeted
expertise in specific markets,
HF&C throve.

In the mid-1960s, the agency
became what is now known as
Haylor, Freyer & Coon, Inc. It is
the largest independent insurance
agency in Central New York and
is ranked among the top 100 independent agencies in the nation.
Although the mid-Atlantic region
is its primary service area, it is
licensed to operate nationwide
and underwrite risks worldwide.
The agency is currently headquartered in Syracuse, and maintains

15 branch offices across New York State and two additional offices in Maryland and New Hampshire.

Pride in Product Expertise

HF&C represents more than 50 insurance carriers and employs more than 200 insurance professionals. These resources and the focus on niche or target marketing have prompted the establishment of units and divisions within the agency. The HF&C Commercial Lines Department is comprised of the Transportation Unit, the Construction & Bonding Unit, the General Insurance Unit, and the Manufactured Housing Division. Additional products and services are offered by the Personal Insurance Division, with coverages ranging from home and auto to personal umbrella and life, and by the Employee Benefits Department, offering group health, disability, and estate planning.

The first unit to emerge after the Manufactured Housing Division was the Transportation Unit. In the late 1970s, HF&C identified the transportation industry as an underserved market. Beginning with individual owner/operators and small fleets, the agency began working with the transportation community to gain expertise in the insurance needs of the industry and the insurance carriers to develop products to meet those needs. Programs were developed for long-haul trucking firms, auto dealers, and bus, taxi, and limousine operations, and by the mid-1980s, HF&C was an established leader in the transportation insurance arena. The agency is a current member of the New York State Motor Truck Association and the Automobile Dealers Association.

The Construction Unit was the next niche to follow. Focusing on general contractors and equipment dealers, the unit also worked with various insurance carriers to develop tailored, industry-specific programs. As the unit grew, a bonding department was established for issuance of construction, surety, fidelity, and government bonds. HF&C is a current member of Associated Builders and Contractors Inc. and the National Association of Surety Bond Producers.

Service Excellence

From the beginning, HF&C understood that a product is only as good as the service system established to support it. In an effort to ensure that every client, whether a large trucking firm or an individual purchasing auto coverage, was given the best possible service, the agency formed specialized service units.

The Claims Department was established to offer HF&C clients fast and convenient claim reporting and to expedite claim resolution. The department accepts initial claim reports and has limited draft authority. In addition, the department tracks the status of all claims, allowing claimants to access status reports through the agency's toll-free line 24 hours a day.

Another service offered by HF&C is the Engineering Services Department. This department provides consultation and recommendations on risk exposures, OSHA regulations, state building code regulations, workers' compensation issues, property and fire protection, and valuation for replacement cost estimates.

Staying Ahead of the Competition

Maintaining a competitive edge is a key element in the success of HF&C. To stay ahead of its competition, the agency has gained a presence by establishing

local servicing branches throughout the state for the convenience of its customers. The agency has also invested nearly $1 million in state-of-the-art computer technology that further ensures customer satisfaction by providing prompt billing and coverage information, expedient claim resolution, and other services. Finally, HF&C remains the leader in the insurance industry by staying in touch with the Syracuse community. The agency and its staff are active members in the Metropolitan Development Association, YMCA, United Way, Community Foundation, Little Leagues, and various other community organizations.

After 70 years, Haylor, Freyer & Coon is still growing and learning about the needs of its customers and the community as a whole. "We're proud of our growth, stability, and adjustments to market changes," says James D. Freyer Sr., the agency's CEO and chairman of the board, "but the secret is treating every client, large or small, as if he or she were the only one."

JAMES D. FREYER SR. (LEFT) SERVES AS CHAIRMAN OF THE BOARD AND CEO OF HAYLOR, FREYER & COON. JAMES A. STODDARD SR. IS PRESIDENT AND COO.

HF&C REPRESENTS MORE THAN 50 INSURANCE CARRIERS AND EMPLOYS MORE THAN 200 INSURANCE PROFESSIONALS. THESE RESOURCES, AS WELL AS THE AGENCY'S FOCUS ON NICHE OR TARGET MARKETING, HAVE PROMPTED THE ESTABLISHMENT OF UNITS AND DIVISIONS WITHIN HF&C, TO ENSURE THAT EVERY CLIENT—WHETHER A LARGE TRUCKING FIRM OR AN INDIVIDUAL PURCHASING AUTO COVERAGE—IS GIVEN THE BEST POSSIBLE SERVICE.

perfect a laser technology designed to count garments even faster and more accurately.

Protecting the Environment

I don't think there is anything as important to me as keeping the environment safe for all of us," says Thomas Coyne. "Expense is not an issue in making sure that we're helping—not hurting—the environment. After all, from the very beginning, CTS has been offering environmentally friendly products that can be cleaned and reused many, many times rather than being used once and thrown away."

With this foresight, CTS became the first company in the industry to clean heavily soiled garments and shop towels by a process that eliminates the need to dispose of hundreds of tons of wastewater sludge into valuable landfill space. This process also virtually eliminates future liability to CTS and its customers for improper disposal.

CTS developed a unique process that separates waste oils and solvents from water. This waste is collected and shipped to cement kiln operations, where it is cleanly burned as a supplemental fuel, thus saving energy as it saves the environment by destroying the waste material in an environmentally responsible manner.

A World-Class Delivery Fleet

The sight has become a familiar one throughout the eastern half of the United States: clean, bright, yellow-and-blue CTS delivery trucks crisscrossing towns and cities making deliveries to nearly 40,000 customers every week.

CTS maintains its fleet of more than 500 vehicles in its own

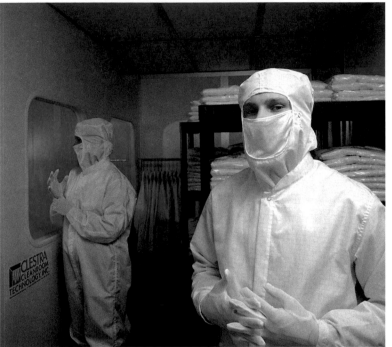

CLOCKWISE FROM TOP LEFT:
CTS SERVES MANY TYPES OF BUSINESSES, INCLUDING THOSE INVOLVED IN HIGH TECHNOLOGY.

CTS IS A LEADER IN PROVIDING BUSINESSES WITH CUSTOM UNIFORMS AND APPAREL TO ENHANCE THEIR COMPANY IMAGE.

EACH BUSINESS DAY, CTS SERVES NEARLY 40,000 CUSTOMERS.

sophisticated maintenance facility in Syracuse. The company designs, builds, and maintains its own vehicles, performing every aspect of vehicle care from body work, painting, and mechanical repair to complete teardown and rebuilding from the chassis up.

Trucks are customized with a special dashboard; rear bumper; additional taillights, for greater safety; and vents, added for extra ventilation. Even the distinctive CTS logos and striping are applied in-house.

Caring for the Community

CTS continues to play an important role in supporting organizations throughout Syracuse and Onondaga County, primarily through its Coyne Foundation. Just as his father did before him, Thomas Coyne is very active with worthwhile fund-raising organizations, helping to raise thousands of dollars each year.

CTS makes its company plane available to the Corporate Angel Network to transport severely ill patients to specialized medical treatment facilities anywhere in the world. "We have a share in this city," says Thomas Coyne.

Anticipating a Bright Future

As the company looks forward to the next century, Thomas Coyne expects CTS to continue its fast-paced growth by providing its customers added value, high quality, and total satisfaction. "We're as excited as ever about the future. The many new technologies that are available to us today are dramatically chang-ing the way we do business," says Coyne. "We intend to be on the leading edge of these technologies for the benefit of our customers. Being a good citizen, enjoying what you do for a living, and helping others to realize their dreams is a philosophy that has helped us to succeed in business. With this continuing philosophy, I believe our future looks brighter than ever."

CLOCKWISE FROM TOP: CTS' NEW PLANT IN BUFFALO IS OUTFITTED WITH THE LATEST IN CLEANING AND HANDLING TECHNOLOGIES, MANY OF WHICH WERE CREATED BY THE COMPANY.

CTS RAISES MONEY FOR AND DONATES ITS OWN DOLLARS TO VALUABLE COMMUNITY SERVICES SUCH AS A NEW ACTIVITIES CENTER FOR THE SYRACUSE RESCUE MISSION.

CTS PRESIDENT THOMAS M. COYNE LOOKS FORWARD TO A FUTURE OF RAPID GROWTH AND TECHNOLOGICAL ADVANCEMENT.

BENJAMIN RUSH CENTER

ENJAMIN RUSH CENTER, THE LARGEST PROVIDER of inpatient mental health services for children, adolescents, and adults in the Central New York region, specializes in treating patients with the most advanced therapies available today. This distinguished

PRESIDENT AND GOVERNING BODY CHAIRMAN FRANCIS J. McCARTHY JR., M.P.A., IS THE VISIONARY FORCE BEHIND BENJAMIN RUSH CENTER'S BECOMING THE PREMIER INPATIENT MENTAL HEALTH FACILITY IT IS TODAY (ABOVE).

ADMINISTRATOR AND CEO NORMAN J. LESSWING, PH.D., BRINGS MORE THAN 20 YEARS OF EXPERIENCE AS A PRACTICING PSYCHOLOGIST TO HIS ROLE AT BENJAMIN RUSH CENTER (ABOVE).

AS PATIENT NEEDS FOR MORE SPECIALIZED CARE HAVE EVOLVED, BENJAMIN RUSH CENTER HAS RESPONDED BY ADDING DIALECTICAL THERAPY APPROACHES TO ITS TREATMENT PROGRAMS OF INDIVIDUAL AND GROUP PSYCHOTHERAPY (RIGHT).

hospital has a long tradition of helping thousands of people back to good mental health. Benjamin Rush Center's origins date back to 1929, when the hospital was founded as a 21-bed private facility to treat adults with depression. Today, almost 70 years later, the modern, 107-bed hospital located on South Salina Street serves patients from age five to 65 and over. Its specialties, besides treating serious mood disorders, now include inpatient programs for anxiety disorders, eating disorders, traumatic stress issues, personality disorders, and coexisting mental health and chemical dependency problems.

Perhaps not surprisingly, the hospital treats patients from a 36-county area throughout upstate New York and northern Pennsylvania. That's because Benjamin Rush Center offers many unique treatment programs, which set it apart from the general services offered at other hospitals and clinics.

"Doctors, clinicians, and families often tell us we're the hospital they think of first for highly specialized inpatient mental health care," says

Administrator and CEO Norman J. Lesswing, Ph.D. "We're proud of having a great reputation."

Lesswing continues, "When you've been around as long as Benjamin Rush Center, it's important to let people know our system of care is always evolving. We're planning for the next century—looking at new areas of treatment, more efficient models of inpatient hospitalization, and integration across all areas of behavioral health care."

Pioneering Innovative New Treatment Methods

Under 25 years of leadership by President and Governing Body Chairman Francis J. McCarthy Jr., the hospital was the first private facility in the area to recognize the need for separate programs for both children and adolescents suffering from serious behavioral disorders, developmental disabilities, or traumatic reactions to abuse or neglect. "We have the longest-established children's and adolescent programs in the region available within a private facility," says McCarthy.

Next came the addition of an innovative treatment approach

called centralized programming. Patients choose various psycho-educational groups to complement individual and group psychotherapy plans, delivering more treatment during brief stays.

Today, Benjamin Rush Center is pioneering the use of two other treatment approaches: cognitive and dialectical behavioral therapies. McCarthy adds, "We're also one of the few facilities in the region to provide both neurocognitive and psychological assessments on-site, which patients, managed care organizations, and referral sources find beneficial."

A Special Environment Helps Patients Recover

Board-certified psychiatrists oversee the patient care within the center's separate units for children, adolescents, adults, and the newly remodeled intensive care.

Immediately upon entering Benjamin Rush Center, people often sense something different. The patient environment is warm and soothing. Environmental Consultant Jean Klym chose a pastel color scheme and added beautiful artwork to achieve a homelike feeling. Patient rooms, larger than sizes set by regulations, have attractive furniture and windows overlooking a garden or fountain.

Benjamin Rush Center is named for Dr. Benjamin Rush, known as the Father of American Psychiatry. Today, the staff of 250 mental health professionals at the center still follow his principles. They offer kind treatment, encourage talking about problems, and provide an atmosphere of caring and trust. Says McCarthy, "We believe in delivering healing with dignity."

Chase Manhattan Bank	1930
General Super Plating Co., Inc.	1932
Higbee, Inc.	1932
Byrne Dairy	1933
Blue Cross and Blue Shield of Central New York	1936
Bristol-Myers Squibb Company	1943
O'Brien & Gere Limited	1945
Le Moyne College	1946
Lockheed Martin Ocean, Radar & Sensor Systems	1948
WTVH-5	1948
Niagara Mohawk	1950
Dumac Business Systems, Inc.	1952
Internist Associates of Central New York, P.C.	1953
The Scotsman Press, Inc.	1954
Crouse Radiology Associates	1957
University Orthopedics & Sports Medicine, P.C.	1959
Philips Broadband Networks Inc.	1963
Devorsetz Stinziano Gilberti Heintz & Smith, P.C.	1966
C&S Companies	1968

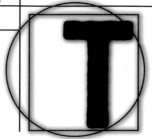

THE CHASE MANHATTAN BANK TRACES ITS CENTRAL New York roots to a group of local business leaders who chartered Lincoln National Bank and Trust Company in Syracuse on January 2, 1930. In the early 1970s, the bank joined the Rochester-headquartered Lincoln First Bank

system. After being acquired by New York City-based Chase Manhattan Corporation in 1984 and operating as a separate subsidiary, Lincoln First Bank merged with Chase Manhattan in 1993, and the Syracuse institution was renamed The Chase Manhattan Bank. Chase merged with the Chemical Banking Corporation in 1996, positioning Chase as the largest banking company in the nation. Chase currently has more than $365 billion in assets.

Proud of its world-class status, Chase succeeds by developing close relationships within the community and offering a wide variety of financial services. Its highly qualified and well-trained staff is equipped with state-of-the-art banking technology to help the bank maintain its leadership position.

Global Reach, Local Touch

With offices in 39 states, Chase is one of the nation's preeminent financial service companies. But it also has a dominant position in global and consumer finance, sustaining relationships with more than 30 million customers in 75 countries. "We're a cor-

poration with a global reach but a local touch," says Jack Webb, regional retail executive in Syracuse.

Chase is the market leader in retail, commercial, and trust businesses in upstate New York, as well as number one in the upstate middle market, which includes businesses with annual revenues exceeding $3 million. Local relationship managers, who serve as liaisons between business clients and the bank, provide one consistent and familiar face to the business customer. Branch managers make major developmental efforts, including maintaining communi-

cation with business prospects and the community as a whole, to better focus on the individual customer relationship. "With Chase, the right relationship is everything," says Webb. "We want to make our customers' financial lives easier."

A Premier Service Provider

In addition to serving middle market businesses, Chase is a premier service provider to small businesses. "This segment of the economy is growing faster than most," says Webb. Recognizing the fast pace of business today, the bank has introduced a streamlined credit process and has significantly shortened turnaround times for credit decisions on small-business loans under $50,000. Individual financial statements are not required. "If we can make a $30,000 car loan decision in four minutes, we should be able to make a $30,000 business loan decision in the same amount of time," says Webb. "Our goal is to make processes easier and less expensive for both the bank and its customers."

With that in mind, Chase has invested more in technology than any other bank in the world: $1.8 billion annually. The corporation is a leader in automated, telephone,

THE CHASE MANHATTAN BANK'S LOCATION ON 7TH NORTH STREET IN SYRACUSE IS ONE OF 15 BRANCHES IN THE CITY SERVING THE CENTRAL NEW YORK REGION.

"WE'RE A CORPORATION WITH A GLOBAL REACH BUT A LOCAL TOUCH," SAYS JACK WEBB, REGIONAL RETAIL EXECUTIVE IN SYRACUSE.

on-line, and debit card banking services, offering convenience for customers and reducing the cost of processing. Free on-line banking, a proprietary product, gives customers access to select deposit accounts.

Customers can also contact Chase's customer service representatives via E-mail 24 hours a day. Internally, Chase's computer system tracks its customers' transactions and provides an improved and more comprehensive range of services, including cash management and foreign exchange.

Chase also invests heavily in its employees and their training to ensure they are qualified to give the highest-quality service to customers. As an employer of choice, Chase offers attractive benefits, incentives, and career advancement opportunities to help foster healthy, profitable, long-term relationships with its employees.

A Variety of Financial Solutions

Chase is a worldwide leader in managing personal and corporate trust relationships. The bank's 15 branches in Syracuse are dedicated to providing extensive financial solutions for its customers.

Chase Personal Bankers are knowledgeable and poised to guide customer choices from the variety of checking, overdraft protection, savings, home equity credit, and mortgage products offered by the bank. Additionally, mutual fund and other investment alternatives are available from Chase Investment Services Corporation, which operates out of existing Chase branches.

Fostering a Spirit of Giving

Although Chase is headquartered in New York City, it maintains a strong presence across upstate New York and Syracuse. "We are people who live and work in Central New York—many of us all our lives," says Webb. "We have a sincere commitment to every community we call home." Chase's 260 Syracuse-based employees volunteer approximately 5,000 hours to the community each year—not as a condition of employment, but rather a continuation of the infectious corporate spirit. Chase backs this with a contributions program in which it will match up to $10,000 in donations made by any employee.

Chase in Syracuse is among the top five per capita contributors to the United Way among Chase Corporation affiliates. Additionally, the Chase Manhattan Foundation offers a competitive grants program focused on arts and culture, precollegiate education, and com-munity revitalization. Although grants typically range from $1,000 to $5,000, some grants of up to $25,000 are given to organizations of larger scope.

Looking to remain on the cutting edge, Chase is one of the few banks currently establishing its name as a brand identity. "We want people to immediately think Chase when they think financial services," says Webb. Based in New York City, but deeply involved in the Syracuse community, The Chase Manhattan Bank continues working to enhance the quality of life of its customers and the residents of Central New York.

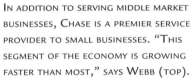

IN ADDITION TO SERVING MIDDLE MARKET BUSINESSES, CHASE IS A PREMIER SERVICE PROVIDER TO SMALL BUSINESSES. "THIS SEGMENT OF THE ECONOMY IS GROWING FASTER THAN MOST," SAYS WEBB (TOP).

SELECT BANKING TELLER BONNIE PURCELL TALKS WITH A CUSTOMER (BOTTOM).

GENERAL SUPER PLATING CO., INC.

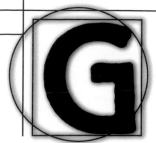

GENERAL SUPER PLATING CO., INC. (GSP) HAS A LONG and rich history in Central New York, with a strong commitment to its hometown of Syracuse. Originally founded in 1932, GSP began as a part-time chrome plating operation in its founder's garage. Today, still a family-owned operation, GSP is one of the largest and most experienced plating companies in the nation, with a reputation for quality, innovation, and responsiveness to the customer's needs.

GSP provides metal finishing and electroplating services to many industries, including automotive, electronics, appliance, plumbing, health and beauty, electrical, and the military. In addition to enhancing a product's appearance, conductivity, and durability, the company's finishes provide protection from adverse environmental conditions, and electromagnetic interference. While the vast majority of GSP's clients are based in the United States, the company's products reach the global marketplace. Because of this worldwide success, the firm is listed among the top 25 plating firms in the nation by *Products Finishing* magazine.

Innovation and Adaptation

General Super Plating was one of the first companies in 1962 to use Borg-Warner Chemicals' process of coating plastic surfaces with metal plating. The original plated plastic products were knobs for General Electric televisions being assembled in Liverpool, New York. GSP continues today as one of the leaders and innovators in the industry to provide electroplating of plastic components.

With the company's ability to quickly adapt to its customers' ever changing requirements, General Super Plating has become a leader in the health and beauty industry. The firm has plated components to be used on products for such companies as Victoria's Secret, Avon, Gillette, Calvin Klein, and Halston, to name a few. Additionally, General Super Plating provides finishes that meet the rigorous standards of the defense and aerospace industries. Products featuring such finishes include metallic skins that are deposited on components for EMI (electromagnetic interference) and RFI (radio frequency interference) protection that are used in the military's night-vision goggle and communications headsets. Additionally, GSP provides such finishes to IBM, Motorola, Mitsubishi, AMP, and others.

General Super Plating considers its more than 200 employees to be essential to the success of the company. With a growing workforce that includes people with 30-year-plus longevity, GSP strives to keep its employees abreast of technical developments, and provides ongoing training to promote teamwork and motivation.

Committed to Syracuse

Throughout its 60-plus years, General Super Plating has maintained a strong commitment to the city of Syracuse. With the help of resources in Central New York, GSP will maintain its leadership position in the plating industry by adhering to its philosophy of customer-driven adaptation, represented by the inscription on a sign in the office of GSP Chairman H.N. "Duff" Gerhardt: "When you are through changing, you are through."

CLOCKWISE FROM TOP LEFT: GENERAL SUPER PLATING IS A SUPPLIER OF FINISHES FOR VARIOUS COMPONENTS USED BY COMPANIES IN INDUSTRIES SUCH AS HEALTH AND BEAUTY, MEDICAL, AUTOMOTIVE, PLUMBING, ELECTRONICS, AND OFFICE PRODUCTS.

THE FIRM IS EQUIPPED TO MEET A DIVERSITY OF METAL FINISHING REQUIREMENTS.

GENERAL SUPER PLATING IS PROUD OF ITS REPUTATION FOR QUALITY FINISHES THAT PROVIDE SOLUTIONS FOR A VARIETY OF CUSTOMER NEEDS.

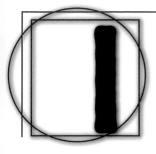

I N 1932, LYMAN F. HIGBEE AND HIS UNCLE MILES Higbee formed Higbee Rubber Company in downtown Syracuse to sell rolls and sheets of rubber, rubber gloves and hats, and other rubber products. In 1998, the 60-employee company, now known as Higbee, Inc., will manufacture 500 million gaskets from its 58,000-square-foot facility in Syracuse.

According to President Larry Higbee, Lyman Higbee's son, the company made its first fabricated part—a flexible coupling for a local washing machine company—in 1939. Then, Lyman Higbee and a machinist decided to convert a printing press to manufacture gaskets. "Dad's first big gasket customer was Crouse Hinds," recalls Higbee. More than 50 years later, Crouse Hinds—a Syracuse-based manufacturer of electrical products—remains a staunch Higbee customer.

In 1975, Lyman Higbee changed the company's name to Higbee Gaskets and Sealing Products. After his son James became president in 1978, the company entered the international market to accommodate the needs of its expanding U.S.-based customers. Larry Higbee became president in 1991, and changed the company name to Higbee, Inc. in 1997.

Today, Higbee, Inc. specializes in custom die-cut gaskets for compressors, pumps, valves, outdoor lighting, the automotive aftermarket, and other applications. The corporation fabricates rubber, sponge, fiber, paper, and engineered plastics for high-volume original equipment manufacturers. Higbee also distributes O-rings, extrusions, lathe-cut gaskets, custom-molded elastomers, thermal/electrical barriers, and a complete line of sheet and roll goods. As a certified supplier for many companies, Higbee has established dock-to-line, dock-to-stock, just-in-time, blanket, and consignment relationships with its industrial customers.

Higbee's client list includes local companies—such as Carrier Corporation and Crouse Hinds—and other businesses in the eastern half of the United States, including Pennsylvania-based York International. In addition, the company serves international clients in France, England, Korea, India, and Israel. Higbee is committed to meeting the requirements of the ISO 9000 and QS 9000 quality standards set forth by the International Organization for Standardization (ISO).

The Team Approach

B etween 1991 and 1992, Higbee, Inc. received a grant from New York State to implement continuous-flow manufacturing and a team-based structure. According to Larry Higbee, the goal was to educate employees by allowing them to share business decisions, including the company's strategic plan and budget. "We have no supervision on the production floor, and we empower teams to both interview and hire employees," says Higbee. As a result of its achievements in this area, the company received the first Yenawine Institute Award of Syracuse University School of Social Work for creativity in the workplace. "With the team system, our employees go out of their way to meet the needs of our customers," says Higbee.

Voted the 1993 Business of the Year by the Greater Syracuse Chamber of Commerce, Higbee also was one of six 1994 winners of the Blue Chip Enterprise Award. As a quality, customer-driven company for more than 65 years, Higbee, Inc. forms a vital link in the Syracuse manufacturing community.

HIGBEE, INC. HAS A NEW HIGH-SPEED PRECO PRESS ROOM (LEFT).

THE COMPANY HAS THE CAPABLITIES TO HANDLE ALL OF ITS CUSTOMERS' DIE-CUTTING NEEDS (RIGHT).

BYRNE DAIRY HAS BEEN PROVIDING AREA FAMILIES with only the freshest dairy products since 1933. Over the years, Byrne has grown from delivering to a few local homes to serving schools and colleges, hospitals and nursing homes, restaurants and convenience stores, and independent supermarkets throughout Central and western New York. Local farms still supply the company with milk, and some have been doing so for 50 years or more.

Matthew V. Byrne, a native of Syracuse, started bottling and delivering high-quality milk to local families at the height of the Great Depression. Byrne realized that, no matter how hard the times, people would always need fresh milk. The success Byrne Dairy achieved is due to its founder's dedication to providing quality products and dependable service.

A History of Growth

The first Byrne milk processing plant was located on West Genesee Street in Syracuse. Soon, the yellow-and-brown Byrne delivery wagon became a familiar sight. In 1938, the company introduced homogenized milk to area families, and by 1940, the growing business had added several trucks to its fleet of horse-drawn wagons.

In 1948, a new milk plant was built on Oneida Street that featured the most modern equipment available at the time. The year 1952—when the last horse-drawn wagon was retired—marked the end of an era for Byrne Dairy.

The 1950s saw the grand opening of the first Byrne Dairy store. Two more stores opened later in the decade—beginning the chain of convenience stores that are a fixture in most Central and western New York communities—bringing fresh dairy products, snack foods, and ice cream to thousands daily. In 1955, ever increasing demand compelled the company to double the size of its Oneida Street plant.

William M. Byrne Sr., son of the founder, became president of the company in 1972—a post he held until his death in 1979, when his brother C. Vincent Byrne took the helm. Another era for Byrne Dairy ended in 1977, when the energy crisis and modern food merchandising practices finally ended the home delivery of milk for Byrne Dairy.

In 1978, Byrne introduced its own brand of ice cream. Byrne Butter was launched in 1981, packaged in one-pound bricks, the old-fashioned way. The product has received numerous awards for its exceptional quality, including both first- and second-place awards at the New York State Fair in 1991 and first place in 1992.

A small dairy in Hornell, New York, was acquired in 1986. This initiative allowed Byrne Dairy to expand into western New York and the Southern Tier. Further expansion and modernization of the Syracuse plant was completed in 1989 and 1997 to meet the growing company's production requirements.

Much of Byrne Dairy's growth can be attributed directly to its employees, who participate in the company's success through a profit-sharing program. Their ongoing commitment to exceptional quality has remained the cornerstone of Byrne Dairy's business philosophy since its inception, and as a result, the company has earned the trust of its millions of customers throughout upstate New York.

SINCE 1933, BYRNE DAIRY HAS BEEN SUPPLYING NEW YORK RESIDENTS WITH FRESH MILK—MUCH OF WHICH ORIGINATES FROM LOCAL DAIRY FARMS—AND OTHER DAIRY PRODUCTS.

THE YEAR WAS 1943. AMERICAN TROOPS BATTLED their way up the Italian peninsula, President Franklin D. Roosevelt signed a bill initiating payroll withholding, and the Yankees downed the Cardinals to win their 10th baseball world championship. And in Syracuse, a small

manufacturer of proprietary drugs became one of the first companies chosen by the government to begin large-scale production of a then-new miracle drug: penicillin. This became Washington's number two priority, second only to the Manhattan project to develop the atom bomb.

For the company that would become Bristol-Myers Squibb in Syracuse, it was the start of a half century of remarkable achievements in discovery, development, and distribution of one lifesaving drug after another.

Bristol-Myers had received approval to manufacture penicillin shortly after purchasing Cheplin Biological Labs on West Taylor Street in Syracuse. To handle the government's demand for the drug—as much and as fast as possible—the company began construction of new facilities on Thompson Road in March 1944. The same month also marked the production of the first commercial batch of penicillin at the Taylor Street plant.

Within three months, Bristol-Myers and other newly established penicillin manufacturers had produced enough of the antibiotic to treat all the Allied soldiers wounded during the D day invasion of Normandy. But while the war of guns eventually would end, the global war against bacterial illness would not. In 1945, Bristol-Myers in Syracuse began systematizing and enlarging operations for civilian production.

Breakthroughs Save Lives

Through the years, other breakthroughs followed that resulted in many lives being saved, while establishing Bristol-Myers in the forefront of the pharmaceutical industry. Within the first two decades of Bristol Laboratories' history, the company and the en-

tire industry scored unprecedented advances against diseases, slashing the U.S. death rate from infectious illnesses by 92 percent and raising Americans' life expectancy by 10 years. And the company never stopped looking forward.

Today, as part of the worldwide business now known as Bristol-Myers Squibb Company (BMS), the Syracuse facility continues to manufacture lifesaving antibiotics. As the only penicillin maker in the United States, the company enjoys a 70 percent share of the nation's antibiotic marketplace. The company's Syracuse employees continue to identify new strains to fight infectious illnesses.

Beyond the antibiotic business, the Syracuse facility is most known in the BMS network as a development center for new drugs. The majority of the company's breakthrough medicines in the categories of cancer and cardiovascular, metabolic, and infectious diseases have at some point gone through the hands of employees in Syracuse.

Community Commitment

Boasting a workforce of nearly 1,000, BMS's commitment

to the community is undaunted. The company's pledge mandates "conscientious citizenship, a helping hand for worthwhile causes, and constructive action in support of civic and environmental progress" in the communities where the company has plants and offices.

In fulfilling this pledge, the Syracuse operation has been particularly active throughout the 1990s. In addition to major corporate and employee contributions to United Way, the company's highly visible community activities support a wide range of cultural, human service, health care, and civic organizations, as well as educational sponsorships, academic scholarships, and special programs for local school districts and institutions of higher learning.

As a committed corporate citizen and a major regional employer of Central New York, Bristol-Myers Squibb in Syracuse will continue to maintain a level of community involvement that reflects its stature as a world leader with a local point of view.

THE SYRACUSE FACILITIES OF BRISTOL-MYERS SQUIBB COMPANY MANUFACTURE LIFESAVING ANTIBIOTICS. AS THE ONLY PENICILLIN MAKER IN THE UNITED STATES, THE COMPANY ENJOYS A 70 PERCENT SHARE OF THE NATION'S ANTIBIOTIC MARKETPLACE.

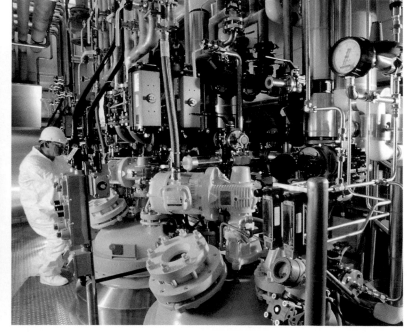

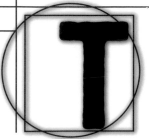

HE NUMBER ONE RATING FOR HEALTH INSURANCE that Blue Cross and Blue Shield of Central New York (BCBSCNY) received from physicians of the Onondaga County Medical Society in 1997 testifies to the company's unwavering dedication to its mission of supporting local health care, its strong awareness of community needs, and the deep-rooted loyalty it has earned from Central New York physicians. As further proof, the New York State Insurance Department's annual complaint survey rated BCBSCNY the best in the not-for-profit category for 1996.

Traditional Indemnity to Managed Care

The model for Blue Cross originated in 1929 in Dallas, when a former high school superintendent named Justin Ford Kimball devised a plan to help local schoolteachers keep up with their hospital bills. He found that by charging the schoolteachers 50 cents per month, he could assure them coverage for 21 days of hospitalization in a semiprivate room. The idea was successful and spread

to other areas of the United States, including Syracuse. In 1939, the first plan to provide a cash benefit to cover medical and surgical expenses took root and evolved as Blue Shield.

Blue Cross established its presence in Syracuse with the formation of the Syracuse Health Service Corporation in 1936. By 1940, the plan had expanded to its present 10-county service area and was called Blue Cross of Central New York. Five years later, Blue Shield of Central New York opened, and in 1985, it merged with Blue Cross to form Blue Cross and Blue Shield of Central New York.

As an independent licensee of the Blue Cross and Blue Shield Association, BCBSCNY offers a diverse line of quality managed care and traditional health care products. As managed care gains momentum in Central New York, the plan has introduced managed care products through its subsidiary, HMO-CNY, Inc. Subsidiary BC&S Associates, Inc. serves as a full-service administrator of benefit programs, including self-funded medical, dental, prescription drug, and/or vision care plans, as well as providing COBRA and flexible spending and parking reimbursement account services.

BCBSCNY has launched innovative products that have taken hold in the arena of managed care. One is the point-of-service plan called BluePoint®, in which enrollees choose their own physician and reimbursement level. BluePoint is unique because it offers enrollees three, rather than two, levels of reimbursement. Members may choose between primary network (level one), extended network (level two), and out-of-network (level three) coverage. With level one, members receive managed care coverage under a primary care

SCOTT BEACHAM SERVES AS PRESIDENT OF BLUE CROSS AND BLUE SHIELD OF CENTRAL NEW YORK.

BLUE CROSS AND BLUE SHIELD OF CENTRAL NEW YORK—HEADQUARTERED IN SYRACUSE—OFFERS A DIVERSE LINE OF QUALITY MANAGED CARE AND TRADITIONAL HEALTH CARE PRODUCTS.

physician. At level two, members receive extended network coverage with no referral requirement to consult a specialist. And level three allows enrollees to consult out-of-network physicians.

HealthGuard Blue[SM] is another successful new product that offers cost-effective HMO coverage through an alliance with selected local providers. Care Directions offers long-term multilevel care coverage. Workers' CompChoice, a workers' compensation managed care product, and MSA Blue, a medical savings account product, are also available.

As a nonprofit, private insurance company, BCBSCNY offers several advantages to its members. One is that state law requires that 12.5 percent of revenue be placed in reserve to pay claims to victims of a catastrophe. This assures that BCBSCNY will always meet its financial commitments. Another advantage is that administrative costs are less than 10 percent of total revenues, compared to 25 percent in for-profit companies. This low administrative expense ratio is a hallmark of BCBSCNY, which has made a substantial investment in technology to achieve this goal. In addition, the company played a major role in developing QuickLink, an electronic claims clearinghouse system designed to eliminate paper in processing claims.

The Health Insurance Legend

BCBSCNY takes great pride in its achievements in support of local health care. In 1989, BCBSCNY saw a need to provide coverage for needy children and founded the Caring Program for Children Foundation. This program served as the model for New York State's Child Health Plus (CHP) program, which was introduced in 1991. BCBSCNY continues to offer Child Health Plus throughout its 10-county service area and is sole administrator of the program in seven of these counties. Also in 1991, BCBSCNY funded a public information effort to address the high rate of infant mortality in Syracuse and Central New York. By educating young women in prenatal and postnatal care, the program succeeded in reducing infant mortality over a two-year period.

In 1997, BCBSCNY became affiliated with Blue Cross and Blue Shield of the Rochester Area under a holding company now known as Excellus, Inc. Later that year, Blue Cross and Blue Shield of Utica-Watertown became affiliated with the Rochester and Central New York plans, increasing the combined Excellus service area to 31 counties in upstate New York with more than 1.7 million subscribers.

The grandfather of modern health insurance is not destined for a nursing home. The national Blue Cross and Blue Shield system, created during the Great Depression, has grown to be a major force in health care, with more than 67 million subscribers. With its market-driven products, strong local presence, leadership position in the use of technology, steadfast loyalty from local physicians, and staunch commitment to its mission, Blue Cross and Blue Shield of Central New York will remain the market leader in health care financing well into the 21st century.

BLUE CROSS AND BLUE SHIELD OF CENTRAL NEW YORK'S CUSTOMER SERVICE DEPARTMENT STAFF CONSISTS OF LOCAL PEOPLE HELPING LOCAL PEOPLE.

T

HE YEAR 1945 BROUGHT MORE TO SYRACUSE THAN the end of World War II. It also heralded the establishment of Holmes, O'Brien & Gere, a full-service engineering and construction firm today known as O'Brien & Gere Limited. Starting with three engineers committed

to delivering innovation, reliability, and excellence in consulting engineering, O'Brien & Gere is currently a full-service, vertically integrated family of nine companies headquartered in Syracuse.

Although originally focused on sanitary engineering, the firm now boasts a widely diverse pool of talent that includes civil, environmental, mechanical, electrical, structural, and chemical engineers; environmental ecologists, geologists, and hydrogeologists; construction, fabrication, and operations specialists; scientists, chemists, and laboratory technicians; computer-aided design and drafting (CADD) technicians; and health and safety specialists. O'Brien & Gere also has been a leader in wastewater treatment and hazardous waste handling, but its services also range from engineering design, construction, fabrication, and operation to laboratory analysis and scientific consulting.

O'Brien & Gere's client base is just as diverse as its services. The firm has worked for large national corporations, such as Nabisco, Dow Chemical, IBM, Bristol-Myers Squibb, and Kraft Foods; major utility companies like AT&T and Niagara Mohawk; and cities and counties in New York and elsewhere. Federal government agencies, such as the Environmental Protection Agency and the U.S. Air Force, also have relied on the firm's expertise. In addition, O'Brien & Gere has a significant global presence, with offices across North America and in Mexico, and additional clients in China, the United Kingdom, and Venezuela.

THE YEAR 1945 BROUGHT MORE TO SYRACUSE THAN THE END OF WORLD WAR II. IT ALSO HERALDED THE ESTABLISHMENT OF HOLMES, O'BRIEN & GERE, WITH HEADQUARTERS ON JEFFERSON STREET (TOP).

O'BRIEN & GERE SERVES THE COMMUNITY FROM ITS BRITTONFIELD PARKWAY HEADQUARTERS IN EAST SYRACUSE (BOTTOM).

A Quality Organization

T

he quality of O'Brien & Gere and its services is recognized by the company's clients, peers, and 900-plus employees. Already ranked among the nation's Top 200 Environmental Firms, Top 500 Design Firms, and Top 20 Firms in Construction/Remediation by *Engineering News-Record*, O'Brien & Gere spent more than $4 million on upgrading its computers and networks in the late 1990s in an effort to better communicate with its offices and clients.

O'Brien & Gere believes that listening carefully to the client is the key to giving the highest caliber of service. To that end, the company provides regular in-

struction in communication and listening skills to its workforce. Classes are given every spring and fall to reinforce written business communication skills, and every few years, employees attend an effective-communications course to refine their speaking and listening skills.

A unique aspect of O'Brien & Gere is its employee-driven focus. "Our people have shaped the organization more than anything else," says Cornelius B. Murphy Jr., PhD, president. "As our people and their interests change, our interests change." The average tenure for the company's corporate officers is approximately 23 years, and for staff members, eight to 10 years. Employee satisfaction can be attributed largely to O'Brien & Gere's effort to de-emphasize corporate structure and hierarchy. Says Murphy, "We want people who are willing to build their careers with us, while developing their personal lives." Within the company, which is 100 percent employee owned, staff members are offered extensive benefits, mentoring, training opportunities, and tuition reimbursement.

O'Brien & Gere is a local leader in corporate wellness programs, having designed an effective system to promote the physical and mental health and well-being of its people. An essential component in the company's wellness program is its spacious office building. "This office was not designed for business efficiency," says Murphy, "but as a comfortable place for our people to work." For the convenience of its employees, O'Brien & Gere has an in-house

fitness center and an on-site day care facility that is licensed by the New York State Department of Social Services and certified by the National Association for the Education of Young Children. The scope of the program also includes coverage for regular physical examinations and seminars on nutrition, first aid/CPR, and stress management.

Contributing to the Community

O'Brien & Gere also takes pride in what it has contributed to the community over the years. As individuals, many of its 450 local employees are active volunteers in local and national nonprofit organizations. The firm sponsors the United Way, Success by Six, Hiawatha Council, Red Cross, Museum of Science and Technology, and many others in the Syracuse community, and, in 1995, was the sole sponsor of the Syracuse Symphony Orchestra's production of *The Nutcracker*. In both 1995 and 1996, O'Brien & Gere purchased all of the Thanksgiving turkeys for the Rescue Mission and helped deliver the meals to needy individuals unable to leave their homes. O'Brien & Gere and its family of employees continue to contribute to the well-being of Central New York outside of the office.

Beyond philanthropic efforts, much of O'Brien & Gere's work improves the overall quality of life in the community. One of its first projects, in the 1950s and 1960s, was handling the expanding sanitary infrastructure of Onondaga County, including sewage systems

and treatment, as well as the freshwater supply from Otisco Lake. In addition, the company has been the major player in initiatives to treat and convey water from Lake Ontario to Central New York, allowing companies and communities access to a nearly limitless supply of clean water. O'Brien & Gere is also a consultant to major companies, dealing with environmental issues and helping industry to be more productive.

According to Murphy, the future of O'Brien & Gere will be in the expansion of its global market and the growth of its domestic environmental management systems services. O'Brien & Gere looks forward with its New Millennium plan, which seeks to incubate ideas and avenues of growth to 2015. Says Murphy, "We are an example of what a group of dedicated, well-educated, innovative, and career-oriented people can accomplish. However, we still have a long way to go."

CLOCKWISE FROM TOP LEFT: O'BRIEN & GERE USED ITS DESIGN-BUILD SERVICES TO COMPLETE BRISTOL-MYERS SQUIBB'S $30 MILLION WASTEWATER PRETREATMENT PLANT.

"OUR PEOPLE HAVE SHAPED THE ORGANIZATION," SAYS CORNELIUS B. MURPHY JR., PHD, PRESIDENT OF O'BRIEN & GERE.

HELPING EMPLOYEES BALANCE WORK AND FAMILY, O'BRIEN & GERE OFFERS AN ON-SITE CHILD CARE CENTER.

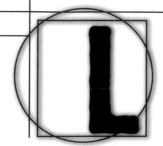

E MOYNE COLLEGE'S 150-ACRE CAMPUS IS COMfortably nestled in the forested suburban hills of Syracuse. Established in 1946 by the Society of Jesus, the college has its roots in the 450-year-old Jesuit tradition of excellence in education. ■ With its nationally

recognized quality and value, Le Moyne offers a unique educational experience for students living in an era of conflicting values and increasingly specialized education. The college's comprehensive liberal arts curriculum offers a values-based education that stresses one-on-one attention, service to others, and the ability to think and communicate clearly.

Affordable Academic Quality

At Le Moyne, students may choose from a wide variety of major fields ranging from accounting to psychology. In addition to its undergraduate program, the college offers preprofessional programs in education, a variety of medical and health-related fields, engineering, law, and environmental science. The college has also enjoyed recent growth with the addition of graduate programs in business administration and education, and offers the only physician assistant program in Central New York.

As testimony to Le Moyne's academic quality, the college was rated number three among the top 10 regional liberal arts colleges in the North according to *U.S. News & World Report*'s America's Best Colleges for 1998. With a 14-to-1 ratio of students to faculty, in-

structors can help each of the school's 1,900 undergraduate and 990 graduate students develop his or her physical, emotional, intellectual, and spiritual capabilities in a lifelong learning environment.

Following the Jesuit tenet of service to others, many Le Moyne students become active in the community. Students can select from a variety of service projects through the Campus Ministry Office, which constantly updates its database of available service programs.

The value of Le Moyne's financial aid package is shown by the college's listing among *Money Guide* magazine's Best College Buys in the Northeast for the past eight years. Highly trained staff members carefully evaluate the qualifications of each student and award various forms of financial aid, including scholarships; in the latest figures available, more than 94 percent of students had received some form of financial assistance.

A Vital Part of the Syracuse Community

The quality of a Le Moyne education is evident from the 97 percent success rate for alumni in obtaining employment or acceptance to graduate schools within one year of graduation. Many

choose to stay in the Syracuse area, continuing to contribute successfully to the college and community. Some participate in Le Moyne's internship and externship programs, through which students gain valuable workplace experience.

The college recently received a $1 million gift from Michael D. Madden, a member of the class of 1971, to create and endow the Michael D. Madden Institute for Business Education. The family of Noreen Reale Falcone (class of 1953) donated $1 million in her honor, and the Jesuits at Le Moyne recently gave a $1 million gift to underscore their commitment to Le Moyne.

Le Moyne employs nearly 500 people and exerts a significant economic impact on the local community. For fiscal year 1997, salaries and fringe benefits totaled nearly $19 million, and revenue exceeded $33 million.

Graduates of Le Moyne—many of whom have entered business, accounting, medicine, law, education, and other professional fields— often comment on the excellent preparation they received for their professions, and the skills they acquired to successfully handle challenges they meet at work, in society, and within their personal lives. It's an education, in the Jesuit tradition, that has prepared them for life.

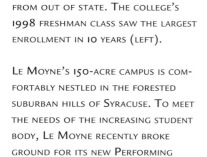

LE MOYNE'S NATIONAL RECOGNITION CONTINUES TO ATTRACT MORE STUDENTS FROM OUT OF STATE. THE COLLEGE'S 1998 FRESHMAN CLASS SAW THE LARGEST ENROLLMENT IN 10 YEARS (LEFT).

LE MOYNE'S 150-ACRE CAMPUS IS COMFORTABLY NESTLED IN THE FORESTED SUBURBAN HILLS OF SYRACUSE. TO MEET THE NEEDS OF THE INCREASING STUDENT BODY, LE MOYNE RECENTLY BROKE GROUND FOR ITS NEW PERFORMING ARTS CENTER AND CAMPUS CENTER (RIGHT).

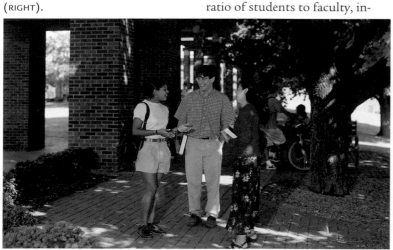

DAVID REVETTE

WHEN HARRY S TRUMAN WAS ON THE VERGE OF leaving office, in 1952, William C. McCarthy and Hugh O. Duskee of Syracuse took office as partners in a new business: the service of NCR Cash Registers. Their founding philosophy—to take full responsibility for their

work—is echoed in Truman's own words, "The buck stops here."

As it approaches the 21st century, the still growing firm, now called Dumac Business Systems, Inc., lives by that philosophy. When a client calls on Dumac to resolve a problem, the company never blames the malfunction on the manufacturer. "We solve the problem with the manufacturer and don't quit until the customer is satisfied," says William McCarthy's son, current Chairman and CEO David McCarthy. "That's why the bulk of our work is repeat business," he says.

Keeping pace with ever changing technology, Dumac offers point-of-sale systems—hardware, software, and service for NCR, Panasonic, and Digital Dining equipment—to independent supermarkets, restaurants, and retail stores. With 43 full-time employees and field offices in Rochester, Gouverneur, and Jamestown, the firm has installed more than 150 systems in independent supermarkets across New York State and more than 600 systems in restaurants nationwide. Dumac's success has not gone unrecognized: For five years running, the company has held a prestigious position on the Syracuse 100, compiled by the Greater Syracuse Chamber of Commerce.

Fostering Long-Term Relationships

Dumac's sales and service relationships with its suppliers, spanning more than four decades, originally focused on the company's strategic location in Central New York. An outstanding record with NCR paved the way for Dumac to expand sales and service statewide (excluding New York City). In 1991, the company established its association

with Panasonic, which soon named Dumac its statewide master dealer. These achievements have made the Syracuse firm the recognized industry leader in the sale, support, and installation of supermarket systems in New York and of quick-service restaurant systems on a nationwide basis.

With the goal of helping customers become more competitive and profitable, Dumac professionals regularly attend exhibits and trade shows to learn about the industry's latest technological innovations. "Our customers know what technology they need, but have no resources to implement it," says David McCarthy. "By

keeping abreast of new developments, we provide them with this service." Once a sale is made, Dumac follows through with the proper training, installation, and service. "We are like a consulting firm that applies the solutions," says Howard McCarthy. "We sell our service as a by-product."

Dumac's principals are nationally recognized leaders in their profession. David McCarthy has served on NCR's Retail Business Partner Advisory Council since its inception in 1991, and is the 1998 president elect of the Independent Cash Register Dealers Association. His brother, Howard, Dumac's president and COO, is one of five people in the United States selected to serve on the Panasonic Dealer Advisory Board.

The company takes great pride in the industry and product knowledge and quality of the Dumac people who serve its customers. In addition, Dumac has maintained a significant growth rate for five years in a row. The McCarthys attribute this solid record to the firm's focus on service, which encompasses not only field engineers, but also front office, sales, technical support, and training staff. After more than 45 years, the buck still stops at Dumac.

TOP: WHEN HARRY S TRUMAN LEFT OFFICE IN 1952, WILLIAM C. McCARTHY (RIGHT) AND HUGH O. DUSKEE OF SYRACUSE TOOK OFFICE AS PARTNERS IN A NEW BUSINESS: THE SERVICE OF NCR CASH REGISTERS. THEIR FOUNDING PHILOSOPHY—TO TAKE FULL RESPONSIBILITY FOR THEIR WORK—IS ECHOED IN TRUMAN'S OWN WORDS, "THE BUCK STOPS HERE."

BOTTOM (FROM LEFT): DAVID McCARTHY, CHAIRMAN AND CEO; SHAUN O'BRIEN, EXECUTIVE VICE PRESIDENT; AND HOWARD McCARTHY, PRESIDENT AND COO, STAND WITH AN NCR MODEL 452 CASH REGISTER FROM 1909, RESTORED BY WILLIAM McCARTHY. EVEN AS THEY KEEP PACE WITH THE EVER CHANGING TECHNOLOGY, THE CURRENT PRINCIPALS HOLD ON TO THE COMPANY'S FOUNDING PHILOSOPHY— TO TAKE FULL RESPONSIBILITY FOR THEIR WORK.

YSTEMS THAT LISTEN AND SEE VERY WELL AND very fast—sometimes even around corners, over mountains, and deep in the sea—are the masterworks of the men and women of Lockheed Martin Ocean, Radar & Sensor Systems in Syracuse, New York. On any given day just about

anywhere in the world, an Ocean, Radar & Sensor Systems high-technology system might be sounding a hurricane evacuation call, moving ship traffic efficiently, giving a sailor real-time danger warnings, locating undersea mines, or even pinpointing disaster survivors. These systems are designed to provide customers with situation awareness. These are part of the family of Lockheed Martin future-making technology that includes the X-33 space plane, C-130J jumbo cargo jet, Mars Pathfinder, and F-16 and F-22 aircraft. Ocean, Radar & Sensor Systems leads in this proud tradition of quality and innovation.

To make its customers "the first to know" is the company's motto today, and the culmination of a long and rich tradition in state-of-the-art information collection. This tradition began with

the development of a stethoscope-like listening device used on surface ships in World War I, and included the development of the first radar and surface ship sonars by General Electric (GE) engineers working on the most sensitive, classified products in the campus-like atmosphere of Electronics Park. These breakthrough devices, advanced acoustic technologies, and systems integration capabilities served the United States during World War II. Some believe this helped win the cold war, with radars that provided air surveillance from the East to the West blocs, and along the North American DEW (distant early warning system) line. Such technology also created the foundation for maintaining the U.S. Navy's superiority at sea with surface ship sonars and integrated combat systems, and

NATO-based listening devices, including two generations of radar systems protecting the United States and countries around the world. For much of the post-World War II years, commercial endeavors expanded, as well, with Electronics Park the nation's hub for production of high-technology television picture tubes. With the GE aerospace business purchased by Martin Marietta in 1993, the business assumed its present form with the merger of Lockheed and Martin Marietta.

Since the pioneering days of radar and sonar development, Ocean, Radar & Sensor Systems has had many firsts, including airborne early-warning radar, over-the-horizon radar, solid-state long-range radar, weather radar, variable depth sonar, hull-mounted active and passive sonar,

CELEBRATING 50 YEARS AT ELECTRONICS PARK IN SYRACUSE, LOCKHEED MARTIN OCEAN, RADAR & SENSOR SYSTEMS IS THE RADAR CENTER FOR ITS PARENT COMPANY.

long-range passive tactical towed sonar, next-generation sonar, and a host of similar inventions.

Exciting new commercial uses for this technology are here today and on the horizon, including vessel-traffic management systems for ports and waterways around the world, creating a new age in shipping safety, commerce, and environmental protection.

Computerization and systems integration to make these products work are the hallmarks of the business. The Syracuse facility is one of only 14 companies worldwide to have achieved a Level IV designation from the Software Engineering Institute. The company has also proudly achieved ISO 9001 and 14001 certifications, along with countless awards for its environmental work, including achievement of STAR in the Occupational Safety and Health Administration's Voluntary Protection Program (VPP) and the New York State Governor's Award for Pollution Prevention.

The talent of the 2,200 workers who call Syracuse home base is only eclipsed by their dedication to the community. Actively participating in the United Way, American Red Cross, Junior Achievement, Explorers, and a host of other volunteer

organizations is their passion and pleasure. Lockheed Martin employees and the company combine to support community organizations with approximately $500,000 dollars a year contributed to community agencies. The firm is also a leading supporter of children's programming through WCNY, Syracuse's public broadcasting station. Sponsorship of the regional International Science Fair with the Museum of Science and Technology and other educational partnerships is the focus

for the company's extensive philanthropic activities.

According to Michael Smith, Ocean, Radar & Sensor Systems president, "No matter how large or small the task, meeting our commitments to our customers and our community is key to our continuing success. As pioneers, we are always seeking the new, fresh, and innovative in ourselves and in the systems we develop. This is our goal and our passion. We look forward to the future with excitement and anticipation."

WTVH-5

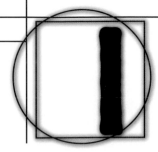

IN 1948, MEREDITH CORPORATION, PUBLISHER of *Better Homes & Gardens* and *Ladies' Home Journal* magazines, entered the television broadcast medium by launching Central New York's first station: WHEN, channel 8. Today, with call letters WTVH and channel

5, the station serves Greater Syracuse and the surrounding area within a 65-mile radius. In addition, the station provided a training ground for NBC's *Today* show weatherman Al Roker and ESPN's Mike Tirico.

In 1952, Meredith Corporation purchased radio station WAGE and changed its call letters to WHEN. By the early 1960s, the radio and television stations had moved to the company's present facility, which offered additional studio space for live commercials, public affairs programs, and other productions. The advent of videotape in the 1970s made production simpler and more cost effective. In 1976, Meredith sold its radio station to Park Communications and changed the television station's call letters to WTVH.

Granite Broadcasting Corporation purchased WTVH-5 in 1993. The corporation already owned stations in Fort Wayne, Duluth, San Jose, and Peoria. It has since acquired stations in Fresno, Austin, Grand Rapids, Buffalo, Detroit,

and San Francisco. WTVH-5's present facility, built to accommodate both radio and live television, is the largest of any in the Granite group.

Fifty Years of Achievement

Since it began broadcasting, WTVH-5 has accumulated a list of notable accomplishments. For example, it was the first station in Central New York to offer

closed captioning of local news programming for the hearing impaired. In the 1970s, it was the first to switch from film to videotape programming, as well as the first to broadcast live remotes when its Live Eye remote truck covered the 1976 election returns. And in 1989, WTVH-5 became the first station in upstate New York to receive a New York State Emmy award for its live newscast the day after the

KLINEBERG INC.

CLOCKWISE FROM TOP: WTVH-5'S CURRENT BROADCAST FACILITY IS LOCATED AT 980 JAMES STREET IN SYRACUSE.

SHOWN HERE IS THE CAST OF *THE MAGIC TOY SHOP*, ONE OF THE EARLIEST TELEVISION PROGRAMS FOR CHILDREN. THE SHOW AIRED FOR 27 AND A HALF YEARS.

THE ORIGINAL BUILDING FOR WTVH-5, THEN KNOWN AS WHEN TELEVISION, WAS LOCATED AT 101 COURT STREET IN SYRACUSE, WHERE THE STATION BROADCAST ITS PROGRAMMING FROM 1948 TO 1962.

Pan Am Flight 103 disaster in Lockerbie, Scotland.

Still another first in Central New York is WTVH-5's Web site, which features frequently updated news headlines, sports, weather, program schedules, classifieds, community events, community service information, a homework home page, a link to the CBS Network home page, and employment opportunities. The station's Web site newsroom tour includes a surprise from WTVH-5's Play Lady of *The Magic Toy Shop*, one of America's longest-running children's shows, which the station aired from 1955 to 1982. Generations of Central New Yorkers remember "the smile that is the magic key to the magic door that leads to the wonderful magic toy shop." Once inside, young viewers met regular characters, including Merrily, Eddie Flum Num, Mr. Trolley, and Twinkle.

Serving Clients and the Community

WTVH-5 takes great pride in the quality of service it provides to local and national clients. The station holds forums to show advertising clients how to tell the story of their businesses and works closely with them to improve the effectiveness of their television commercials. On the technology side, WTVH-5 makes substantial investments in equipment to produce more effective advertising. Today, the station is actively responding to an FCC directive to convert all analog equipment and infrastructure to accommodate digital signals by 2002.

As part of its Companies That Care program, the station annually receives and evaluates nominations for the Jefferson Award for outstanding service to the Greater Syracuse community. The nationally recognized award was established in 1972 with the support of Jacqueline Kennedy Onassis and Senator Robert Taft Jr. Each year, WTVH-5 presents five Jefferson awards.

Recognizing the special needs of hospitalized people and other shut-ins, the station secured permission from the Vatican in Rome in 1966 to broadcast videotaped Catholic masses. The Vatican consented with the stipulation that the station would not edit the services, which WTVH aired until 1993. In addition, the station provides a growing community archive, having preserved numerous historical documents, such as its original Teletype for President Kennedy's assassination.

Technology and Journalism

Although broadcasting technology is constantly changing, WTVH-5 journalists believe that the basics of good journalism do not change, and they take pride in the high quality of their reporting. To them, a house that burns down is a home burned down, and it is more important to interview the homeless people than to present a graphic video of the disaster.

In everything it broadcasts—news, investigation, and entertainment—WTVH-5 is at the heart of the Syracuse community. Staff members have a stake in the station because they live in the Syracuse area and are proud that their station is the first to tell the personal stories of Central New Yorkers.

RON CURTIS AND MAUREEN GREEN HAVE BEEN COANCHORS LONGER THAN ANY CURRENT TEAM IN THE SYRACUSE AREA.

NIAGARA MOHAWK PROVIDES ELECTRICITY TO HOMES and businesses across 24,000 square miles of upstate New York, and natural gas to customers occupying 4,500 square miles of the central, northern, and eastern parts of the state. But there's much more to this utility than just providing

energy; it also conducts an award-winning environmental program, operates two nuclear power facilities, assists neighboring utilities in repair work, is restructuring itself to lower energy costs, and partners with economic development agencies to keep existing businesses and attract new ones to Central New York.

Evolution with Technology and Trade

Niagara Mohawk evolved from hundreds of local gas and electric companies into a single, integrated system for power generation and distribution. The first seed was sown in 1823, when the Oswego Canal Company diverted the waters of the Oswego River to generate power for parts of upstate New York. Other water power companies emerged and, as cities, towns, and industries proliferated along New York's rivers, local power companies began to manufacture gas to light streets, stores, and homes.

Thomas Edison's invention of the incandescent lamp in 1879 set the stage for lighting with electricity rather than gas. While

NIAGARA MOHAWK EVOLVED FROM HUNDREDS OF LOCAL GAS AND ELECTRIC COMPANIES INTO A SINGLE, INTEGRATED SYSTEM FOR POWER GENERATION AND DISTRIBUTION. RELIABLE SERVICE—COUPLED WITH ENVIRONMENTAL ACHIEVEMENTS, LEADERSHIP IN UTILITY RESTRUCTURING, ECONOMIC DEVELOPMENT, AND RESEARCH—TESTIFIES TO THE UTILITY'S COMMITMENT TO SERVE BOTH THE PUBLIC AND ITS SHAREHOLDERS.

▲ RENATE GADDIS

◄ BRUNO TILLS/RANDY CALKINS

▲ RENATE GADDIS

gas company shares plummeted on Wall Street, the development of gas ranges for cooking and gas heating for homes enabled the companies to survive and later join forces with electric companies for economy and efficiency of service. Efforts were also under way to convert waterfalls to electric power throughout the state.

By 1900, the new steam turbines were driving electrical generators to supplement water power. Steam-driven generating plants developed in Buffalo, Utica, Amsterdam, Albany, Oswego, and Dunkirk. As the power industry developed, the need for a business organization to operate it grew, and the larger public utilities appeared. Numerous mergers and consolidations culminated in the creation of Niagara Mohawk in 1950.

More Than Just a Utility

Niagara Mohawk is particularly proud of its environmental program, which has been recognized by the president, the U.S. Department of Energy, and several environmental organizations. The company was the first utility nationwide to achieve certification from the International Organiza-

tion for Standardization for the ISO 14001 environmental management standard, which represents universal quality standards for the global marketplace. In the mid-1990s, improved operations at the company's two nuclear power plants ranked those plants among the world's top performers.

Niagara Mohawk is a leader in the quality and timeliness of repair and maintenance work. The company's research and development team has created a detection system that more rapidly pinpoints the precise site of a lightning strike, significantly reducing the time to restore power

the utility industry. Under the plan, Niagara Mohawk will reduce average electricity prices, give customers a choice of electricity suppliers, and restructure Niagara Mohawk into a leaner, more competitive company. The five-year plan will sharply reduce industrial electricity prices, which, in turn, is expected to create more than 8,000 new jobs in upstate New York. In addition, environmental and low-income programs will be preserved and enhanced.

Niagara Mohawk is focused on rebuilding shareholder value and helping upstate New York grow economically. The company is exploring new opportunities in regulated and unregulated services as a new era dawns in the utility industry. In the meantime, the company continues to be engaged in research and development projects to find new ways to use electricity to enhance customer efficiency, to make delivery of power safer and more reliable, and to find economical ways to use renewable energy sources.

Niagara Mohawk's reliable service—coupled with its environmental achievements, leadership in utility restructuring, economic development, and research—testifies to the utility's commitment to serve both the public and its shareholders. "Our primary goal is to make Central New York a better place to live and work," says Davis. "We will do whatever it takes to make that happen."

CLOCKWISE FROM TOP LEFT:
A NIAGARA MOHAWK TEAM WORKS TO SYNCHRONIZE THE STREETLIGHTS IN SYRACUSE.

NIAGARA MOHAWK PROVIDES NATURAL GAS TO CUSTOMERS OCCUPYING 4,500 SQUARE MILES OF THE CENTRAL, NORTHERN, AND EASTERN PARTS OF THE STATE.

NIAGARA MOHAWK PROVIDES ELECTRICITY TO HOMES AND BUSINESSES ACROSS 24,000 SQUARE MILES OF UPSTATE NEW YORK.

in its own service area. In addition, Niagara Mohawk is highly regarded by other utilities with whom it has mutual assistance agreements. According to William E. Davis, chairman and chief executive officer, "These companies continually commend our crews, who don't quit until a problem is solved."

Niagara Mohawk maintains a multifaceted community action program for each community it serves. For example, the corporation sponsors Earth Day cleanup programs, and is active in charitable and civic organizations across its service area. In addition, company employees teach electrical and natural gas safety in settings ranging from classrooms to state fairs.

In partnership with environmental groups, the utility produces the Earth Generation, an interactive environmental education program delivered to thousands of secondary school students in upstate New York. The Niagara Mohawk Foundation, established in 1992 and funded by shareholders, distributes $1 million annually in small grants to support nonprofit organizations for eco-

nomic development, conservation and the environment, youth and education, health care, human services, and cultural organizations.

Lowering Energy Costs

Niagara Mohawk was one of the first utilities in America to propose a plan for creating a competitive utility market. That plan became a nationally recognized model for restructuring

INTERNIST ASSOCIATES OF CENTRAL NEW YORK, P.C.

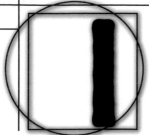

N 1953, AT A TIME WHEN MANAGED CARE AND HMOs were unheard of, Dr. William A. Schiess, an internist, opened a solo practice in Syracuse and began a long tradition of providing the highest-quality patient care in a courteous, professional, and efficient manner. He formed a partner-

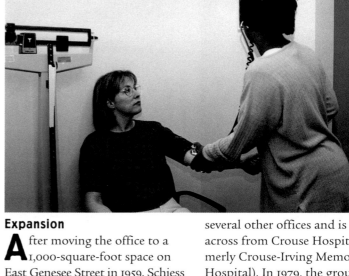

ship with Dr. John J. Duggan in 1956, and the two physicians opened a practice offering internal medicine and cardiology while also making rounds at all Syracuse hospitals.

Schiess, who had been the chief of medicine at the original Crouse Irving Hospital, continued in that role after Crouse Irving and Memorial Hospital merged in 1968. Schiess continued as chief until 1984. Since then, Dr. Paul J. Kronenberg has served in this appointed position.

INTERNIST ASSOCIATES' STAFF APPRECIATE THAT TECHNOLOGY IS ENHANCED WHEN USED IN TANDEM WITH ONE-ON-ONE PERSONAL SERVICE.

Today, the organization known as Internist Associates of Central New York, P.C. is the largest independent group practice for internal medicine in Central New York (CNY). The 14 staff physicians—all of whom are certified by the American Board of Internal Medicine—treat 18,000 patients annually in both the Syracuse office and a satellite location in nearby Manlius. In addition to its physicians, Internist Associates employs 55 nurses, nurse practitioners, technologists, medical assistants, and secretarial, business office, and administrative people. Additional services include treatment of endocrinology, rheumatology, and pulmonary diseases.

Expansion

After moving the office to a 1,000-square-foot space on East Genesee Street in 1959, Schiess and Duggan decided to expand their practice by adding the most highly qualified physicians available. The partnership increased to four by the mid-1960s with the addition of Dr. John H. Sipple and Dr. Philip J. Speller. As new doctors joined the practice over the next three decades, they brought a need for larger quarters. In 1976, the office relocated to the much larger Crouse Irving Memorial Physicians Office Building (CIMPOB) on Irving Avenue, which houses

several other offices and is located across from Crouse Hospital (formerly Crouse-Irving Memorial Hospital). In 1979, the group became a professional corporation, changing its name to Internist Associates of Central New York, P.C.

Physicians at Internist Associates who provide general internal medicine services include Kronenberg; Ray T. Forbes, M.D.; James P. Blanchfield, M.D.; Eileen D. Stone, M.D.; Anne G. Bishop, M.D.; Louis M. Green, M.D.; Erik S. Daly, M.D.; Daniel L. Carlson, M.D.; and Caroline W. Keib, M.D. Those physicians having additional

NURSE PRACTITIONERS AND PHYSICIANS WORK CLOSELY TOGETHER TO DELIVER COMPREHENSIVE MEDICAL CARE IN REVIEWING A MEDICAL CHART (LEFT) AND CONSULTING ON A CHEST X RAY (RIGHT).

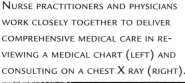

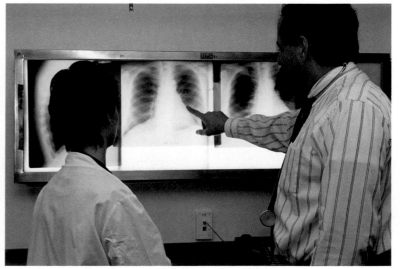

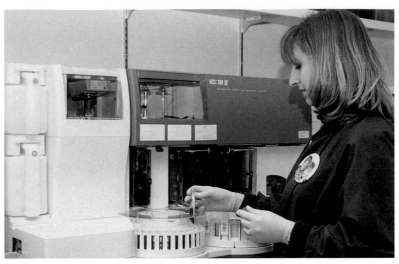

subspecialty training include Sipple; Speller; Mitchell R. Lebowitz, MD; Linda J. Warnowicz, MD; and Ami C. Milton, MD. The Manlius satellite office was added in 1994, and in 1997, the CIMPOB office moved to the newly constructed Central New York Medical Center, an even larger building adjacent to CIMPOB. The new office was designed to provide patients with the familiarity and personal touch of a small practice while offering the services of a large group practice. In addition, Central New York Medical Center's enhanced communication infrastructure provides an efficient flow of medical data and a smooth, safe transition to the electronic medical record.

The Team Approach

In 1987, professional administrator Chris Tirabassi joined Internist Associates to oversee operations and to assemble a team of administrative professionals, nurse practitioners, nurses, medical laboratory technologists, and radiology technologists who could provide on-site services. Today, a distinguishing feature of Internist Associates is its unique team approach to treating primary care patients. Patients typically see not only the same physician with each visit, but the same secretarial and clinical people, as well.

As part of its commitment to high-quality patient care, Internist Associates operates a laboratory certified by Medicare and licensed by the New York State Department of Health. "As the first of a few CNY group practices with a New York State permit, our laboratory provides the same high-quality

testing results as any New York hospital or commercial laboratory and accepts referrals from physicians outside the practice," says Tirabassi. To ensure timely testing results, highly trained technologists utilize state-of-the-art instruments, which, with the aid of computers, allow physicians and staff ready access to laboratory results.

For additional convenience to patients, Internist Associates performs comprehensive radiology testing in-house with timely interpretation by an on-premises radiology group. Services include bone densitometry to assist in the prevention, diagnosis, and treatment of osteoporosis. The group was the first internal medicine practice in Central New York to open an osteoporosis treatment and prevention center.

Education for Patients, Students, and Physicians

Internist Associates is actively involved in patient education, offering instruction in diabetes, hypertension, weight control, osteoporosis, and other adult conditions. "Our program is conducted by certified diabetes educators with additional training and experience in osteoporosis education," says Tirabassi. "And our physicians teach both medical students and resident physicians at the Health Science Center." In 1997, Internist Associates began a clinical research program to explore new treatment modalities for known medical conditions.

Internist Associates is an integral part of the Crouse Hospital Physician-Hospital Organization (PHO), an alliance composed of

the hospital and local physicians from many specialties. Each PHO physician is on staff at nearby Crouse Hospital. Some have received training from the Health Science Center, contributed to medical journals, and held offices in professional organizations. Tirabassi is a former president of the New York State chapter of the Medical Group Management Association and is certified as a medical practice executive.

More Than Medicine

In addition to educational services, Internist Associates employees traditionally host a family for the Christmas holidays. They also participate in United Way, Easter Seals, corporate challenges, health fairs in local malls, and softball tournaments. In 1997, employees contributed money to Amber's Room at the local YWCA, which serves children of homeless, battered, and drug-addicted women. "The children's playroom was established by the YWCA in honor of the late Amber Reilly, former YWCA president and mother of one of our employees," says Tirabassi.

For the future, Internist Associates maintains a focus on customer service and increased access to services, preventive medicine, staff development, improved cost-effectiveness of administration, and pursuit of an additional satellite office in the northern or western suburbs of Syracuse. As the preeminent group practice for internal medicine in Central New York, Internist Associates will continue to provide the highest-quality patient care into the 21st century.

INTERNIST ASSOCIATES BELIEVES THAT ONGOING PATIENT EDUCATION IS INCREASINGLY IMPORTANT IN ACHIEVING VALUE IN HIGH-QUALITY MEDICAL CARE (LEFT).

STATE-OF-THE-ART TECHNOLOGY IS INCORPORATED INTO ACCURATE TESTING IN THE NEW YORK STATE-LICENSED CLINICAL LABORATORY (RIGHT).

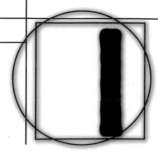

THE SCOTSMAN PRESS, INC.

IT'S ACTUALLY A SHORT TRIP FROM THE GARAGE where a young entrepreneur published the first *Scotsman— Your North Side Shopper* to its new facility on West Genesee Street. However, it's a journey that started for the Scotsman Press in 1954 and continues today with weekly

publications delivered throughout Central New York, as well as commercial printing products and services produced for clients statewide and beyond.

The concept behind that first edition—delivered to some 11,000 northside Syracuse homes—today remains intact in the 18 zoned Scotsman Community Publications that reach more than 211,000 homes and businesses each week. It's a commitment to deliver news of community interest and neighborhood shopping information to virtually every home in the area. Readers enjoy a publication that's devoted to their community, while advertisers welcome the ability to target and saturate potential customers living near their stores and businesses. It's made Scotsman Community Publications the largest print medium in Central New York today.

This philosophy of efficiency and value led the company's founders to employ the Scotsman name and theme. Many loyal readers still refer to the weekly papers as the *Pennysaver* or one of the various other titles by which each of the local editions may have been known. Over the last several years, though, all editions have come to bear the Scotsman Community Publications banner in order to help readers easily identify these popular papers.

Value, efficiency, and quality are also hallmarks of the Scotsman commercial printing division. The company produces a wide variety of webfed and sheetfed printed products for a growing number of clients. While thousands of people are exposed to the Scotsman name through its publications, even more people come in contact with the company's products through

the many publications, brochures, catalogs, and flyers produced for its commercial printing customers.

Growing with the Community

The original *Scotsman—Your North Side Shopper* was produced with very few hands on board. Those first staffers sold and designed ads, wrote articles, printed and delivered the paper, and more. As Syracuse city residents moved to the budding suburbs, they looked for their *Scotsman* to follow. Thus, the number of zones and papers the company produced steadily increased. Today, the Scotsman Press employs about 130 people in its offices and printing facilities, as well as more than 200 people who assist in delivery of the publications each week.

To better accommodate this growing staff and product line, the company recently moved into improved facilities on West Genesee Street on Syracuse's near west side. According to publisher Loren Colburn, "This is a great opportunity for the Scotsman Press to improve and add to the services we currently offer our commercial printing and publications customers. The new facility has had a very positive impact on both our printing capacity and quality while providing the space to accommodate our aggressive growth plans." The Scotsman Press's commercial printing capacity is further augmented by Our Press, Inc., a webfed printing facility the company owns and operates in Chenango Bridge, New York, serving Southern Tier customers.

Much of the Scotsman Press's growth and progress has occurred since it was acquired by Badoud Communications in 1990. Badoud

SCOTSMAN PUBLISHER LOREN COLBURN (RIGHT) AND ASSOCIATE PUBLISHER TOM CUSKEY LEAD A CUSTOMER SERVICE TEAM OF 130 MARKETING, DESIGN, AND PRODUCTION PERSONNEL.

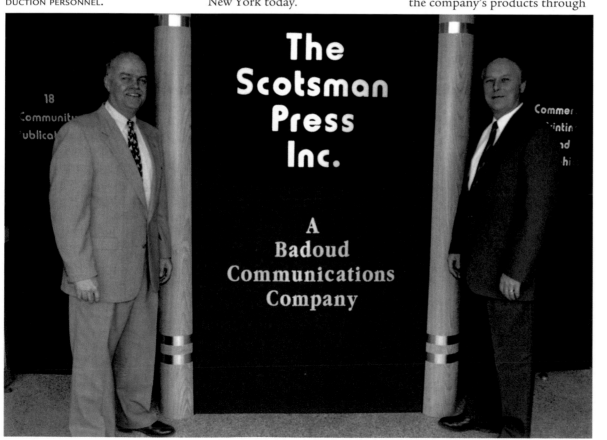

GREATER SYRACUSE

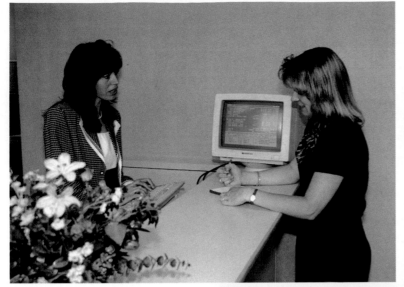

also publishes weekly newspapers in Grand Rapids, Michigan.

An Industry Leader

Since the early days, its peers have regarded the Scotsman Press as an innovator and pioneer in the free paper industry. While paid circulation dailies and weeklies around the country continue to lose subscribers and readers, free papers like the *Scotsman* have experienced steady growth and unprecedented recognition in the marketplace.

Individual recognition for Scotsman Community Publications reached a zenith in 1992 when the papers were chosen number one in general excellence by the Association of Free Community Papers, an international trade group. Since then, the papers have consistently placed annually in the top three selections for general excellence at the national and state (Free Community Papers of New York) levels. Since 1996, Scotsman papers have received more than 30 awards for excellence in editorial, photography, community service, creative design, and graphics. "Our reputation has given us credibility with our audience," says Colburn. "And the awards are due to our dedicated employees, who are motivated by the pride they have in their product."

Once referred to as "the best kept secret in Syracuse," the Scotsman Press's commercial printing division has seen its reputation for quality and unparalleled service extend beyond the borders of New York State. Scotsman is one of only a few area printers to offer both webfed printing, which is used for newspapers and larger publications, and sheetfed printing. This enables the Scotsman to effectively handle almost any type of printing project. Colburn says, "We often attract a customer because of our flexibility and competitive pricing. We keep them with our quality and outstanding customer service."

Capable of producing everything from single-sheet, one-color flyers to complex process color catalogs, brochures, and publications, the Scotsman Press is committed to continually expanding its capabilities. The new facility includes additional press units and the space needed to grow all the related areas of the business, including graphic production, mailing, and bindery services.

The company also recently committed its resources and talents to include state-of-the-art digital image setting in its printing repertoire. "This new equipment allows us to produce even better results for our customers, in both printing and our own publications," according to Colburn. "It's a commitment we intend to keep as technology continues to grow."

An Eye on the Future

The Scotsman Press is solidly committed to technology throughout its publications, as evidenced by the company's Internet presence. "We were the first in the area to offer our classified ads and more on-line to our readers," Colburn points out. "Our staff is working to ensure that our products are ready for the marketplace in the coming years, no matter what that marketplace looks like." It's this spirit of entrepreneurship and vision that has made Scotsman a household word in Central New York over the last 44 years, and will for many years to come.

CLOCKWISE FROM TOP LEFT:
BOTH BUSINESSES AND PRIVATE CONSUMERS SELL GOODS AND SERVICES THROUGH SCOTSMAN CLASSIFIED ADVERTISING. SCOTSMAN "AD-VISORS" ASSIST CUSTOMERS IN WORDING EFFECTIVE ADS.

SCOTSMAN COMMUNITY PUBLICATIONS REACHES A LARGE AND DEMOGRAPHICALLY DESIRABLE AUDIENCE OF READERS EACH WEEK.

A BLEND OF SERVICE, TECHNOLOGY, AND QUALITY RESULTS IN A HIGH LEVEL OF SATISFACTION AMONG SCOTSMAN'S VARIED COMMERCIAL PRINTING CLIENTELE.

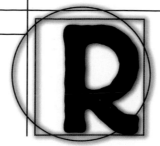

ADIOLOGY IS A MEDICAL SPECIALTY THAT USES X rays, ultrasound, radioactive isotopes, and magnetic energy to produce images of the human body that can be used to diagnose and treat disease. Radiologists are physicians with specialized training in the use of the

highly sophisticated equipment and techniques such as computerized axial tomography (CAT scanning), magnetic resonance imaging (MRI scanning), and angiography (blood vessel X rays) that allow today's physicians to view hidden abnormalities that previously were difficult or impossible to detect without surgical exploration.

Crouse Radiology Associates (CRA) is a 19-member partnership of board-certified radiologists whose mission is to maintain the highest standard of radiologic practice and patient care while continuing to keep pace with the ever changing scientific and socioeconomic aspects of health care. In addition to providing inpatient services at Crouse Hospital, CRA offers outpatient services at the new Crouse Imaging Center (CIC) adjacent to the hospital, the Medical Imaging Center (MIC) in Syracuse, Advanced Medical Imaging (AMI) in nearby Fulton, and all eight sites of Syracuse-based HMO Prepaid Health Plan (PHP).

To accomplish its mission, CRA radiologists utilize state-of-the-art technology in all procedures, including mammography, diagnostic

CLOCKWISE FROM TOP: MICHAEL OLIPHANT, M.D., MEDICAL DIRECTOR OF CROUSE RADIOLOGY, SERVES WITH ASSOCIATE RADIOLOGISTS (CLOCKWISE) R. ROZANSKI, M.D.; B. SCHNEIDER, M.D.; S. SINGER, M.D., M. CONNOLLY, CEO; E.M. LEVINSOHM, M.D.; AND D. THOMPSON, M.D.

CROUSE RADIOLOGY INTERVENTIONAL RADIOLOGISTS R. ASHENBURG, M.D., CAQ-IR; K. TAYLOR, MS, RNCS, ANP; K. SYMINGTON, M.D., CAQ-IR; AND J. CUCINOTTA, M.D., CAQ-IR, STAND IN FRONT OF STATE-OF-THE-ART SIEMENS MULTI STAR T.O.P. ANGIOGRAPHIC EQUIPMENT.

S. MONTGOMERY, M.D., DIRECTOR OF BREAST IMAGING, AND KIMBERLY KIEFL, RT(RM), MAMMOGRAPHY SUPERVISOR, WORK WITH THE FISCHER MAMMOTEST BREAST BIOPSY UNIT.

X ray, ultrasound, CT scanning, nuclear medicine, bone densitometry, interventional radiology, and MRI scanning. As new technologies become available, they are promptly considered for addition to the diagnostic armamentarium.

The Trend to Outpatient Care

The partnership that is now CRA began in 1957 when two radiologists, Dr. Paul Riemenschneider and Dr. Alfred Berne, joined together to provide X-ray services to Syracuse Memorial Hospital. In the late 1960s, Memorial Hospital consolidated with its near neigh-

bor, Crouse-Irving Hospital, to form what is now Crouse Hospital. During this period, the field of radiology was expanding rapidly with many significant new technological developments. The practice grew steadily in size and scope of services, and added radiologists as many new subspecialties came into being.

During the mid-1980s, it became clear that both referring physicians and patients preferred to obtain radiology examinations in a setting outside the walls of acute care hospitals. The trend toward expanded outpatient radiology service had

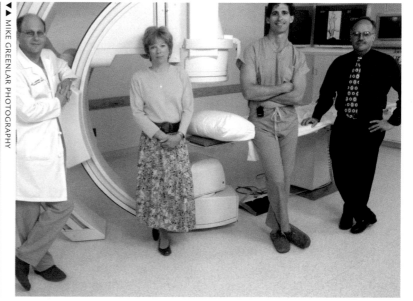

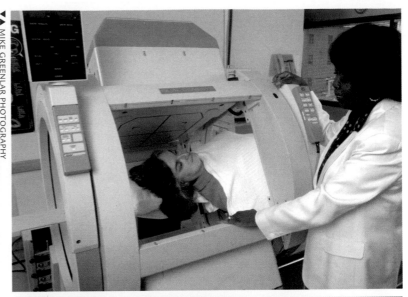

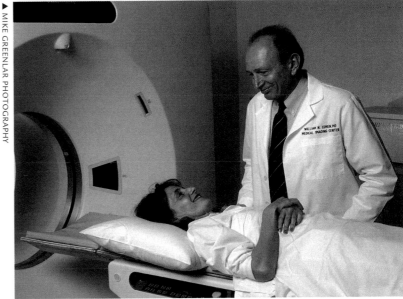

begun. In response to this growing demand, CRA opened its first outpatient office, the Medical Imaging Center, in Syracuse. The success of that center prompted physicians in Oswego County to request CRA to open and develop a second outpatient facility, Advanced Medical Imaging, in Fulton.

CRA currently employs 75 people at MIC in Syracuse and AMI in Fulton. The staff includes general and specialty-registered radiological technologists, registered coders for billing and diagnosis, medical transcriptionists, and administrative staff. Both facilities provide reports to referring physicians on a same-day basis, and emergency cases are accepted and evaluated immediately.

High Quality through Continuing Education and High Tech

Patients are assured of high-quality service by the superior training and skills of the CRA radiologists and their commitment to continuing education of both medical and technical personnel. All CRA radiologists are board certified and many hold subspecialty certification. Most also hold academic appointments at the State University of New York Health Science Center at Syracuse. CRA radiologists have published numerous scientific papers and textbook articles, and they continue to educate students and peers at conferences and seminars. In 1993, CRA achieved full accreditation of all of its components from the American College of Radiology. At that time, CRA was the only radiology

practice in Onondaga County and one of only 10 practices in New York State to hold this distinguished status.

CRA physicians are leaders in Central New York in the practice of interventional radiology. This is an exciting and cost-effective way of treating abnormalities such as blocked arteries and internal fluid collections using special imaging techniques that replace traditional surgery. Many of these procedures can be performed in the outpatient setting and have been made available at the Crouse Imaging Center in addition to Crouse Hospital.

CRA has long been active in providing a high-quality, comprehensive mammography program. Working with Crouse Hospital and its surgical staff, CRA physicians were first in the Central New York area to introduce the technique of stereotactic breast biopsy. This procedure allows the patient to have a breast biopsy performed as an outpatient with local anesthesia and minimal discomfort, with results available the same day.

CRA, together with Crouse Hospital and Health Care Data Systems, has developed a computerized radiological information system (RIS) that links the hospital, the three CRA outpatient facilities, and all PHP centers. Using a single patient identifier, an attending physician can call the system from his or her office or home and learn the results of an imaging procedure performed at any CRA location as soon as the report has been completed. The RIS speeds physicians' access

to vital information while preserving patient confidentiality.

In the future, CRA will continue to seek new ways to provide state-of-the-art care. The development of a picture archiving and communication system (PACS) is one of the next major undertakings being considered by the group. The PACS stores not only examination reports but also the actual radiological images in digital form in a computer, so that they may be instantly retrieved, studied, and even transmitted electronically between facilities, eliminating the need for costly and time-consuming storage and transport of bulky film jackets.

In this and many other ways, CRA remains committed to the success of its strategic partner—Crouse Hospital—and looks forward to the continued development of high-quality radiological services for the residents of Central New York.

CLOCKWISE FROM TOP LEFT: V. KALIKA, M.D., REVIEWS ULTRASOUND IMAGES TAKEN WITH THE NEW ACUSON SEQUOIA UNIT, GIVING CROUSE RADIOLOGY THE LEADING EDGE IN DIAGNOSTIC ULTRASOUND TECHNOLOGY.

Z. SMALL, M.D., DISCUSSES WITH A PATIENT THE NUCLEAR MEDICINE SPECT PROCEDURE UTILIZING THE ADAC GENESYS PEGASYS SCINTILLATION CAMERA.

B. SCHNEIDER, M.D., ATTENDS TO A PATIENT BEFORE COMPLETING A COMPUTERIZED TOMOGRAPHY PROCEDURE. CROUSE RADIOLOGY ASSOCIATES IS DEDICATED TO QUALITY AS WELL AS PATIENT COMFORT.

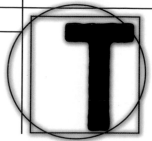

THE FORERUNNER TO UNIVERSITY ORTHOPEDICS & Sports Medicine, P.C. began in 1959, when Dr. Mark Harwood asked Dr. Charles Linart to join him in his private practice in downtown Syracuse. Their goal was to provide the highest-quality orthopedic surgery and treat-

ment to the people of the community—a mission that still drives the practice today.

What started with two doctors and two employees has since grown to include 55 employees and eight board-certified physicians entirely dedicated to the treatment of orthopedic and sports medicine conditions. Orthopedic surgery is a medical specialty devoted to the treatment of injuries to muscles, bones, tendons, ligaments, and nerves. Sports medicine is a related field focusing on the prevention, diagnosis, treatment, and rehabilitation of sports and athletic injuries.

After careful evaluation of a patient's past history and present physical problems, from arthritis to major knee damage, several methods of treatment are available. Areas of practice at University Orthopedics include spinal, arthroscopic, foot and ankle, and hand and upper extremity surgery; electrodiagnostic medicine; and pediatric orthopedics. The practice also provides rehabilitation and post-treatment pain management.

University Orthopedics also employs specialty practitioners, including a registered physician assistant, certified nurse practitioner, licensed practical nurses, registered radiologic technologists, and certified physical therapists. In addition, the practice has access to a variety of diagnostic services, including X-ray, electromyography, CAT and MRI scanning, and laboratory blood testing.

After relocating in 1959 from the State Tower Building in downtown Syracuse to a larger facility on East Genesee Street, and adding services to accommodate a growing business, Dr. Harold Weichert—who is currently the practice's senior partner—was invited to join the practice in 1967. In 1976, Dr. David Hootnick became a member after completing two training fellowships, and Dr. Glenn Axelrod joined the practice in 1982.

In 1984, the practice relocated to a larger suite of offices at the North Medical Center on Buckley Road in Liverpool, a suburb of Syracuse, to serve a growing suburban patient base. That same year, Dr. Stephen Robinson was brought on board, bringing several years of experience as a private practitioner in Pennsylvania. A satellite office was opened at the Clay Medical Center on Oswego Road in 1987, and in 1988 the base facility moved to the newly rebuilt North Medical Center on West Taft Road in Liverpool.

After Dr. Seth Greenky joined the group in the summer of 1989, two additional surgeons entered the practice in 1990: Dr. Nicholas Ricciardi, who had maintained an orthopedic private practice for

GATHERED IN THE LIBRARY OF THE UNIVERSITY AVENUE OFFICE ARE FIVE OF THE EIGHT PARTNERS OF UNIVERSITY ORTHOPEDICS & SPORTS MEDICINE, P.C.: (SEATED FROM LEFT) STEPHEN C. ROBINSON, M.D., SETH S. GREENKY, M.D., (STANDING FROM LEFT) SAAD G. SOBHY, M.D., BRETT B. GREENKY, M.D., AND DAVID R. HOOTNICK, M.D.

several years, and Dr. Brett Greenky, who had just completed his residency and fellowship training. In the summer of 1991, the practice purchased and renovated a large medical office building on University Avenue in downtown Syracuse. By June 1992, the 9,000-square-foot facility was completed, becoming the primary clinical and business office for University Orthopedics, while the West Taft Road site was retained as a satellite office.

In 1996, the practice further expanded in size and scope with the addition of Dr. Saad Sobhy. A specialist in physical medicine and rehabilitation, Sobhy brought electrodiagnostic medicine and pain management experience to the practice.

Service to Central New York

Serving Onondaga and five surrounding counties, University Orthopedics is affiliated with St. Joseph's Hospital Health Center, Community-General Hospital, and Crouse Hospital, as well as most major Central New York health maintenance organizations (HMOs) and preferred provider organizations (PPOs).

University Orthopedics considers service and promotion of awareness in the community a priority. The practice is on call for area ath-

letic and sporting events, and also offers trainer and therapy services to high school and college athletic programs. Weekly orthopedic clinics are attended by the staff at St. Joseph's Hospital Health Center for patients who are unable to afford such services.

Appearances by University Orthopedics staff at local health fairs enhance public awareness of orthopedics, as well as the facility and services. Additionally, four-week public seminars on arthritis are given regularly. These free seminars provide explanations of the various forms arthritis takes, as well as diagnostic methods, nutritional guidelines, medical and sur-

gical treatment, and psychological and social rehabilitation for sufferers of the disease.

The physicians at University Orthopedics are also highly involved in education. They actively publish works in the medical community; teach residents, medical students, and nurses; lecture; and attend continuing education meetings.

University Orthopedics & Sports Medicine, P.C. continues to grow, with plans to expand to a fourth facility. Dedication to providing quality comprehensive care with enthusiasm, spirit, respect, and professionalism will drive the practice further as it prepares for the next century.

PHILIPS BROADBAND NETWORKS INC.

NESTLED IN THE COZY HILLS OF MANLIUS just outside of Syracuse, Philips Broadband Networks Inc. designs and manufactures the "invisible" cable technology that delivers broadband video, voice, and data services to millions of homes and businesses throughout the world.

Whether people are cruising Los Angeles' Sunset Boulevard or touring the streets of Shanghai in China, there's a good chance the equipment they see strung along the telephone poles was manufactured by Philips Broadband in Central New York. Most people probably don't think about Philips Broadband when they're watching cable television or using cable-driven telephone and Internet services. And that's the way the company likes it: cutting-edge technology that is invisible to the people who depend on it.

Philips Broadband, which supplies radio frequency (RF) and fiber-optic transmission equipment and systems used by cable operators and telephone companies, is also a leading global provider of advanced systems used to access cable telephone services, the Internet, and other interactive multimedia services.

International Presence

Philips Broadband Network first established its international reputation more than 20 years ago. Since that time, the use of the company's products has spread throughout Europe, the Americas, the Middle East, the Far East, Australia, and Eastern bloc countries. Philips Broadband employs approximately 900 people, and its products are marketed in more than 50 countries. The company also has manufacturing plants in the United Kingdom, France, and Aus-tralia, and is forming Broadband System Centers in key regions throughout the world to provide enhanced training and technical support.

Philips Broadband is a subsidiary of Philips Electronics North America Corporation, one of the 100 largest manufacturers in the United States, with products marketed under such familiar brands as Philips, Magnavox, and Norelco. Both entities are part of Philips Electronics N.V., one of the world's largest electronics companies, with sales of $39 billion in 1997.

"Philips Broadband Networks has a worldwide reputation for providing highly reliable products, and this reputation is mostly due to the strong work ethic of our Central New York employees," says Michael Senken, vice president and general manager of Philips Broadband Network's Manlius facility. "Our successful track record has helped us take advantage of new markets around the world. Today, we export more products than we sell domestically, and as new cable networks are being built in places like Brazil and China, the future looks bright indeed."

Beginning as Craftsman Electronics in 1963 with a handful of employees, the company made

PHILIPS BROADBAND NETWORKS' FULL RANGE OF RADIO FREQUENCY (RF) AND FIBER-OPTIC TRANSPORT EQUIPMENT AND SYSTEMS ARE USED BY CABLE OPERATORS AND TELEPHONE COMPANIES IN MORE THAN 50 COUNTRIES.

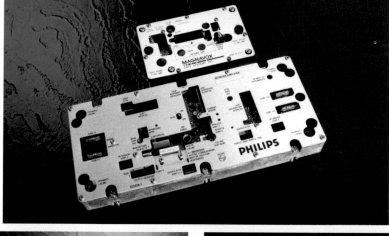

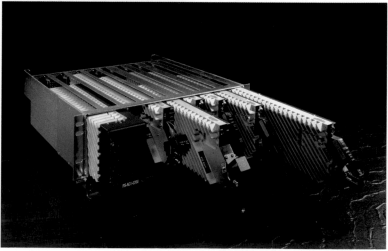

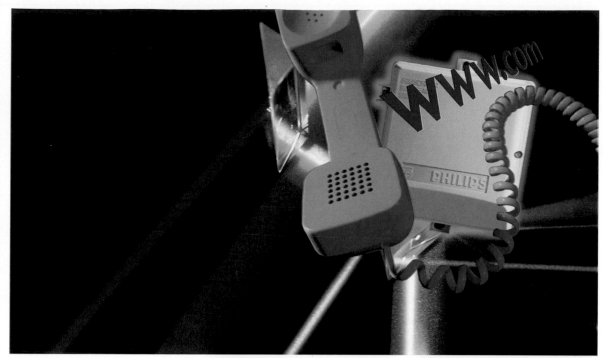

directional taps, splitters, matching transformers, and connectors for the cable television industry. In 1971, Craftsman Electronics was purchased by the Magnavox Company and became Magnavox CATV Systems, Inc., with its principal customer base in the cable television industry. In 1975, Magnavox became a subsidiary of the North American Philips Corporation, and Magnavox CATV changed its name to Philips Broadband Networks in 1992.

Dedicated to Research, Development, and Quality

Backed by Philips Research, one of the world's largest research organizations, and its parent company's multibillion-dollar annual research and development fund, Philips Broadband has access to technical and monetary resources beyond traditional suppliers to the broadband communications industry. After developing the first hybrid amplifier in the cable television industry in the mid-1970s, the company went on to produce the first 330- and 440-MHz amplifiers, as well as the first status monitoring system, power-doubling amplifier, and high-efficiency power supply.

Philips Broadband also supplied the first broadband networks in both China and India, and was the primary equipment supplier for Australia's nationwide cable network, with 6,200 miles of cable connecting 4 million homes throughout the continent. In 1997, the com-

pany introduced its revolutionary Crystal Line™ cable telephone and data system, a unique product that enables telephone and high-speed Internet services to be offered via a cable television network. With a reputation for reliability and strong service, Philips Broadband has earned a place among the most respected companies in broadband distribution electronics.

Philips 2000—An Organization Focused on the Future

In 1997, Philips Broadband introduced Philips 2000, an internal program aimed at creating a proactive, process-oriented working environment at its Manlius and Syracuse facilities. The program initially focused on three critical business streams: product development, world-class manufacturing, and supply chain management. Thus far, the Philips 2000 program has had a very positive impact on the company. In addition to improved employee morale, there have

been significant quality improvements and reductions in product defects.

Philips Broadband's Quality Assurance department and Quality Improvement teams ensure that every product off the assembly line is ready to withstand even the most extreme environmental and operational conditions. Philips Broadband products must meet the standards of the Federal Communications Commission (FCC), as well as those of several international organizations. In 1994, Philips Broadband was granted ISO 9001 certification, which has enabled the company to be more competitive in the global marketplace.

As broadband networks grow in number and become more complex along the way, Philips Broadband is committed to supporting this growth in Central New York with products and services that are turning lines of cable into lines of communication.

DEVORSETZ STINZIANO GILBERTI HEINTZ & SMITH, P.C.

ERVING CENTRAL NEW YORK SINCE 1966, THE Syracuse-based law firm of Devorsetz Stinziano Gilberti Heintz & Smith, P.C. (DSGH&S) began when Sidney Devorsetz, Francis D. Stinziano, and Lynn H. Smith opened their practice in the Hills Building. Partners

William J. Gilberti Jr. and Joshua H. Heintz joined the firm in 1978 and 1982, respectively. The firm, which includes former New York State Senator Tarky Lombardi, is today one of the most highly respected in the community, employing some 60 people and having satellite offices in Harrisburg, Pennsylvania, and Albany, New York.

DSGH&S expanded to MONY Towers in 1972 and remained there until 1983, when the company purchased and refurbished a 20,000-square-foot historical building in Syracuse located at 555 East Genesee Street. An increase in its practice and a need for additional parking compelled DSGH&S to move in

1991 to Bridgewater Place in Franklin Square, but the firm retained ownership of its former office. In 1997, DSGH&S returned to its prior office, making substantial renovations and acquiring an adjacent parcel of land for additional parking. "When we returned to this building, it was as if we were returning home," says Stinziano.

DSGH&S provides legal services to clients in areas of business and corporate law; tax and estate planning; environmental and land use; legislative and government relations; real estate and associated land use; real property tax assessment and condemnation; telecommunications; and civil litigation. The firm is a leader in upstate New York

in certiorari and condemnation law, and boasts a multistate environmental practice.

Going the Extra Mile

We make our clients' business our own business by adopting their goals and their problems," says Stinziano. "We are not a nine-to-five law firm. Every staff member goes the extra mile when called upon. As a part of our representation, we endeavor to learn our clients' businesses to tailor the nuances of the law practice to individual business strategies. We are proud to offer the same quality of service as the New York City or Washington, D.C., firms at a much lower cost due to our upstate location." DSGH&S maintains a constant awareness of legal issues that may affect its clients through the use of technology. This approach allows the firm to keep its clients informed, before problems arise, of trends in legislative rule making or precedent-setting cases from state and federal courts that may affect their own businesses.

Evidence of DSGH&S' strong commitment to service can be found in its Two-Hour Rule. "The purpose," Stinziano says, "is that if a client calls with a question or needs to speak with an attorney who is not available, that client will be called back within two hours by a professional of the firm and will continually be kept informed of the status of their inquiry."

To further assist clients, the firm can provide transportation via its own private plane, a King Air B90, and has a full-time pilot on staff. According to Stinziano, this is not an extravagance, but a convenience and a matter of efficiency in time and dollars. In addition to increasing the mobility and responsiveness of its attorneys, it is often less expensive per billed

◄ DAN VECCHIO PHOTOGRAPHY

THE DEVORSETZ STINZIANO GILBERTI HEINTZ & SMITH (DSGH&S) FAMILY HONORS ITS MANY EMPLOYEE-DRIVEN TRADITIONS.

hour than commercial travel. "It also decreases the time our attorneys are away from the office. In addition to increasing office efficiency, it increases the quality of life for our attorneys, many of whom have families."

An Employee-Driven Tradition

DSGH&S has always valued its employee-driven tradition. "We have dedicated people at all levels of responsibility," says Stinziano. "We promote a family atmosphere by getting involved with our staff. Everyone is part of the team, regardless of their position within the firm." Employees are highly involved in the traditions of the firm, such as the annual Thanksgiving dinner, where the partners provide and serve the turkeys, and everyone brings a dish to pass at the "family" table.

One of the most important traditions at DSGH&S is community involvement. In addition to giving to the United Way, with nearly 100 percent employee participation in 1997, DSGH&S has found many different ways to contribute to its own community. The firm has historically designed and printed the programs for the local chapter of the Make-A-Wish Foundation's Annual Wish Ball. Additionally, the firm's partners match contributions made each month by employees to a fund for Dress Down Fridays. The money goes to a different charity each month chosen by employees. Past recipients have included a local family that was left homeless after a fire, a community center raising money, and a fund drive for a seriously ill child— any place in the firm's own community where there is a need. Another of DSGH&S' traditions is to redirect money the firm would normally spend for a client holiday party as a donation to a different charity each year in the individual names of its clients. Recipients have historically been locally based groups that rely on private funding and that serve the Central New York community. The partners of the firm have consistently shown their leadership through participation in the United Way Campaign; various Catholic, Jewish, and Protestant charities; and Syracuse University's programs.

While DSGH&S has grown steadily over the years, the firm's members consider its modest size an advantage. "Our clients are, for the most part, local businesses, our friends, and our neighbors," says Stinziano. "The genuine concern we have for our clients, our work environment, and our ability to get the job done wouldn't be possible if it were not for our controlled growth."

Stinziano adds, "We're proud that the original partners are still together and that we are the same people that we were 30 years ago." In more than three decades of practice, Devorsetz Stinziano Gilberti Heintz & Smith, P.C. has established a solid tradition of service to both its clients and its employees that will guide the firm's success for many years to come.

THE STAFF AT DSGH&S OFFER A WARM WELCOME TO VISITORS (TOP).

DSGH&S' MAIN OFFICE IS LOCATED IN A HISTORIC BUILDING IN DOWNTOWN SYRACUSE (BOTTOM).

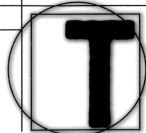

THE HEADQUARTERS BUILDING OF THE C&S Companies, with its tower of black glass, lies quietly on the open flatland surrounding Syracuse Hancock International Airport, site of some of the companies' proudest achievements with a valued, longtime client.

But as commercial airliners make their way to and from Central New York, C&S professionals are not bothered by the frequent jet blasts. That's because the 44,000-square-foot facility, constructed in 1994, was designed with soundproof insulation. C&S provided similarly needed services for some 1,000 residential homes neighboring the airport as part of a comprehensive noise abatement program.

As demonstrated in the example above and in its everyday business, C&S is committed to continually improving the quality of life for the people of Central New York, while contributing to the region's economic growth and development. For more than 30 years, the company has helped implement a wide array of projects to support and strengthen the community fabric.

Four separate but affiliated businesses make up the C&S Companies: C&S Engineers, C&S Design-Build, C&S Technical Resources, and C&S Operations. The oldest and largest enterprise, C&S Engineers, is a Central New York leader in air and ground transportation; municipal/site

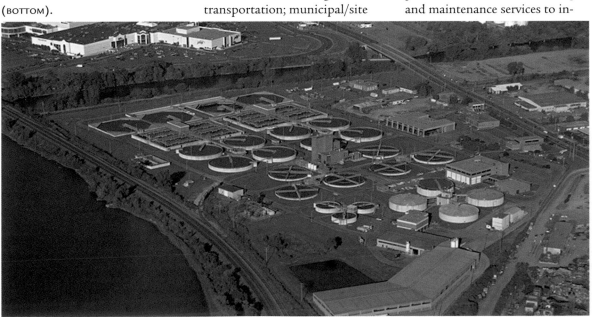

infrastructure; industrial facilities; mechanical, electrical, structural, and architectural disciplines; and environmental management services.

C&S Design-Build combines engineering and construction services for projects that require rapid completion. To achieve that goal, the company offers a single point of responsibility for projects, from concept through construction, thus minimizing delays and saving time and money for clients.

The third company, C&S Technical Resources, was created to provide economical contracting and maintenance services to in-

dustrial clients. Craftspeople and technicians specialize in hands-on systems installation, machinery moving and rigging, process piping and tubing, and preventive maintenance.

C&S Operations, the latest venture, offers contract management services for physical plants, power cogeneration facilities, water/wastewater systems, and airports, allowing industrial and municipal clients to focus their efforts in profitable directions.

These four companies, individually or in combination, deliver the solutions that help industrial, commercial, government/military, and public organizations of all sizes maximize their operations and achieve their business objectives in Central New York and beyond.

A History of Diversification

Professional Engineers Mike Calocerinos and Frank Spina opened for business on January 1, 1968, as a Syracuse-based partnership. Their goal was to provide the more personalized, high-quality service that is typical of a small-to medium-sized company. The six-person firm, named Calocerinos and Spina Consulting Engineers, concentrated on civil engineering (sewage and drainage) for local municipalities. That core business

C&S HEADQUARTERS IS A FAMILIAR SITE TO AIRPORT TRAVELERS IN CENTRAL NEW YORK (TOP).

THE SYRACUSE METROPOLITAN WASTE-WATER TREATMENT PLANT HAS BEEN THE SITE OF SEVERAL C&S PROJECTS (BOTTOM).

remains very much a staple of the engineering company's success today.

It wasn't long before the growing firm moved to a larger building in the Syracuse suburb of Liverpool. Anticipating a market for additional services, Calocerinos and Spina decided to diversify and broaden their base of customers.

In the early 1980s, new environmental regulations precipitated a demand for services in management and compliance, which Calocerinos and Spina met successfully. It wasn't until 1994—not long after Design-Build was formed—that the still-evolving companies, now known as C&S, moved to their present facility, strategically situated near three major transportation arteries: Syracuse Hancock International Airport, Interstate 81, and the New York State Thruway.

Today, the C&S Companies—with New York offices in Buffalo, Binghamton, and Orange County, and additional offices in New Jersey and Texas—is staffed by more than 200 employees, including numerous professionally licensed engineers and other certified specialists. The companies use state-of-the-art equipment and computer software—including GIS (geographic information systems), Intergraph, and AutoCAD design and drafting—for planning, designing, and constructing buildings, roads, bridges, airport runways, water and sewer systems, treatment plants, cellular stations, fiber-optic networks, and more. Environmental services range from industrial compliance plans and air quality programs to municipal waste management, water and waste-water treatment, and hazardous materials remediation.

The Key to Success

C&S' success in the wake of several national and local economic downturns toward the end of the century is no accident. Sound organizational planning and the entrepreneurial spirit of staff, as well as branching into new markets and diversifying services to meet evolving needs, have brought a staying power sure to benefit the Greater Syracuse community for years to come. As the companies continually search for new and better ways to serve their customers and the public at large, they remain true to the core principles that have generated nearly 80 percent of total annual work volume in repeat business. It's a partnership approach that has kept clients such as Onondaga County and the City of Syracuse, among others, coming back for 30 years.

Orrin MacMurray, president of the C&S Companies, maintains a strong desire to provide services that exceed clients' expectations, a business philosophy that was clearly demonstrated when C&S Engineers received the Award for Excellence from the Commercial Builders subgroup of the National Association of Home Builders. The honored project was a new water filtration building, completed $1 million under budget for the nearby city of Elmira in 1996. In addition, the Central New York Professional Engineering Society recognized C&S Engineers' airport achievements with the society's 1993 Project of the Year award for expanding and modernizing Syracuse Hancock International Airport.

The vast majority of the C&S Companies' revenue remains in Central New York because, quite simply, most C&S employees live and work in the area. The engineering company strives to use local contractors on projects, thus contributing further to the growth of businesses in the region. Even as the companies are now expanding into global markets, C&S leaders stress that their roots will always remain in Central New York.

The C&S philosophy is reflected in the words of MacMurray: "It's not just what we do, but how we do it." C&S blends the detail and precision of careful engineering and design with the warmth and friendliness of a personal, custom approach and genuine concern for the specific needs and budgets of clients, whether they are local villages or global, Fortune 500 companies. "Technical accuracy and efficiency are essential in every job," says MacMurray, "but how we treat our customer is the key to our success."

A C&S Tech worker prepares a radar antenna for rooftop installation (top left).

C&S has been a key partner in the growth of the Syracuse Hancock International Airport (top right and middle).

Civil, structural, and geotechnical engineering disciplines are integrated in the inspection, design, and rehabilitation of state and county bridges (bottom right).

Central New York Regional Transportation Authority	1970
Pyramid Brokerage Company, Inc.	1972
Eagle Comtronics, Inc.	1975
V.I.P. Structures	1975
Upstate Administrative Services, Inc.	1976
Genesee Inn: A Golden Tulip Hotel	1977
Syracuse Hematology/Oncology, P.C.	1977
The Widewaters Group	1982
Anheuser-Busch, Inc.	1983
Empire Medical Management, Ltd.	1983
A.J.M. Management Services, Inc.	1984
Götz Puppenfabrik and Götz Dolls Inc.	1985
The Business Journal	1986
Residence Inn by Marriott	1991
TWG Construction Company, Inc.	1991
A.G. Edwards & Sons, Inc.	1993
Time Warner Cable	1995
United HealthCare of Upstate New York	1995
Bell Atlantic	1997
M&T Bank	1998

FOUNDED IN 1970 BY THE NEW YORK STATE LEGISLAture, Central New York Regional Transportation Authority (CNYRTA) coordinates public transportation in 24 county legislative districts, with its 214 service vehicles. As Central New York's "mobility manager," the

independent, nonprofit entity transports handicapped and disabled persons, maintains a carpooling database, operates downtown parking lots, and provides bus transportation to all major shopping areas. Unlike other tax-funded government authorities, CNYRTA generates 35 percent of its own revenue, primarily through its fares.

CENTRAL NEW YORK REGIONAL TRANS-PORTATION AUTHORITY (CNYRTA) OPERATES THROUGH SIX SUBSIDIARY CORPORATIONS, INCLUDING THE REGIONAL TRANSPORTATION CENTER.

CNYRTA operates through six subsidiary corporations: CNY Centro, Inc., serving Syracuse and Onondaga County; CNY Cayuga for Cayuga County; CNY Oswego for Oswego County; Call-A-Bus for the handicapped and disabled; Centro Parking for downtown parking; and a new subsidiary for the Regional Transportation Center (RTC) that began operation in July 1998. At RTC, Greyhound and Trailways buses, as well as Amtrak trains, will stop so that passengers to Syracuse can access local Centro buses directly from a single transportation hub.

Reliable, Safe Public Transportation

The backbone of Syracuse and Onondaga County public transportation is the CNY Centro fleet of 40-foot buses, some of which are air-conditioned and powered by environmentally safe natural gas. In addition to major retail centers,

THE BACKBONE OF SYRACUSE AND ONONDAGA COUNTY PUBLIC TRANSPORTATION IS THE CNY CENTRO FLEET OF 40-FOOT BUSES, SOME OF WHICH ARE AIR-CONDITIONED AND POWERED BY ENVIRONMENTALLY SAFE NATURAL GAS.

Centro routes connect hospitals and major educational centers such as Syracuse University, Le Moyne College, Onondaga Community College, and State University of New York at Oswego.

CNYRTA's involvement is not restricted to bus transportation. Since 1994, the authority (through Centro) has managed Connections, a no-charge carpooling service that matches people offering rides to people needing rides to and from their jobs. For customers who drive to work, CNYRTA operates downtown parking lots where permit holders can park and then ride a bus to the downtown area at no charge.

Local employers, to support their nondriving employees, may take advantage of Centro's Fare Deal program, in which companies re-

ceive a tax-free allowance for providing bus fare in the form of monthly Centro Passports, token packs, or trip tickets to employees. Employees are not taxed for this benefit, and Centro guarantees the Centro Passport holder a safe ride home if he or she works late.

According to CNYRTA Executive Director Joe Calabrese, Central New York is moving from a manufacturing-based economy to a service-based economy. "People used to live in the suburbs and work downtown Monday through Friday, 9 a.m. to 5 p.m.," says Calabrese. "Now, work shifts are irregular and unpredictable, and people work on all days of the week. We are conducting a major study on how to handle this redistribution of workplaces."

With 60 percent of its passengers traveling to and from their jobs, CNYRTA plays a key role in the economic development of the area. In particular, the Regional Transportation Center is an essential gateway to Syracuse and a milestone in transportation efficiency for the city. CNYRTA is particularly proud of its natural-gas-powered vehicles, which will eventually comprise the entire fleet, testifying to the authority's commitment to the environment, the future, and the quality of life for residents of Central New York.

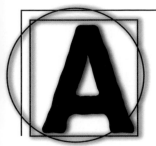

AS THE LARGEST ARCHITECT-LED DESIGN/BUILD COMpany in Central New York, V.I.P. Structures, Inc. provides full architectural, construction, and development services to a variety of clients. The privately held company is headquartered in Syracuse and is licensed or is registered

in 34 states. Founded in 1975 by President David C. Nutting, AIA, the company adopted the motto "architects who build" to describe its role in the construction industry. To date, V.I.P. Structures has completed more than 10 million square feet of manufacturing, distribution, and office space.

V.I.P. Structures is composed of three distinct companies functioning together under one roof. Headed by Vice President James E. Herr, V.I.P. Structures, Inc. is an accomplished general construction company. While performing much of its work with its own crews, the construction company features a solid safety program, a sizable bonding capacity, and a long list of repeat customers. The company also serves as a "supply/erect" steel subcontractor to major national contractors. Led by Director of Project Architecture Thomas C. Malinowski, AIA, V.I.P. Architectural Associates is a fully computerized professional design firm that serves clients both through design/build and architectural design/bid processes. Under the direction of Vice President Charles C. Wallace Jr., V.I.P. Development Associates is a real estate development company that leases facilities to industrial and commercial customers across the United States. V.I.P. Development also conducts national site searches, negotiates economic incentives, and identifies finance sources.

Design/Build

According to Nutting, the design/build approach simplifies communications, increases operating efficiency, shortens construction schedules, and saves time and money by eliminating overlapping overheads. "As a single, responsible entity, we gain a greater understanding of clients' goals,"

says Nutting. Although a full-service company, V.I.P.'s flexibility permits clients to choose only those services that meet their needs.

The company's projects are primarily industrial with about 75 percent manufacturing and distribution and 23 percent medical, offices, and retail. Annual company revenue is approximately $30 million.

The company's design/build expertise enables it to complete projects in record time. For example, the company designed and built a 45,000-square-foot water treatment facility for Gould's Pumps, Inc. in only 74 days, a time considered impossible by all other bidders. "You designed and built our warehouse in 74 calendar days! None of the other bidders were willing to commit themselves to a 120-day completion," said Gould's Pumps Manufacturing Engineering personnel.

V.I.P. Structures also assists Central New York clients in local and out-of-state expansion by analyzing various options, including renovation of existing buildings versus construction of new facilities, and ownership versus leasing of V.I.P.-built facilities.

Recognized as one of the nation's largest metal-building contractors for more than 15 years, V.I.P. Structures has been twice included in *Inc.* magazine's 500 fastest-growing privately held companies, and has ranked among the Greater Syracuse Chamber of Commerce's Syracuse 100 on three occasions, ranking second in 1998.

Through the combined capabilities of the V.I.P. companies in architectural, construction, design/build services, and development, V.I.P. Structures is sure to remain an important contributor to the Central New York area for many years to come.

V.I.P. STRUCTURES, INC. DESIGNED AND BUILT THIS 37,000-SQUARE-FOOT, STATE-OF-THE-ART WELLNESS CENTER FOR CARRIER CORPORATION.

V.I.P. STRUCTURES HAS ENJOYED A LONGSTANDING RELATIONSHIP WITH NATIONALLY RECOGNIZED FURNITURE MANUFACTURER STICKLEY FURNITURE.

EAGLE COMTRONICS, INC.

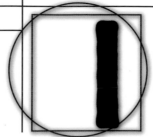

IN 1975, A MECHANICAL ENGINEER NAMED ALAN Devendorf began his business as a basement operation, manufacturing a new product of his own design: a signal filter—a cylindrical trap to maintain electronic signal security—for the burgeoning cable industry. Today, the business

he started has grown into Eagle Comtronics, Inc., a company that designs and manufactures traps, scrambling systems, and general filters for telecommunications systems in the United States and more than 60 countries around the world. Eagle Comtronics, which is the world's largest trap manufacturing facility, holds many patents within the industry, offering a full range of innovative products.

Early Success

Prior to transforming a basement into an entrepreneurial workshop, Devendorf served as a mechanical engineer for General Electric (GE). He had often considered starting his own business, and when GE asked him to relocate after 20 years of employment, Devendorf decided that it was time

for a career move. He thought the best way to ensure success in a new venture was to put himself on the line, so he resigned from GE.

Devendorf had no idea at the time what he might want to build or design, but providence and a little research uncovered a need in the cable industry for a reliable device to filter out pay-television signals before they reached non-subscribers. "Previous traps were weak and prone to malfunction," says Devendorf. "When I went to United Cable in Tulsa, Oklahoma, they said they'd been looking for a product like mine for four years. They put in an order for 129,000 units on the spot."

Working with a few assistants around the clock, Devendorf struggled to deliver his new product. Orders were being filled and

then taken to the airport for immediate, overnight delivery. Adds Devendorf, "I just came out with the right product at the right time."

As the fledgling company grew, increasing revenues provided the capital to move the operations out of the basement and into larger quarters. The current operation in Liverpool comprises more than 150,000 square feet.

A Standard of Excellence

Known industrywide for the unparalleled quality of its products and its ability to deliver them on schedule, Eagle has a success rate of more than 98 percent for orders. The company has high standards for product workmanship and performance, backing all products with guarantees and technical support.

Eagle designers use computer-aided-design technology and state-of-the-art equipment for simulation and measurement. Eagle works closely with its vendors and component suppliers, which are held to the same strict standards of excellence to ensure that they understand product requirements and provide materials that meet or exceed company specifications. Eagle's finished products are tested rigorously to ensure that they will withstand exposure to the environment.

With the largest product selection in the industry, Eagle offers the greatest number of options to the customer, as well as custom design capabilities. The firm keeps more than 750,000 traps in stock at all times. Once an order is placed, sales representatives work to ensure clients receive deliveries in the shortest time possible. Eagle refuses to give unrealistic delivery dates just to secure orders.

CEO ALAN DEVENDORF (RIGHT) AND HIS SON, PRESIDENT WILLIAM DEVENDORF, GUIDE EAGLE COMTRONICS, WHICH MAINTAINS ITS LEAD IN A HIGHLY COMPETITIVE INDUSTRY THROUGH THE QUALITY, PERFORMANCE, AND RELIABILITY OF ITS PRODUCTS, AS WELL AS ITS INTEGRITY IN CUSTOMER SERVICE AND EMPLOYEE RELATIONS.

DAVE REVETTE

DAVE REVETTE

A Quality Workforce

A s one of the largest private employers in Syracuse, Eagle realizes that its workforce is essential to the success of the business. The firm currently employs approximately 900 in the Syracuse area. "I treat every member of this company like family," says Devendorf.

Eagle Comtronics is a horizontal organization. Its hierarchy consists of CEO Alan Devendorf; President William Devendorf, who is Alan's son; five divisional directors; and individual managers and employees, who make many of the company's key decisions. "You hire the best people you can get and then you let them do their jobs," says Devendorf.

The company stresses the importance of open internal communication, and at both Eagle's management meetings and its employee meetings grievances and new ideas can be shared. Everyone's opinion is important at these meetings, which often produce higher morale and innovation. The company's focus on open communication extends to the customer; Eagle maintains a continuous dialogue between its divisions and its clients to ensure the best service possible.

Devendorf feels that the Syracuse community and its excellent

DAVE REVETTE

talent pool are also major factors in Eagle's success. Since its inception, the company has been a member of the Greater Syracuse Chamber of Commerce. In addition, Eagle outsources to other local companies—including component suppliers, machine shops, and contractors—whenever possible.

Always expanding in size, services, and product lines, Eagle recently renovated its engineering, research, and development labs, as well as its corporate offices. An

additional building was purchased in 1997 to further enlarge the firm's manufacturing and administration space, as new product lines are constantly being introduced.

Eagle Comtronics, a pioneer in electronic signal security, maintains its lead in this highly competitive industry through the quality, performance, and reliability of its products, as well as its integrity in customer service and employee relations. "We built this company on two premises: quality and integrity," says Devendorf, "and it works."

UPSTATE ADMINISTRATIVE SERVICES, INC. (UAS) IN Syracuse provides employers and other organizations in six states with cost-effective claims administration for their insured and self-insured benefit plans. UAS is a third-party administrator (TPA) that assists its 150 clients in

benefit plan design, implementation, documentation, cost-containment measures, stop-loss coverage, management reporting, and premium development.

UAS is part of Upstate Insurance Brokerage Service, Inc. (UIBS)—also known as Upstate Companies—and its products and services are available directly from the company and through brokers. UAS' up-to-date technology permits rapid claims processing and data analysis, as well as flexibility for customizing the administration of each employer's plan. Once retained, the company either duplicates the client's present plan or helps to make changes of the client's choosing. For its self-insured clients, UAS pays claims as they occur and does not charge a monthly premium.

According to President Stephen Bennett, UAS can perform its services for a more moderate cost than a traditional insurance firm because the company has fewer managers, lower overhead, and lower profit margins. "Premiums may cost an employer $200,000 per year for only $120,000's worth of claims," says Bennett. "We simply pay the $120,000 and charge an administrative fee, and the client reimburses us for the claims

through its own funds or a trust." To limit the employer's exposure to catastrophic claims or an unusually high incidence of small claims, UAS purchases a stop-loss insurance product.

A History of Growth

With offices in a historical mansion on James Street, founding partners Clifford Watkins, Michael Conway, and Theodora Lohnas opened Upstate Unity Associates, Inc. in 1976 as a life insurance general agent for Unity Mutual Life Insurance Company. The firm provided support services for Central New York independent agents handling life and health insurance, including group insur-

ance, retirement plans, and long-term care insurance. In 1981, the partners founded Upstate Insurance Services, Inc. in Decatur, Georgia, serving clients in North Carolina and Georgia, and along the East Coast. At that time, the firm enjoyed annual revenues approaching $400,000. In 1982, Bennett joined the firm to develop the Syracuse-area client base, and the company name was changed to Upstate Administrative Services, Inc.

The group reorganized in 1987 to form UIBS as a parent company for all operations, transferred claims processing to the James Street offices, and named Bennett an equal partner. During 1988, the company

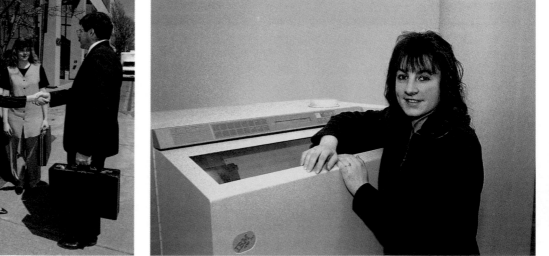

AS PART OF UPSTATE'S ONGOING COMMITMENT TO QUALITY, PRESIDENT STEVE BENNETT MEETS REGULARLY WITH CLIENTS' HUMAN RESOURCES MANAGERS (LEFT).

THE LATEST IN COMPUTER, PRINTER, AND ELECTRONIC DATA PROCESSING EQUIPMENT IS UTILIZED IN UPSTATE'S CLAIMS PROCESSING (RIGHT).

expanded its medical and dental plans by adding flexible spending accounts (FSAs), in which certain employee benefit expenses are paid with pretax dollars. Today, with 130 clients, UAS is a Central New York leader in administering these cafeteria plan accounts. Lohnas has since been approved by the New York State Workers' Compensation Board to administer workers' compensation and disability benefits law (DBL), and the company currently handles DBL benefits for many of its clients.

In 1995, UAS restructured to provide managed care services. The company added its Quality Health Network, Inc., a preferred provider organization (PPO) in which a significant number of area physicians participate. Network users receive a substantial discount that new clients can access without changing their plan design. UAS also added a provider relations department to work with its case management group to provide high-quality but affordable provider network contracts for clients. With 1997 annual revenues exceeding $4 million, UAS relocated to 16,000 square feet of modern office space at 620 Erie Boulevard West, in a reclaimed and graciously refurbished former warehouse.

Personalized Service

Understanding the importance of its staff to its continuing growth, UAS provides its 110 employees with continuing education and customer service seminars on a regular basis. "We encourage our people to think for themselves, which gives them a sense of job ownership," says Bennett.

UAS recently made a $250,000 investment in improved technology to better serve its clients. This has made it possible to report data to clients in a form that fits their needs. By the end of 1998, employees of UAS' client companies will be able to make benefit inquiries during evening hours.

By monitoring claims data, UAS can make cost-effective adjustments for its clients. Using its state-of-the-art technology and clinical reviews performed by registered nurses, the company constantly checks to ensure correct

medical procedure coding and accurate billing for effective cost management. UAS also keeps clients abreast of government regulations and changes in health care trends, providing clients with confidence that their benefit plan is up to date.

According to Bennett, UAS' personal approach to serving clients distinguishes the company from its competitors. "Our clients are employers who want to be closely connected to their people," says Bennett. "Once the client retains us, we explain the plan to the employees, answer their questions, and keep them up to date on changes. They know that we have integrity: We care about them and are not just working for the bottom line."

Quality Comes First

Believing that quality comes first and prosperity follows, UAS is proud of the benefits it has provided to thousands of individuals. "We never expected our company to become a $4 million business," says Bennett. "Our year-to-year revenue and cash flow have grown steadily since we started in the late 1970s, and our services help clients save money through self-funded plans. Our business has become stronger, even during recessions."

Company partners are active in the Society of Professional Benefit

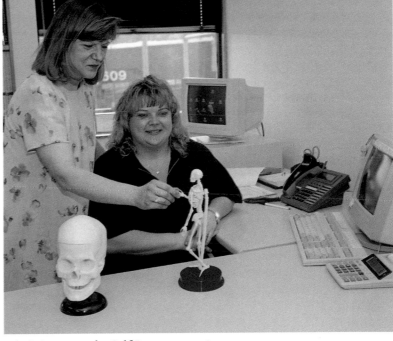

Administrators, the Self-Insurance Institute of America, and the New York State Association of Professional Benefit Administrators. As a midsize company with numerous out-of-state clients, UAS brings millions of dollars into Central New York. "Since it is close to most of our clients, Syracuse is the perfect location for our office," says Bennett. "And it's where we started our business." And with Upstate Administrative Services' dedication to service and quality, the company will continue to be an important part of the Syracuse community for many years to come.

INTERDEPARTMENTAL CONFERENCE SESSIONS ARE A COMMON OCCURRENCE AT UPSTATE (TOP).

PRECERTIFICATION AND UTILIZATION REVIEW BY STAFF REGISTERED NURSES ARE IMPORTANT COST- AND QUALITY-CONTROL FEATURES OF SERVICES OFFERED TO CLIENTS (BOTTOM).

GENESEE INN: A GOLDEN TULIP HOTEL

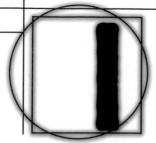

N 1997, THE REOPENING OF GENESEE INN: A Golden Tulip Hotel in downtown Syracuse launched the 19th hotel in the United States for Golden Tulip Worldwide, a prominent international hotel consortium of some 350 locations in 50 countries. Although it has international ties, Genesee Inn remains a locally owned, full-service hotel, offering a unique blend of turn-of-the-century surroundings and up-to-date conveniences for travelers. Like the consortium to which it belongs, Genesee Inn is commited to achieving consistent quality in all services and amenities provided to lodgers.

At Genesee Inn, guests enjoy a home-style, friendly atmosphere enhanced by the elegance of oriental rugs and solid cherry furniture, which has been handcrafted by Syracuse-based Stickley Furniture. Visitors are greeted in a lobby framed by marble, etched glass, and Palladian windows. Designed for short, medium, and extended stays, the hotel features a full-service restaurant, extensive meeting facilities, and convenient access to downtown Syracuse, medical complexes, Onondaga County Convention Center, and performing arts venues. The hotel's proximity to the Everson Museum of Art, Salt City Museum, and other Syracuse cultural offerings is an added attraction.

AS A FULL-SERVICE HOTEL, GENESEE INN PROVIDES MEETING ROOMS OF MANY SIZES FOR CONFERENCES, BANQUETS, CLASSES, AND RECEPTIONS.

Inn-Touch

Many guests who stay at Genesee Inn are relocating physicians or relatives of hospitalized patients. As part of its close association with nearby hospitals, the hotel's Inn-Touch program offers a discounted rate for relatives of patients. Transportation to and from nearby medical facilities is readily available, and Genesee Inn staff members take special care in making guests feel at home by maintaining a strong awareness of their special needs.

Genesee Inn is also in close proximity to Syracuse University, which maintains offices for its International Center at the inn. The university's Department of Global Affairs often houses its international guests at Genesee Inn. In addition, parents and sports enthusiasts often choose Genesee Inn for their lodging during graduation, sporting events, parents weekend, homecoming weekend, and alumni activities.

Antique Buildings Renovated

Prior to its affiliation with Golden Tulip Worldwide, Genesee Inn made its debut in 1977, when owner Norman Swanson realized the potential of a downtown location close to a medical center and Syracuse University. He converted a building on East Genesee Street into an attractive facility with three floors of office space and three floors of efficiency apartments, or minisuites. The 45 minisuites provided a flexible alternative to apartment leasing for relocating

AT GENESEE INN, THE CAPITAL CLUB—A LONG, BRIGHT, AND EXQUISITELY FURNISHED CONFERENCE ROOM—IS DIVIDED BY FRENCH DOORS AND DESIGNED FOR UP TO 50 PEOPLE.

guests and their families. Encouraged by the success of this venture, Swanson purchased, restored, and reopened the nearby Mayflower Building as a hotel with 53 spacious one- and two-bedroom suites. He named the two-building combination Executive Quarters.

In 1984, Swanson added a small, intimate business hotel by purchasing the nearby Treadway Motor Inn and reopening it as Genesee Inn for overnight business travelers to Syracuse. The three buildings became known as Genesee Inn Executive Quarters and offered 96 guest rooms, 98 suites, a restaurant, and meeting rooms. When the 65-employee facility became a Golden Tulip Hotel in February 1997, the name was changed to Genesee Inn: A Golden Tulip Hotel, and major renovations were made to maintain the inn's high-quality accommodations.

Stylish Suites and Conference Rooms

For extended-stay guests, Genesee Inn offers one- and two-bedroom suites with classical high ceilings, spacious living rooms and baths, and specially designed wall beds for more living space. The modern kitchen includes a full-size refrigerator, stove, dishwasher, garbage disposal, toaster, and coffeemaker, as well as utensils, dishes, glasses, and flatware to serve four to eight people. Cable television, free parking, and a remote-control garage are additional services for registered guests.

The 80-seat Tavern at Ten-Sixty restaurant, located on the first floor, provides personal service and accommodations for business entertainment during breakfast, lunch, and dinner. In particular, the restaurant features the culinary expertise of two chefs who happen to be identical twin sisters.

As a full-service hotel, Genesee Inn provides meeting rooms of many sizes for conferences, banquets, classes, and receptions. The Grand Terrace on the first floor can accommodate up to 275 people with its nearly 2,500 square feet of meeting space, which may be divided into private rooms for smaller groups. On the second floor, the Capital Club—a long, bright, and exquisitely furnished conference room—is divided by French doors and designed for up to 50 people.

Genesee Inn has maintained a stable presence in Greater Syracuse through its local popularity and steady inflow of patrons, particularly those associated with the medical center and Syracuse University. In addition, Genesee Inn is very active in recruiting convention groups to Syracuse through its collaboration with the Greater Syracuse Chamber of Commerce.

As part of an international organization with a local focus, Genesee Inn offers the best of both perspectives. It is a true Syracuse business run by people born and raised in Syracuse, and the staff's intimate, personalized service makes guests feel at home, no matter what part of the nation or world they call home. By maintaining the consistent quality that is Genesee Inn's hallmark, the hotel will continue providing accommodations to Syracuse's future visitors.

CLOCKWISE FROM TOP:
GUESTS AT GENESEE INN ENJOY A HOME-STYLE, FRIENDLY ATMOSPHERE ENHANCED BY LOCALLY PRODUCED SOLID CHERRY FURNITURE. FOR EXTENDED-STAY GUESTS, GENESEE INN OFFERS ONE- AND TWO-BEDROOM SUITES WITH CLASSICAL HIGH CEILINGS AND SPACIOUS LIVING ROOMS.

THE GRAND TERRACE ON GENESEE INN'S FIRST FLOOR CAN ACCOMMODATE UP TO 275 PEOPLE WITH ITS NEARLY 2,500 SQUARE FEET OF MEETING SPACE.

THE 80-SEAT TAVERN AT TEN-SIXTY RESTAURANT PROVIDES PERSONAL SERVICE AND ACCOMMODATIONS FOR BUSINESS ENTERTAINMENT DURING BREAKFAST, LUNCH, AND DINNER.

SYRACUSE HEMATOLOGY/ONCOLOGY, P.C. (SHO), located on East Genesee Street in Syracuse, has been treating patients for more than 20 years. Since Dr. J. Robert Smith, one of Central New York's foremost authorities on hematology, established the practice

in 1977, compassion for the patient has been its driving force.

SHO currently treats approximately 1,600 active patients, with more than 13,000 patient encounters per year. Every aspect of the practice's operation is geared towards maximizing patient comfort and minimizing patient stress. "Since we began, we've treated every patient like they're the only one we have," says Sharon Van Marter, practice administrator at SHO. "Our goal is to maintain the best quality of life for our patients and their families."

Originally located in Crouse Irving Memorial Physicians Office Building, SHO has specialized in

hematology and hematologic oncology since its founding. Smith's growing reputation as a compassionate and skilled specialist eventually necessitated expansion of the practice. In 1992, Dr. Frank P. Paolozzi joined the practice, bringing with him expertise and experience in oncology.

In 1994, expanding the practice in both size and scope, another physician, oncologist Dr. Benjamin S. Himpler, was added. That year also marked the relocation of the facility to its present location, increasing the office space from 1,265 square feet to 4,000 square feet. When 2,000 additional square feet of space became available at

the site in 1996, SHO's offices expanded further. In 1997, a 2,500-square-foot satellite office was opened in the North Medical Plaza in Liverpool.

Meeting the Needs of Patients

SHO's full-service hematology and oncology centers house laboratory facilities, which handle blood work, as well as infusion units, where various forms of chemotherapy and support therapies are administered. Since patients may receive treatment for up to eight hours at a time, the infusion areas are furnished with recliners, rather than clinical tables and chairs, and are decorated in soft

SYRACUSE HEMATOLOGY/ONCOLOGY, P.C. (SHO), LOCATED ON EAST GENESEE STREET IN SYRACUSE, HAS BEEN TREATING PATIENTS FOR MORE THAN 20 YEARS. THE PRACTICE'S TWO LOCATIONS HOUSE LABORATORY FACILITIES, WHICH HANDLE BLOOD WORK, AS WELL AS INFUSION UNITS, WHERE VARIOUS FORMS OF CHEMOTHERAPY AND SUPPORT THERAPIES ARE ADMINISTERED.

colors. A selection of magazines, books, and audios, as well as televisions and VCRs, are provided. Patients are welcome to bring whomever or whatever they need during treatment, and every effort is made to give patients freedom movement.

In addition to quality medical care, procedures—such as phlebotomies, bone marrow testing, and hydration—are performed regularly at both locations. SHO is fully accredited and has memberships in the Association of Community Cancer Centers (ACCC) and the National Cancer Institutes (NCI) treatment protocol programs.

According to Van Marter, one of the more difficult aspects of running such a practice is finding the right people to hire. "It's not because qualified people aren't out there, but because they must share SHO's philosophy of care," says Van Marter. "We're not here to see as many patients as we can in as short a time as possible, making as much money as we can. We're here to treat patients."

It is every employee's responsibility to help SHO meet the physical and emotional needs of its patients. "They need special care every day, from the minute they walk through the door to the minute they leave, and every single time they call us. Maintaining a patient's optimism makes treatment easier on everybody," Van Marter says.

SHO's highly educated staff also provides nutritional and emotional counseling to give the best support and understanding to patients and their families. The practice employs 20 people—including certified oncology nurses, lab technicians, and support personnel—and is growing.

Unlike many other group practices, SHO does not use ancillary personnel, such as physicians' assistants or nurse practitioners, in lieu of physicians. Each physician gives time and personal attention to patients, involving them and their families in every aspect

PHOTOS BY FINE-MANLIUS, NY

THE STAFF AT SHO INCLUDES (SEATED) SHARON VAN MARTER AND (STANDING, FROM LEFT) DR. J. ROBERT SMITH, DR. BENJAMIN S. HIMPLER, AND DR. FRANK P. PAOLOZZI.

of treatment. Physicians discuss diagnosis and all treatment options in great detail with each patient to ensure that he or she makes fully informed decisions regarding care.

Putting the Patient First

Since SHO was founded, there have been many changes in the health care field—especially with the introduction of managed care. SHO thrives in this new environment because it has always had a responsible and conservative philosophy regarding treatment, according to Van Marter. "We've never had to make cutbacks because we have always believed in treating the patient judiciously. When you put the patient first, you make the right management decisions."

SHO serves Medicare and Medicaid patients, as well as those with no ability to pay whatsoever. "We advocate for our patients," says Van Marter. "Never does a patient's ability to pay have anything to do with what kind of treatment they receive. Sometimes, the physician's expertise is free, and we contact the drug companies to get necessary drugs for these people at no cost to anyone. The pharmaceutical companies have never turned us down."

Success at SHO always has been the result of putting the patient first. "The physicians here don't believe in advertising, as a rule," says Van Marter. "They believe that if you practice good, compassionate medicine and maintain high ethical standards, people will find out about it."

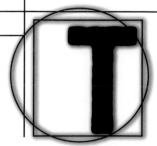

THE WIDEWATERS GROUP (WWG) IS A DIVERSE REAL estate development and management company based in the Syracuse suburb of DeWitt. Joseph T. Scuderi founded the company in 1982 to develop quality real estate products for long-term ownership. Since then, WWG has built a

reputation on a firm foundation of experience and financial strength. Through its total service approach, WWG carries a project from conception to successful completion and operation through its comprehensive in-house services, which include design, planning, construction, leasing, accounting, legal, property management, and maintenance. WWG has successfully applied these wide-ranging services to the development of millions of square feet of office, retail, and hotel projects throughout the eastern United States.

Office Development

WWG owns and operates an extensive inventory of Class A office space, including the Widewaters Office Park in DeWitt and the Woodcliff Office Park near Rochester. As the largest office complex in Central New York, the 65-acre Widewaters Office Park provides more than 700,000 square feet of office space for Fortune 500 companies, as well as locally owned up-and-coming businesses. The multibuilding Widewaters facility includes a health and fitness club with indoor tennis and racquetball courts, swimming pool, spa, saunas, weight training equipment, aerobics, running track, and day care center. The park's proximity to I-690 and I-481 offers convenient commuting from Syracuse and its suburbs. Additionally, the park is three minutes from the New York State Thruway (I-90), six minutes from downtown Syracuse and I-81, and 15 minutes from Hancock International Airport.

The 285-acre Woodcliff development is a mixed-use project housing the 800,000-square-foot Woodcliff Office Park, as well as a hotel conference center with nine-hole golf course, residential community, hiking/jogging trails, and full-service health club with tennis courts. The I-490 expressway and Route 96 lead directly to the park's main entrance, while the New York

FOUNDED IN 1982, THE WIDEWATERS GROUP (WWG) IS A DIVERSE REAL ESTATE DEVELOPMENT AND MANAGEMENT COMPANY BASED IN THE SYRACUSE SUBURB OF DEWITT. WWG OWNS AND OPERATES AN EXTENSIVE INVENTORY OF CLASS A OFFICE SPACE, INCLUDING THE WIDEWATERS OFFICE PARK IN DEWITT.

State Thruway (I-90) is just three minutes away.

WWG also has extensive experience with build-to-suit Class A office developments for such tenants as Metropolitan Life, Kemper Insurance, Xerox, NEC, Peerless Insurance, and various medical facilities.

Retail Development

WWG retail center developments—which range in size from 15,000-square-foot neighborhood centers to 500,000-square-foot regional centers—are located throughout the Northeast. WWG's retail development team creates opportunities for local and national retailers by providing profitable locations in growing markets. WWG's ability to identify sites with superior sales potential and develop these sites in a timely and cost-effective manner has led to projects with retailers such as Home Depot, JC Penney, Kmart, P&C Food Markets, Price Chopper Markets, Sears, and Wegmans.

While maintaining its presence in upstate New York, the WWG retail development division is active throughout New England and the mid-Atlantic states.

Hotel Development

In addition to its office and retail projects, WWG is developing limited-service, upscale-compact, and extended-stay hotels throughout the Northeast. Widewaters Group hotel developments include Hampton Inns, Hampton Inn & Suites, Hilton Garden Inns, Courtyard by Marriott, Marriott Residence Inns, and Embassy Suites. As with all its projects, WWG hotels are developed and managed with the same philosophy of providing customers with quality, value, and service.

Total Approach to Real Estate Development

The Widewaters Group's total approach applies to all areas of real estate development, including design, planning, construction, and property management. Utilizing in-house staff rather than outside vendors to perform specific development tasks ensures that each facet receives ongoing attention from concept to completion and beyond. By providing clients with comprehensive ongoing services, WWG ensures maximum quality control through each phase of every project. This is the key to the success of the Widewaters Group.

WWG RETAIL CENTER DEVELOPMENTS—WHICH RANGE IN SIZE FROM 15,000-SQUARE-FOOT NEIGHBORHOOD CENTERS TO 500,000-SQUARE-FOOT REGIONAL CENTERS—ARE LOCATED THROUGHOUT THE NORTHEAST. WWG'S RETAIL DEVELOPMENT TEAM CREATES OPPORTUNITIES FOR LOCAL AND NATIONAL RETAILERS BY PROVIDING PROFITABLE LOCATIONS IN GROWING MARKETS.

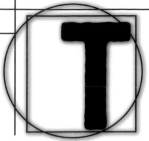

TWG CONSTRUCTION COMPANY, INC., AN AFFILIATE of The Widewaters Group, was formed in 1991 to provide construction management and general constructing services for clients. The company specializes in retail, office, hospitality, educational, and pre-engineered building projects. TWG provides pre-construction phase services, including client needs analysis, design coordination, preliminary budgeting, and value engineering. Construction phase services include construction management, safety compliance, computerized scheduling, and cost control.

Rooted in Service to Owners

Because TWG evolved from an owner's perspective, it is well prepared to assist owners with their project goals. Having completed millions of square feet of new projects, TWG has developed a track record for achieving high client satisfaction, which is the company's ultimate goal.

State-of-the-Art Technology

TWG strives to stay on the leading edge of technology and to apply it to construction projects. This, in turn, allows TWG project managers to be more efficient in the field. The company's network communications system allows project managers from the field office to be linked to the home office via laptop computers. This system allows them to access centralized programs, including scheduling, estimating, Internet E-mail, and a correspondence database.

Value Engineering

TWG's expertise in evaluating the most cost-effective methods and materials for a project often results in a design that allows for quality while maximizing value for its owners.

Single-Source Responsibility

TWG can be a single-source entity to handle all aspects of a construction project. From design management to construction management, TWG's extensive resource of in-house services can be tailored to meet any client's needs. As a construction company, one of TWG's most important tasks is to address client concerns before a project begins and to develop project goals that are specifically aligned with what the owner wishes to accomplish. It is TWG's responsibility to ensure that these goals are met.

TWG CONSTRUCTION COMPANY, INC., AN AFFILIATE OF THE WIDEWATERS GROUP, PROVIDES CONSTRUCTION MANAGEMENT AND GENERAL CONSTRUCTING SERVICES FOR CLIENTS. TWG—WHICH SPECIALIZES IN RETAIL, OFFICE, HOSPITALITY, EDUCATIONAL, AND PRE-ENGINEERED BUILDING PROJECTS—HAS CONSTRUCTED A VARIETY OF RETAIL AND OFFICE FACILITIES IN THE GREATER SYRACUSE AREA AND BEYOND.

SINCE ITS ESTABLISHMENT IN 1972, THE SYRACUSE-based Pyramid Brokerage Company, Inc.—with offices in Buffalo, Rochester, Utica, and Albany—has become upstate New York's largest full-service commercial broker. This fact testifies to the company's adherence to its mission:

"To be a superior supplier of real estate services and information with an absolute commitment to ethics and integrity where the client's interest is best served."

Pyramid Brokerage Company buys, sells, and leases nonresidential real estate for landlords, tenants, buyers, sellers, and individuals. Each area office has its own executive and specialty councils in the real estate disciplines of industrial, office, retail, and investment sales and leasing. Council members maintain up-to-date knowledge of current market conditions; local, regional, and national trends; and lease and purchase economics within their respective areas. Pyramid Brokerage Company clients range from local service stations and pizza shops to the largest, most prestigious international companies.

Teaming with the Client

Pyramid Brokerage Company establishes a client relationship by first keying in on the client's specific goal, while working in the strictest confidence with companies seeking or contemplating relocation.

Pyramid Brokerage Company is proud of its success in bringing companies to the Greater Syracuse area, thus creating jobs and promoting economic growth. The firm initially developed the Syracuse market, later expanding to Rochester, Buffalo, Utica, and Albany.

Pyramid Brokerage Company has taken over the real estate departments of many companies, and publishes data on all served markets through its Market Research Services Group. As a member of New America International (NAI), Pyramid Brokerage Company offers an international scope of services extending to South America. With

its expertise in corporate strategies, the Pyramid Advisory Services Group—a division of Pyramid Brokerage Company—provides clients with services in asset/portfolio management, acquisition/disposition, financial analysis, and lease review.

New America International

Pyramid Brokerage Company's history of success and reputation for integrity and high business ethics helped the company gain affiliation with New America International, an organization in which membership is limited to the most outstanding regional brokerage firms located in more than 220

markets in North and South America and Europe.

Pyramid Brokerage Company regularly invests in advanced technology to better communicate with clients and administer international real estate transactions. To keep abreast of new developments, the company frequently sends its full-time technology professionals to seminars across the country.

With its technology, teams of agents, and support staff, Pyramid Brokerage Company is easily distinguished from its competitors. The company will continue to grow because its willingness to improve attracts good employees and creates satisfied clients.

◄ PHOTOS BY FINE-MANLIUS, NY

◄ PHOTOS BY FINE-MANLIUS, NY

PYRAMID BROKERAGE COMPANY BUYS, SELLS, AND LEASES NONRESIDENTIAL REAL ESTATE FOR LANDLORDS, TENANTS, BUYERS, SELLERS, AND INDIVIDUALS. IN ADDITION TO SERVING NEW YORK STATE THROUGH ITS SYRACUSE HEADQUARTERS AND OFFICES IN BUFFALO, ROCHESTER, UTICA, AND ALBANY, THE COMPANY OFFERS AN INTERNATIONAL SCOPE OF SERVICES EXTENDING TO SOUTH AMERICA, HONG KONG, GERMANY, PUERTO RICO, AND OTHER LOCATIONS THROUGHOUT THE WORLD.

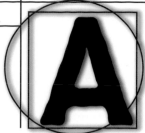

ANHEUSER-BUSCH, INC.—THE WORLD'S LARGEST producer of beer—began as a tiny brewery on St. Louis' South Side in 1852. Founded by Eberhard Anheuser and Adolphus Busch, the brewery still operates on this original site. Busch is credited as the driving force that took a

CURRENTLY, ANHEUSER-BUSCH, INC.—A SUBSIDIARY OF ST. LOUIS-BASED ANHEUSER-BUSCH COMPANIES, INC.—EMPLOYS APPROXIMATELY 1,100 PEOPLE AT ITS BALDWINSVILLE FACILITY, MAKING IT ONE OF THE LARGEST PRIVATE EMPLOYERS IN ONONDAGA COUNTY.

THE FAMOUS BUDWEISER CLYDESDALES HAVE BECOME A WORLDWIDE SYMBOL OF ANHEUSER-BUSCH'S FLAGSHIP PRODUCT.

struggling local brewery and transformed it into an industry giant.

Known for his vision and innovation, Busch set out to change an industry that consisted primarily of local beers, which were brewed and sold locally. Young Busch's goals were focused on creating a beer for the national beer market that would appeal to virtually every taste. This was accomplished through technical innovations that led the industry to such inventions as icehouses that were used to cool railcars of beer being shipped long distances. In the 1870s, Busch launched the industry's first fleet of refrigerated freight cars. Additional technical innovations were still required to ensure freshness in transit over long distances, and in response, Busch pioneered the use of pasteurization in the brewing process.

In 1876, Busch's foresight led him to collaborate with his close friend Carl Conrad to create a new brand—Budweiser—by using time-consuming, traditional methods and only the finest barley malt, hops, and rice. Today, more than 120 years later, Budweiser continues to be brewed to the same high standards that Busch employed in creating the King of Beers.

A Modern World Leader

Today, St. Louis-based Anheuser-Busch Companies, Inc. is a $13 billion global corporation that includes the world's largest brewing organization, the second-largest U.S. manufacturer of aluminum beverage containers, and one of the largest theme park operations in the country through its Busch Entertainment subsidiary. Better known to many consumers by such icons as Budweiser, Bud Light, Michelob, Sea World, Busch Gardens, and the Clydesdales, the 146-year-old company—headed by Chairman of the Board and President August A. Busch III—is synonymous with quality and leadership in everything it does. Since 1957, the company has been the U.S. industry leader.

In 1997, Anheuser-Busch produced more than 30 brands of beer and three nonalcoholic beverage lines at 12 nationwide breweries, and imported six other beers for domestic distribution. That same year, its flagship Budweiser family of brands accounted for 32 percent of all beer sold in the United States. Anheuser-Busch holds a leading world market share of 8 percent—almost twice the share of the second-largest brewer. The company now brews Budweiser under license, contract, or joint venture in eight

countries, and exports Budweiser and other brands to more than 80 others—accounting for nearly half of all American beer shipped abroad.

Company profits have increased from $85 million in 1975 to $1.2 billion in 1997. During that same time frame, company beer sales grew 159 percent, compared to industrywide growth of only 34 percent. Anheuser-Busch's corresponding share of the U.S. beer market has nearly doubled, from 23 percent in 1975 to more than 45 percent in 1997, with a 23 share-point lead in 1997 over the nearest competitor.

Through its Metal Container Corporation subsidiary, Anheuser-Busch is also a leader in the nation's packaging industry. This division has captured an increasing share of this market by providing the highest-quality, lowest-cost cans, lids, labels, and beverage can recycling in the industry. With 11 plants nationwide, Metal Container Corporation has grown from a start-up in 1973 to the country's second-largest producer of aluminum beverage containers in 1995. In addition, Anheuser-Busch Recycling Corporation, launched in 1978, has become the world's largest recycler of used aluminum beverage containers.

In addition, Anheuser-Busch is recognized as one of America's leading corporate citizens. It has provided long-standing and aggressive support for the communities in which it operates through alcohol awareness efforts, environmental conservation, educa-

tional opportunities, and disaster relief.

The Baldwinsville Brewery

Currently, Anheuser-Busch employs approximately 1,100 people at its Baldwinsville facility, making it one of the largest private employers in Onondaga County. Under the leadership of Plant Manager Brian J. McNelis and Resident Brewmaster Mark P. Sammartinio, the brewery produces 8.6 million barrels annually, representing approximately 27 brands of beer.

Since opening in 1983, Anheuser-Busch has invested nearly $200 million in improvements to the 1.5 million-square-foot Baldwinsville facility. The plant is also one of three business administration hubs for Anheuser-Busch Companies, Inc., handling administrative tasks for breweries in Newark, New Jersey; Columbus, Ohio; and Merrimack, New Hampshire.

The Baldwinsville brewery has contributed more than $1 million over a five-year period to a number of local organizations, including the United Way, Onondaga County Operation Brightside, Urban League, Boys and Girls Club of Syracuse, Junior Achievement, American Red Cross, Burnett Park Zoo, and other organizations. Furthermore, the brewery is actively involved in the Greater Syracuse Chamber of Commerce, Metropolitan Development Association, Business Council of New York State, Manufacturer's Association of Central New York, Baldwinsville Chamber of Commerce, and Radisson Community Association.

The Baldwinsville brewery has a significant impact on the local economy through its warehousing, packaging, and supplies operations. "Five years from now, I see us as a very healthy operation," says McNelis. "I see us as a more modernized brewery and still in upstate."

ANY SUCCESSFUL CORPORATIONS WERE BEGUN BY one person who followed through with a great idea. Back in 1979, Dr. Harvey Y. Lewis had just such an idea. While working in Flint, Michigan, he determined that employers needed independent and timely medical consultation

services. When his first client—General Motors (GM)—asked him to provide this service, he responded with a simple yes, and then determined the best way to do it. His Syracuse-based organization—called Riverfront Medical Services, PC—now has 3,000 clients, including casualty and life insurance carriers, multinational corporations, and government agencies, to name a few. In fact, with 14 sites across New York State, Riverfront requires a separate management arm, Empire Medical Management, Ltd., which is co-owned by Peter Clark and Lewis' daughter, Sherry Lewis.

Growth by Saying Yes

Harvey Lewis' 1979 involvement with the General Motors Independent Medical Opinion Program was part of a negotiated agreement between GM and the United Auto Workers in Flint. If a worker reported sick for a non-work-related injury, the shift supervisor could quickly refer the individual to an independent physician to determine the worker's fitness for the next shift. The timeliness of the evaluation minimized time lost from work, and the program's success prompted GM to provide the same service at its plants in the Buffalo area. When

asked to relocate and launch the New York program, Lewis again said yes, and left Michigan in 1981 to establish the Riverfront East Medical Center, which later became part of Riverfront Medical Services, PC.

Lewis soon became aware that insurance companies were frustrated with the time—sometimes months—required to schedule a medical examination with a private physician for a bodily injury claim. Seizing the opportunity, Lewis announced that he could provide an independent examination for the insurance companies in 10 days. Then he hired physicians to do the job.

Formation of Empire Medical Management

By the mid-1980s, Riverfront had opened offices in Syracuse (1983), Rochester, and Binghamton. It was then that Lewis and Clark formed Empire Medical Management to administer the rapidly growing business. A primary task of Clark's, who was then Empire's director of operations, was to lay a solid foundation for management and future growth by securing an automated information system. Using the UNISYS Make and Prepare Executive Reports (MAPPER) system, he hired specialists to develop in-house programs that became proprietary within Empire.

As comptroller, Sherry Lewis was charged with developing sound fiscal policy and creating a competitive benefit package for Riverfront's employees. Once these objectives were met, Empire established a marketing department based on the directive "Grow the business in response to customers' needs." In 1991, Clark and Sherry Lewis purchased Empire from Harvey Lewis, and Clark became CEO.

Today, Riverfront physicians annually conduct some 30,000 independent and timely physical examinations for carriers of work-

CLOCKWISE FROM TOP:
SHERRY LEWIS AND PETER CLARK, OWN-ERS OF EMPIRE MEDICAL MANAGEMENT, LTD., MEET REGULARLY WITH THE FIRM'S MANAGERS FOR TRAINING AND DISCUSSION OF BUSINESS OPPORTUNITIES. STRATEGIC RESULTS ARE SHARED WITH ALL THE STAFF, AND SUCCESS IS SHARED THROUGH A VARIABLE PAY PLAN.

SUE ALTIERI, CAPITAL DISTRICT MANAGER, REVIEWS EMPIRE'S FORTHCOMING WEB PAGE.

CLARK, CO-OWNER AND CEO, REVIEWS THE COMPANY'S STRATEGIC VALUES AND DIRECTION WITH TEAM MEMBERS.

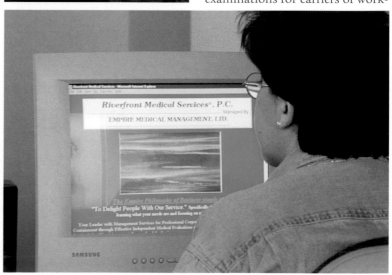

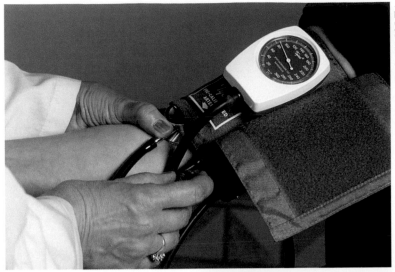

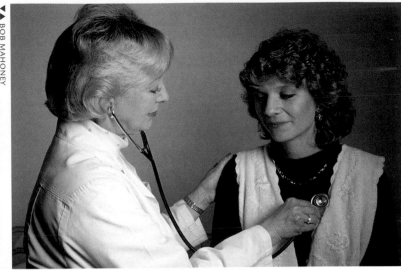

▼▲ BOB MAHONEY

▶ BOB MAHONEY

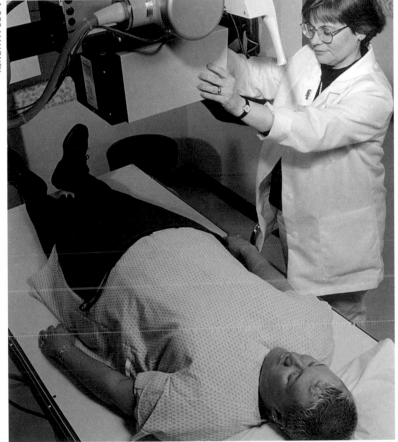

ers' compensation; independent medical exam (IME) businesses; self-insured employers; and attorneys. Medical professionals from 32 specialties are under contract with Riverfront to accomplish this enormous task. As proof of its preeminence in the industry, Riverfront was one of the first two companies, nationally, to be certified by the International Association of Industrial Accident Boards and Commissions.

Empire, in turn, provides operations management, financial administration, management information systems, training and development, and marketing for Riverfront. In particular, Empire delivers a communication system that meets the requirements of medical specialists, the business community, and other claims-resolution parties, such as legal representatives, adjudicators, and the medical community.

A leader in the management of independent medical practices, Empire has been listed for many years among the Syracuse 100, compiled by the Greater Syracuse Chamber of Commerce. Clark attributes this success to the firm's strong belief in its highly trained and motivated staff. "We are not the least expensive provider of our services," says Clark. "What sets us apart is that clients prefer to work with our people, who take great pride in their ability to listen to our clients, as well as to each other." Empire employees, who are empowered to make decisions on their own, observe two tenets of equal importance: "Always look to work smarter and not harder," and "Do it with the customer in mind."

Further differentiating itself, Empire is the only independent medical consultation management group that employs a full-time, certified recruiter to thoroughly check the credentials of examining physicians. "The exam we give a worker is not just a routine physical," explains Clark. "Our physicians act as evaluators who must identify inconsistencies and render an objective opinion for both the insurance company and the worker. This requires a fine balance to give everyone a fair shake. And since all our reports could eventually go to arbitration or workers' compensation court, we must do a top-notch job."

Empire's corporate objective, "to delight people with our service," along with Empire 2001, its vision for the future, helps employees focus on the company's goals for the next decade. "The cost of workers' compensation is a small part of the overall health care bill, but it's growing very fast," says Clark. "We will stay in contact to see what changes are around the corner, and we will adapt to that. We will continue to work with businesses to prevent workplace accidents and to facilitate communication—all with the goal of making the bodily injury claims process much smoother and more efficient."

CLOCKWISE FROM TOP LEFT: HEALTHY COMPANIES NEED HEALTHY EMPLOYEES, AND A GROWING PORTION OF EMPIRE'S AND RIVERFRONT'S REFERRALS COME THROUGH EMPLOYEE PHYSICALS FROM FORWARD-THINKING COMPANIES.

MEDICINE IS A PEOPLE BUSINESS AND ALL EMPIRE STAFF MEMBERS WORK HARD TO PUT THE EXAMINEES AT EASE.

EACH EMPIRE LOCATION FEATURES STATE-OF-THE-ART TECHNOLOGY.

The German poet Johann Wolfgang von Goethe once noted, "The important thing in this world is not where we stand, but in what direction we move." Since the 1970s, the direction of health care delivery in Central New York has moved in an innovative path under the visionary leadership of A. John Merola, M.D. A family practice physician, Merola realized the need for a comprehensive, convenient, state-of-the-art medical facility in the northern suburbs of Syracuse. In 1973, the first phase of Merola's plan was actualized when a 40,000-square-foot building, housing 20 physicians from a variety of specialties, was erected in Liverpool.

Since that time, the direction Merola has taken continues to be on the leading edge of health care delivery. Instrumental to implementing Merola's dream is A.J.M. Management Services, Inc., which he founded in 1984. Currently a 450-employee health care organization, A.J.M. Management Services was the driving force in building North Medical Center and Northeast Medical Center.

North Medical Center

In 1983, Merola formulated plans for the 200,000-square-foot North Medical Center (NMC), which was developed on a condominium basis, enabling physicians to invest in the project. After breaking ground in 1986, Merola completed the medical center—a 32-suite facility of 200 physicians who offer both primary and specialty care ranging from allergy to urology. In essence, virtually any medical specialty or support service can be found on the campus, including, but not limited to, medical imaging, physical therapy, rehabilitation, and on-site laboratories. NMC now serves 35 percent of the Onondaga County population and 65 percent of the people living within 10 miles of the medical complex. For the many patients who use the campus, free parking is particularly convenient and economical. Also, the center is a major source of tax revenue and a significant employer in the Central New York region.

A cornerstone of NMC is the Urgent Care facility, which opened in 1989. Merola was a pioneer with Urgent Care, and since its inception, other similar centers have opened in the county. The 24-hour Urgent Care center is staffed by board-certified physicians who treat non-life-threatening conditions, such as lacerations, fractures, sore throats, and skin rashes, regardless of the patient's ability to pay. According to Merola, about 95 percent of the patients seen in a hospital emergency room could be treated in an urgent care center.

Another important entity at NMC is St. Joseph's North Surgery center. In addition to providing clinical services, the majority of physicians at NMC serve on the faculty at the State University of New York Health Science Center in Syracuse. These physicians stay abreast of new developments in medicine and teach medical students and residents.

Finally, unlike most practices, North Medical Family Physicians (NMFP) has extended hours of operation and uses no answering service. Instead, telephones automatically switch to the Urgent Care center after hours.

Northeast Medical Center

Merola continued to move in new directions when he designed and opened the Northeast Medical Center (NEMC), a 202,000-square-foot facility devel-

A.J.M. Management Services, Inc. was the driving force in building North Medical Center, which serves 35 percent of the Onondaga County population and 65 percent of the people living within 10 miles of the medical complex.

RON TRINCA PHOTOGRAPHY

oped in collaboration with St. Joseph's Hospital Health Center through a $51 million, privately funded initiative. Offering the same services as NMC, the NEMC condominium in Fayetteville was constructed to provide quality health care to the eastern suburbs of Syracuse. Leading the way in health care for women, the new complex also includes the Women's Place, which offers a broad spectrum of female services in gynecology, mammography, and surgery, among others.

Over the next decade, NEMC is projected to pay $2.6 million in school taxes, contribute more than $1.4 million to the local tax base, and create more than 1,000 full- and part-time jobs for Central New York.

According to Merola, his privately owned facilities bear sophistication comparable to those of large not-for-profit hospitals. "Unlike most medical practices, we offer one-stop medical care that includes everything but the hospital." says Merola. "We provide comprehensive services 24 hours per day because people don't get sick on the clock, but rather, need immediate attention when illness occurs."

A Complete Range of Services

In addition to the two medical centers, A.J.M. Management's broad umbrella includes A.J.M. Building Corporation, Merola's construction arm; NM Communications, Inc., which is the communications link between the two medical centers; and Medical Decorating Services, Inc., which provides suite furnishings at wholesale prices through group co-op purchasing. Another entity on the NMC campus that is moving in a progressive direction is Janus Park, a nursing home alternative that allows for dignified residential living with its private apartments and nursing services. The NMC campus also includes a radiotherapy center; medical support facilities offering home health care; pharmacy; office management and billing; optometry; and a bank. Additionally, Franciscan Management—a wholly owned division of St. Joseph's Hospital Health Center—is located on the site and provides home care, durable medical equipment, and respiratory therapy services.

To keep pace with the advent of managed health care in Central New York, A.J.M. Management offers the New York-licensed North Medical Community Health Plan, Inc. (NMCHP), an HMO serving Onondaga and Oswego counties that is managed by the North Medical Health Network. Listed by *Managed HealthCare* magazine as the "fastest-growing MCO [managed care organization] in upstate New York," NMCHP makes medical decisions at a local level for its subscribers. The HMO remains focused on preventive care and wellness. Because it puts people first, the HMO has been recognized by Citizen Action of New York for its outstanding performances in providing information to current and prospective customers. Additionally, for physicians through-

out the Northeast, Merola recently established PhyLinc Practice Management to provide economies of scale in purchasing, billing, and contract negotiation.

Finally, A.J.M. Management Services takes pride in moving in new directions in the health care field by developing its sophisticated health care delivery systems. "When patients are ill, they need the finest health care available," says Merola. Health care, now and in the 21st century, requires the integration of numerous health care professionals. Moreover, patients with serious ailments are frequently treated by several physicians with specific areas of expertise. At NMC and NEMC, the cooperative health care delivery model for the future can be found. As Merola states, "Health care is truly a team game—unlike the past when the single country doctor could meet most of your needs. North Medical Center and Northeast Medical Center are prepared to meet the challenges of the 21st century."

CLOCKWISE FROM TOP LEFT: THE MAIN LOBBY AT NORTH MEDICAL CENTER GREETS LOCAL RESIDENTS VISITING NORTH MEDICAL FAMILY PHYSICIANS.

A. JOHN MEROLA, M.D.—FOUNDER OF A.J.M. MANAGEMENT SERVICES, INC.—CONSULTS WITH A PATIENT.

JANUS PARK—A NURSING HOME ALTERNATIVE THAT ALLOWS FOR DIGNIFIED RESIDENTIAL LIVING WITH ITS PRIVATE APARTMENTS AND NURSING SERVICES—IS LOCATED ON THE NMC CAMPUS.

GÖTZ PUPPENFABRIK AND GÖTZ DOLLS INC.

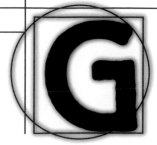

GÖTZ PUPPENFABRIK OF BAVARIA HAS LONG BEEN renowned for creating the finest vinyl dolls in the world. The recipient of several doll and toy industry nominations and awards, including the esteemed Doll of the Year (DOTY®) Award and the Dolls Award of Excellence®, Götz

Puppenfabrik has held steadfast to its mission of creating beautiful, durable, and lifelike play and designer dolls of the highest quality for children and collectors around the world.

Proud to be the exclusive U.S. distributor for Götz Puppenfabrik, Götz Dolls Inc. is America's source for the world's most beautiful dolls. Located in Baldwinsville, Götz Dolls Inc. distributes these extraordinary dolls nationwide while educating the public about their special features.

GÖTZ DOLLS' MODERN DOLL MANUFAC-TURING AND DISTRIBUTION FACILITY IS LOCATED IN BALDWINSVILLE.

What Makes Götz® Play and Designer Dolls So Special?

While there are indeed many brands of dolls on the market for children, there are no substitutes for Götz play dolls, which are so realistic in appearance that they often seem to resemble the family members and friends of many an admirer. In fact, like real people, the Götz play doll characters all have their own distinct appearances. Their wide variety of

faces and expressions range from innocent gazes to mischievous, toothy grins. Their skin, eye, and hair colors are equally diverse and are available in many combinations. They may be fair, tan, or freckled; blonde, red-haired, or brunet. While no two play doll characters are exactly alike, all Götz play dolls do share some common features. For example, they are all constructed from the highest-quality vinyl. Their virtually tangle-free, rooted hair (made of a synthetic fiber ex-

clusive to Götz) looks, feels, and acts much like human hair to withstand hours of styling. Their stylish outfits are made from only the finest fabrics and, like most play dolls themselves, can be machine washed using the gentle cycle.

Discerning collectors forever cherish their Götz designer dolls. The work of a variety of gifted European doll artists, Götz designer dolls are indeed art. These poseable vinyl sculptures may be the elaborate products of the artists' imaginations or the stunning likenesses of real children. In fact, the award-winning Götz artists have developed such precision in their art that many will no longer sculpt from photographs; rather, they travel the world to sculpt the children who inspire them. Once the artists have sculpted their original dolls (usually in porcelain), they work with Götz to create precise vinyl reproductions for worldwide distribution. Götz designer dolls, like the play dolls, are made from the highest-quality vinyl. Their hair, however, is often a wig of human hair or mohair, and their eyes are hand painted or are made from mouth-blown glass. The dolls' clothing and jewelry are typically authentic cultural or regional reproductions. These characteristics of their detailed

THIS GÖTZ FAMILY PHOTO FEATURES (CLOCKWISE FROM TOP RIGHT) COMPANY FOUNDERS FRANZ AND MARIANNE GÖTZ WITH DAUGHTER ANKE GÖTZ-BEYER AND HER HUSBAND, UWE BEYER.

design and workmanship make the designer dolls most suitable for collecting and display.

The Götz Doll Makers

Götz Puppenfabrik (Götz "doll makers"), a privately owned German company, was founded May 1, 1950, by Franz Götz and his then fiancée, now wife, Marianne. While Marianne designed all of the faces, hairstyles, clothing, and accessories for the dolls (which were originally papier-mâché), Franz handled production and sales. The village of Rödental—located in the German state of Bavaria, a classic toy making region—was home to Götz Puppenfabrik.

In the early Götz years, parts for the papier-mâché dolls had to be purchased from the more established doll makers in the area and assembled to produce the Götz doll line. Then, in 1957, Götz Puppenfabrik became one of the first German doll makers to purchase a vinyl rotocasting oven. This technology enabled Götz to produce virtually all its own components for an innovative line of completely lifelike vinyl dolls. In

1976, the company moved to a new facility in Rödental, leading to more efficient and higher-quality production, while maintaining the hand-crafted character of the dolls.

Götz Puppenfabrik undertook a major step toward establishing its international market position in 1985 by opening an American office and distribution center in Syracuse. As an indication of the success of its American operations, the Götz Dolls Inc. (USA) operations were moved in 1987 to a new facility in Baldwinsville that has subsequently evolved into a large, modern, and efficient distribution, manufacturing, and retail facility.

The Next Generation

As a child, Anke Götz (the daughter of Franz and Marianne) grew up with and among her parents' dolls, and provided her input and ideas along the way. In 1989, Anke officially joined the family business, innovating and broadening the Götz product line by introducing the designer doll collection alongside the more traditional play doll collection. Today, the Götz de-

signer doll collection is widely acclaimed by collectors around the world.

In 1993, Anke's husband, Uwe Beyer, joined Götz in a key management capacity. With the team of Anke Götz-Beyer and Uwe Beyer representing the second generation of family doll makers, and with the combined creativity and loyalty of employees and the support of doll customers around the world, the international Götz companies look forward to a bright and successful future in celebration of exquisite doll making.

PAMELA, A GÖTZ PLAY DOLL, HAS A BEAUTIFUL, CURIOUS EXPRESSION AND EYEGLASSES—JUST LIKE A REAL LITTLE GIRL (TOP LEFT).

TWELVE-YEAR-OLD JANINA LINDNER POSES WITH DOLLS AWARD OF EXCELLENCE® RECIPIENT JANINA II. JANINA'S MOTHER, GÖTZ DOLL ARTIST ELISABETH LINDNER, SCULPTED THIS GÖTZ DESIGNER DOLL IN HER DAUGHTER'S LIKENESS (TOP RIGHT).

DOTY® AWARD-WINNING GÖTZ DOLL ARTIST PHILIP HEATH POSES WITH AARON TYSON, HIS INSPIRATION FOR THE AARON I DOLL (BOTTOM LEFT AND RIGHT).

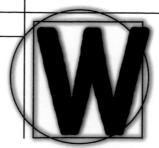

WITH HIS NOTEBOOK, A BRIDGE TABLE, AND A FEW chairs, Norman Poltenson opened his Syracuse office in 1986 and began to recruit staff to create a newspaper with information that would make businesses in Central New York more successful. Today, Poltenson is publisher and editor of *The Business Journal*, an editorially driven source of information that reaches thousands of businesses—from one-person enterprises to large corporations—through its biweekly printed publication, television commentaries, other publications, events, and seminars.

Poltenson originally tried to merge two competing Syracuse-based business publications in 1985. However, a deal was never consummated. Instead, Poltenson established his own newspaper, whose first issue was launched successfully in 1986. Poltenson's newspaper, then called *The Central New York Business Journal*, began as a monthly publication. As circulation grew, Poltenson increased the paper's publication schedule to twice a month, then biweekly. He shortened the name to *The CNY Business Journal*, and eventually to *The Business Journal* to reflect his company's growing reputation as the most comprehensive source of business information in the 16-county area.

Providing Valuable Information to Businesses

The Journal's 14 employees are divided into six departments: editorial, advertising, circulation, business, seminars, and events. According to Poltenson, his employees have but one responsibility: to do their jobs professionally. "All departments work together as a team to get the job done," he says.

To keep abreast of appropriate topics, the editorial staff meets regularly with editorial boards composed of area business executives, academics, government officials, and consultants. The groups evaluate the quality of previous articles and suggest topics to be covered in future issues. Periodically, the staff also conducts and commissions readership surveys, evaluating the results and making recommendations.

The Business Journal regularly includes additional sections devoted to health care, manufacturing, small business, telecommunications, international business, energy, and other topics of interest. The publication also reports regularly on new developments in banking/finance, education and training, construction, insurance, and other areas of interest to business owners and managers.

Each edition contains at least one list of companies within a category, such as banks, credit unions, hotels, engineering firms, colleges, Internet providers, or benefits specialists. Each list contains complete information for each company, such as address, phone, fax numbers, and E-mail contacts; number of employees; assets; principals; and the year founded in Central New York. At year's end, the 40 to 50 lists are compiled into a separate publication, *The Book of Lists*, which is available at no charge to subscribers of *The Business Journal* and to individuals who wish to purchase it.

Poltenson's newest publication, *The Healthcare Provider*, offers an editorial section and a 600-entry directory of health care providers in Central New York. As the only comprehensive source of health care facilities information in the area, *The Healthcare Provider* offers valuable information to physicians, facility administrators, patients, insurance companies, and vendors.

Total Media Coverage

In addition to its printed publication, *The Business Journal* uses radio, television, and the World Wide Web to deliver information. To reach specialized audiences, the company organizes and sponsors seminars, conferences, and forums that feature distinguished speakers from Central New York

THE BUSINESS JOURNAL'S STAFF MEETINGS KEEP THE VARIOUS DEPARTMENTS WORKING TOGETHER AS A TEAM.

and other areas of the nation. *The Business Journal* also sponsors major events like industry trade fairs to offer members of the business community another venue in which to exchange information and to sell their products and services.

Since 1990, the company has sponsored more than 40 seminars on the environment, strategic planning, estate planning, family business, mergers and acquisitions, technology, health care, human resources management, deferred compensation, and investments.

The Business Journal also hosts editorial roundtables—informal gatherings in which the editorial staff explores a specific topic with a group of local experts. Participants, representing diverse views, share their positions, which are captured on tape and transcribed into a lively discussion that is edited and printed in the newspaper.

The Business Journal has enjoyed steady growth, even through the recent national recession. "The need for business information never stops," says Poltenson. "We grew 15 percent last year and expect a 37 percent increase in 1998." Although *The Business Journal* has lots of competition for readership, Poltenson stays with

the paper's core mission: To provide area businesses with useful readable information. Independent surveys clearly show that *The Business Journal* is the leading source of business information in Central New York.

As for the future, Poltenson will continue to focus on business information that will help *The Business Journal*'s readers succeed in their businesses. In addition to planning several new seminars and major events in 1998, *The Business*

ness Journal will introduce a new publication directed to executives of regional midmarket corporations with annual sales of $5 million to $200 million.

In spite of the constant pressure of meeting deadlines, Poltenson maintains his perspective by taking his work in stride. "It's fun," he says. "I enjoy the relationships with a wonderful staff and our clients. It is an exciting business, and I hope it continues like that."

PRODUCTION MANAGER LAWRENCE SECOR VIEWS THE NEWLY DESIGNED COVER OF THE *1998 BOOK OF LISTS*.

NORMAN POLTENSON, EDITOR AND PUBLISHER OF *THE BUSINESS JOURNAL*, DISCUSSES SALES FIGURES WITH MARY EISERT, AN ACCOUNT EXECUTIVE.

RESIDENCE INN BY MARRIOTT

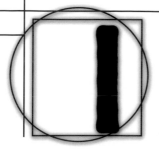

N 1974, TWO MEN NAMED JACK P. DEBOER AND G. Ronald Tyler came up with a concept to build an all-suite, extended-stay hotel—an idea that would come to fruition in Wichita, Kansas, one year later, when the first Residence Inn was constructed. During the next six years, the two

men added six more such inns nationwide, as Residence Inn caught on and became increasingly known for quality service and accommodations.

In 1981, DeBoer and Tyler sold their company to the Brock Hotel Corporation, which set up a franchising system and sold the company back to DeBoer and Tyler in 1985. Then, in 1987, they again sold the chain, this time to Marriott Corporation. And in 1992, when Marriott Corporation split into Marriott International and Host Marriott, Residence Inn and all other lodging brands became divisions of Marriott International. Today, Residence Inn by Marriott is known industrywide as the leader in extended-stay lodging.

In 1995—after having expanded widely throughout the nation with 188 hotels in 42 states—Residence Inn began to look outside the United States, opening the Real del Mar Residence Inn by Marriott in Tijuana, Mexico. The following year, the company expanded to Canada, opening hotels in Montreal, Quebec, and Whistler, British Columbia. Despite its now global outlook, however, Residence Inn has continued to build locations domestically. Today, there are more than 260 locations in 43 states.

A Home Away from Home

Designed primarily for travelers who need lodging for more than just a few nights, Residence Inn by Marriott creates a home away from home for its guests. To that end, the hotel includes an inviting environment with an out-

door barbecue, weekly social hours, an outdoor pool with heated spa, and sport court for outdoor activities. The studio and two-bedroom suites have 50 percent more space than traditional hotel rooms.

The guest-room suites have all the conveniences of home, including a comfortable living room and work space with a desk. In addition, each suite has a completely furnished kitchen with a full-size dishwasher, stove, refrigerator, and microwave oven; counter space; garbage disposal; coffeemaker; toaster; and serving dishes and utensils for four people. Other features include cable and On-Command video television, and telephones with data ports. Some suites even have a wood-burning fireplace. Each two-bedroom suite has the same amenities as the stu-

RESIDENCE INN BY MARRIOTT, WHICH RESEMBLES A RESIDENTIAL SETTING, CONSISTS OF 16 SEPARATE BUILDINGS, HOUSING 78 STUDIO AND 24 TWO-BEDROOM SUITES.

dio suites, with the added amenity of two separate bedrooms. In addition, the two-bedroom suite has three color televisions, two full bathrooms, and three telephones.

Residence Inn also offers many conveniences that are not usually found at home, but that are vital to business travelers, such as a fax, dry cleaning, and safety deposit box services. In addition, there are a number of complimentary services, including daily housekeeping, newspapers, and continental breakfast; a weekly barbecue; voice mail; an exercise room; evening hospitality hours Monday through Thursday; free grocery shopping and restaurant delivery service; and a sport court for volleyball, paddle tennis, and basketball. Laundry facilities are also available. Residence Inn also participates in the Marriott Rewards program—the world's largest frequent guest program.

Residence Inn in Syracuse

When Residence Inn came to Syracuse in 1991, it was the first hotel of its kind in Central New York. Since then, Residence Inns have sprung up in Albany, Binghamton, Rochester, Buffalo, and White Plains.

The hotel, which resembles a residential setting, consists of 16 separate buildings, housing 78 studio and 24 two-bedroom suites. For meetings or seminars, it offers a 560-square-foot, 35-person-capacity room complete with audiovisual equipment. Already unrivaled among Marriott brand hotels in guest satisfaction—thanks to the consistent quality of the accommodations, amenities, and hospitable treatment of guests—the Syracuse hotel recently completed a renovation to update suite and public space decor and amenities.

A distinctive feature of the Syracuse Residence Inn is its friendly, informal atmosphere produced by 35 highly motivated employees. As testimony to their commitment, the hotel has received two silver and three gold awards for achieving budgeted sales, exceeding Marriott standards for quality service and employee satisfaction. When not attending to the needs of guests, the Residence Inn and its staff support the Salvation Army, United Way, and Children's Miracle Network.

Marked by comfortable accommodations, top-notch service, and strong commitment to the community, the Syracuse Residence Inn by Marriott provides a warm welcome to guests on business assignment or who are relocating to the area.

A.G. EDWARDS & SONS, INC.

WITH NEARLY 2 MILLION INVESTMENT CLIENTS, A.G. Edwards & Sons, Inc. has earned a reputation for excellence in the financial industry. The St. Louis-based corporation offers expertise in securities and commodities brokerage, investment banking, asset management, and retirement plans.

The Syracuse office of A.G. Edwards & Sons, Inc. was opened in 1993 by four investment brokers to serve the needs of individual investors. The local firm's initial, six-person staff has grown to include nearly 50 people today.

Serving Clients, Serving the Company

Relying on word-of-mouth advertising, A.G. Edwards brokers across the nation put the interests of their clients first, and the Syracuse professionals, or brokers, are no exception to this rule. "Whatever is good for the client is good for us," says Bill Branson, vice president of the Syracuse branch.

According to Branson, the corporation as a whole maintains its customer-focused perspective by being based far from Wall Street. With the firm's long-standing refusal to pressure brokers to recommend a particular stock, bond, or mutual fund, brokers are free to tailor investments to the needs

of each client. This approach, combined with the company's conservative approach to investing, constitutes the A.G. Edwards formula for success.

A Family Business

A.G. Edwards has been successively managed by five family members since its inception in 1887. Founder General Albert Gallatin Edwards served the Union during the Civil War, and was later appointed by President Abraham Lincoln to the post of assistant secretary of the Sub-Treasury Bank in St. Louis.

After retiring from this assignment, Edwards opened a brokerage company with his son Benjamin Franklin Edwards. Another son, George Lane Edwards, joined the partnership in 1890, and in 1898,

A.G. EDWARDS & SONS, INC. WAS FOUNDED BY GENERAL ALBERT GALLATIN EDWARDS, WHO SERVED THE UNION DURING THE CIVIL WAR.

PICTURED HERE IS A PORTION OF THE 1.4 MILLION-SQUARE-FOOT HOME OFFICE FACILITY FOR A.G. EDWARDS & SONS, INC. IN ST. LOUIS.

HIGHLY SELECTIVE IN ITS HIRING,
A.G. EDWARDS' REPUTATION AS
A GREAT PLACE TO WORK SERVES TO
ATTRACT QUALITY PEOPLE. BROKERS
ARE TREATED AS TEAM PLAYERS, AND
OPEN COMMUNICATION WITH EMPLOYEES
IS ENCOURAGED. PICTURED HERE IS A
PORTION OF THE FIXED-INCOME TRADING
AREA IN ST. LOUIS.

they bought their first seat on the New York Stock Exchange.

George Edwards took over the reins at the company in 1891, and became the first president of the St. Louis Stock Exchange. This legacy of leadership continued with another brother, Albert Ninian Edwards, who took command of the business in 1919.

With the record sale of Liberty bonds during World War II, a new investor base had emerged. The company pursued the individual investor, carving a niche that would later expand to include smaller communities throughout the Midwest. Today, A.G. Edwards has nearly 600 branch offices nationwide.

Measures of Success

The century-old firm is regularly and generously praised by others in the financial industry. A 1996 survey by the National Council of Individual Investors ranked A.G. Edwards number one among the nation's brokerage firms, based on its commissions and fees, investment performance, breadth of services, and disciplinary history. And, although Edwards' conservative approach to the brokerage business might be considered boring by some, it's a label the midwestern giant views as a compliment. If boring means stable,

trustworthy, and a steady producer, then Edwards has rightfully earned the designation.

The firm believes strongly in enjoying its business, and has incorporated these thoughts into its operating philosophy: "To enjoy what we are doing, we must like those with whom we work. In order to do this, we must respect each other and work together in mutual trust. We should try to do our jobs better each week and to have fun doing them."

This weaving of ambition, trust, and optimism characterizes the corporate culture at A.G. Edwards. The firm has resisted the current trend of luring prospective employees with large signing bonuses like

free agents in the sports world, believing that the practice does little to foster the kind of loyalty and long-term relationships that A.G. Edwards enjoys with its people.

Highly selective in its hiring, A.G. Edwards' reputation as a great place to work serves to attract plenty of quality people. Brokers are treated as team players, and open communication with employees is encouraged. In 1998, A.G. Edwards was featured in *Fortune* magazine's listing of the 100 best companies to work for in America. Monthly sessions with current Chairman and CEO Ben Edwards via the firm's internal voice communications network are a ritual throughout all the firm's branches.

Over the years, A.G. Edwards has witnessed the commercial and industrial development of the United States, the birth of the Federal Reserve System, the Great Depression, World Wars I and II, and the globalization of financial markets. Yet, through all of its 111-year history, A.G. Edwards & Sons has maintained its uniquely midwestern character. And by following in its parent company's footsteps, A.G. Edwards' Syracuse branch looks forward to continued growth in the future.

BEN EDWARDS SERVES AS CHAIRMAN
AND CEO OF A.G. EDWARDS.

NITED HEALTHCARE IS ONE OF THE NATION'S largest health and well-being companies, serving individuals and families in all 50 states, the District of Columbia, and Puerto Rico. In fact, 45 of the top 100 ranked Fortune 500 companies offer United HealthCare

to their employees. United Health-Care recognizes that each customer is different—ranging from large corporations to small companies and individuals, newborns and retirees, and urban and rural residents. Locally, according to Marc Rothbart, vice president of sales and marketing, United HealthCare of Upstate New York currently offers health care options to more than 500 employers.

United HealthCare provides health care services to members on an individual basis, through employers, and through various government programs, such as Medicare and Medicaid. In addition to its core health care services, United HealthCare offers mental health care and substance abuse services, workers' compensation and disability management, pharmacy management, employee wellness programs, third-party administrative services, and health information management.

FOR MORE THAN 20 YEARS, UNITED HEALTHCARE HAS UNDERSTOOD WHAT IS IMPORTANT IN HEALTH CARE. THE COMPANY PROVIDES HEALTH CARE SER-VICES TO MEMBERS ON AN INDIVIDUAL BASIS, THROUGH EMPLOYERS, AND THROUGH VARIOUS GOVERNMENT PROGRAMS.

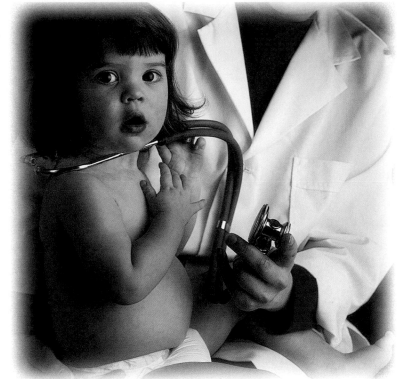

According to Dave Barker, president and CEO of United HealthCare of Upstate New York, the company has grown nationally through the acquisition of other health care companies. In 1995, United HealthCare purchased MetraHealth, the combined health care operations of Travelers Group and Metropolitan Life Insurance Company.

Innovative Approaches to Health Care

For more than 20 years, United HealthCare has understood what is important in health care. United HealthCare is known for innovation, working to achieve the delicate balance of access, quality, cost management, and accountability for its customers. United HealthCare has developed many approaches that are now industry standards.

United HealthCare pioneered the open access plan more than 20 years ago—when members began to demand no-hassle access

to specialists without referrals from a primary physician—with very little effect on costs. Today, the company offers United Health-Care Choice Plus, an open access plan, in 28 states representing more than 70 markets, and growing. Locally, United HealthCare of Upstate New York initiated the open access plan in June 1998.

The patient-physician relationship is the foundation of health care, and United HealthCare is working to make that relationship better. Health education initiatives help members become more informed and confident health care consumers. United HealthCare provides participating physicians with objective information about their own practice patterns and the best medical practices. Armed with better information, patients and physicians are able to reach the right treatment decisions together.

United HealthCare is committed to broad panels of high-quality

providers. Locally, John Evancho, vice president of operations, states that United HealthCare of Upstate New York's network includes almost 90 percent of physicians and all area hospitals. United HealthCare holds high standards for all providers on its panels. The network has embraced a set of consistent national values that are implemented locally to achieve the best health care solutions in the market. United HealthCare recognizes that most health care services are delivered locally and that health care resources vary from location to location. United HealthCare also knows that individual needs vary across geographies and throughout all stages of life.

Health and Well-Being

According to Frederick Goldberg, M.D., local medical director, "United HealthCare's fundamental belief is that we must increase quality in order to reduce costs." In order to achieve this, United HealthCare of Upstate New York has implemented many local initiatives aimed at both physician and member education. Several examples include immunization, mammogram and cervical cancer reminders, and a specific focus on the health and well-being of members with asthma and cardiac conditions. The asthma and cardiac disease management programs boast one-to-one member assessment by a health care professional, and educational interaction in the home to reduce secondary events and to maximize productive lifestyles.

United HealthCare of Upstate New York is also launching an innovative program for physicians in Central New York that provides them with clinically important information about their current practice patterns in comparison with nationally accepted best practices in medicine. For the first time ever, physicians will be able to review reports that focus on medical conditions for which accredited medical organizations have established a broad treatment consensus and that are supported in literature.

Goldberg says, "Some companies make decisions from other states. We have locally qualified health care professionals working with physicians to assure appropriate care for our members." Goldberg has also formed the first ethics committee at a health plan in Central New York. This committee is comprised of United HealthCare employees and community representatives who provide guidance on ethical issues concerning the administration of health care delivery.

Community Involvement

United HealthCare of Upstate New York is active in the local chamber of commerce and supports a significant number of charities in Central New York, including the American Heart Association, Leukemia Society, Make-a-Wish Foundation, Vera House, Think First, and Success by 6.

United HealthCare of Upstate New York has taken a strong interest in events focused on families and children. United HealthCare has sponsored the local Kids Fair, which focuses on children's fun and well-being; 2 Smart 2 Smoke, which emphasizes smoking prevention for grade school children; and the Festival of Races 3K Fun and Fitness Run, which promotes children's fitness.

Additionally, the focus on families and children was affirmed by New York State's selection of United HealthCare to offer Child Health Plus, a state-funded plan that offers free or low-cost health insurance to children under age 19. Since beginning Child Health Plus in November 1997, United HealthCare has been a leader in reaching families and assisting them to obtain affordable health insurance.

Outstanding Reputation

Jay Fischer, chief financial officer for United HealthCare of Upstate New York, notes that the company's success, financial strength, and innovative approach to business have earned United HealthCare prestigious honors. *Fortune* magazine's annual sur-

vey ranked United HealthCare as one of the nation's most admired health care companies for four years running, 1994 through 1997. The company also maintains a Web site at www.uhc.com.

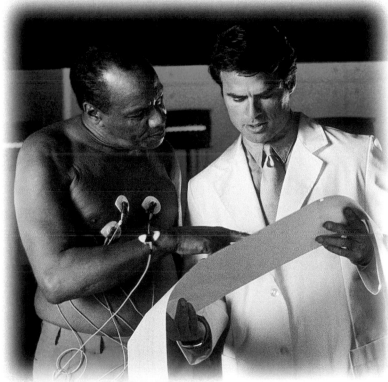

United HealthCare holds high standards for all providers on its panels. The network has embraced a set of consistent national values that are implemented locally to achieve the best health care solutions in the market.

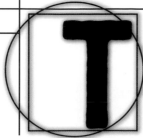

TIME WARNER CABLE IS BRINGING ITS CENTRAL NEW York customers a new future of television and telecommunications services. The Syracuse Division of Time Warner Cable was created in 1995 as the result of a partnership formed between Time Warner Entertainment

and Advance/Newhouse. Several additional systems have since joined the division, which now provides service to more than 325,000 customers in 15 cable systems. The company serves a territory reaching north to the Canada-Vermont border and south to Ithaca, and maintains more than 6,500 miles of a technologically advanced hybrid fiber-coaxial distribution network. After a five-year, $50 million investment, Time Warner Cable's customers enjoy the benefits of a fiber-rich architecture delivering greater reliability, improved reception, and, soon, digital programming services.

Time Warner Cable launched Road Runner—its high-speed on-line service—in its Syracuse, Oswego, and Oneida systems in 1998, with plans to deploy this exciting new service in other systems as engineering upgrades are completed. Road Runner provides on-line access at speeds up to 100 times faster than traditional telephone dial-ups.

"It's much more than a high-speed link to the Internet," says Mary L. Cotter, president of the Syracuse Division. "We deliver an exclusive, comprehensive service

TIME WARNER CABLE SERVES A TERRITORY REACHING NORTH TO THE CANADA-VERMONT BORDER AND SOUTH TO ITHACA, AND MAINTAINS MORE THAN 6,500 MILES OF A TECHNOLOGICALLY ADVANCED HYBRID FIBER-COAXIAL DISTRIBUTION NETWORK (TOP).

EMPLOYEES OF TIME WARNER CABLE ARE ELIGIBLE FOR VOLUNTEER PROJECT GRANTS OF UP TO $500 TO SUPPORT THEIR VOLUNTEER COMMITMENTS AT COMMUNITY AGENCIES AND ASSOCIATIONS (BOTTOM).

◄ KLINEBERG PHOTOGRAPHY

that is a treasure trove of local, national, and global information, with content provided by the best local partners we can find, backed by the rich news, information, and entertainment resources of Time Warner, Inc. and other best-of-brand on-line providers."

With its state-of-the-art production facilities, Time Warner Cable offers local cable advertising to a growing business and customer base. Digital insertion allows businesses and retailers to target their customers demographically on more than 20 different cable networks. The company's commitment to local programming has garnered more than 25 local CableACE (Association for Cable Excellence) awards.

A Commitment to Community

Time Warner Cable has repeatedly demonstrated its commitment to its communities through programs like Cable in the Classroom, which provides free cable service to more than 400 schools; it also supports organizations from the Boy Scouts of America to Hospice of Central New York, and from arts groups to hospitals.

The company donates production and airing of public service announcements for numerous nonprofit organizations, and employees are eligible for Volunteer Project Grants of up to $500 to support their volunteer commitments at community agencies and associations.

Service Comes First

First and foremost, we're a customer-service company," says Cotter. "Our customers are very important to us, and we're always looking for ways to enhance our services to and for them." Time Warner Cable offers customers free, same-day service calls; an on-time guarantee; stringent telephone and technical standards; and extensive training for its 600 employees to ensure that their services remain state of the art.

Time Warner Cable's future will bring continued community support and an exciting array of new products and services for its customers. Says Cotter, "Our customers can be assured that as technology makes new services available, we'll make sure they will be among the first to enjoy them."

**F**OLLOWING ITS APRIL 1, 1998, MERGER WITH OnBanCorp, M&T Bank became the leading bank in Central New York, as well as the largest independent bank headquartered in upstate New York. ■ M&T Bank was originally founded in 1856 in Buffalo, where it

is still headquartered. In the past decade, M&T's entrepreneurial philosophy and strong customer focus have made it possible for it to pursue a course of well-managed growth, allowing the bank to strengthen its base and serve an expanding customer market through steadily increasing market share.

At the time of the merger with OnBanCorp, M&T's parent company, M&T Bank Corporation, became the country's 37th-largest publicly traded bank holding company with assets of approximately $20 billion. M&T now operates more than 250 branches in New York State and northeastern Pennsylvania, including more than 50 branches in Central New York.

M&T's entry into the Syracuse market brings Central New York consumers the stability of one of the nation's leading regional banks, as well as the experience of a local institution singularly positioned to understand the particular needs of its upstate customers. Through local decision making, consistent lending practices, and a complete range of products and services offered through knowledgeable financial services professionals, M&T develops strong and lasting customer relationships by meeting the needs of individual consumers and businesses.

The approximately 6,000 employees of M&T Bank consistently demonstrate their dedication to providing superior customer services through teamwork and commitment, and extend that professional dedication into their communities through their leadership efforts on behalf of hundreds of civic and nonprofit causes.

M&T has proven its commitment to business with repeated designations as the leading Small Business Administration lender

across New York State. As the state's foremost State of New York Mortgage Agency lender, M&T Bank's subsidiary, M&T Mortgage Corporation, has made it possible for thousands of New York State residents to realize the dream of home ownership.

In all of its markets across New York State, M&T Bank has contributed significantly to wide-ranging programs in the form of grants, community service leadership, and lending to low-to-moderate-income households. As a result, the company has consistently received the highest possible Community Reinvestment Act rating through the past decade by the New York State Banking Department and the Federal Reserve Bank of New York—ratings from the latter of which is an achievement attained by fewer than 10 percent of banks nationwide.

M&T Bank looks forward to providing Syracuse the same quality service, financial strength, and commitment to community that have become its hallmarks. With M&T's impressive track record, the promise is as good as kept.

THE LOBBY OF **M&T BANK**'S REGIONAL HEADQUARTERS IN SYRACUSE FEATURES A CELESTIAL MAP AND MURALS DEPICTING LOCAL HISTORY.

M&T BANK IN SYRACUSE BRINGS CENTRAL NEW YORK CONSUMERS THE STABILITY OF ONE OF THE NATION'S LEADING REGIONAL BANKS, AS WELL AS THE EXPERIENCE OF A LOCAL INSTITUTION.

BELL ATLANTIC

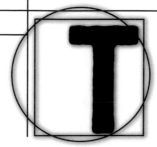

THE NEW BELL ATLANTIC—FORMED THROUGH THE merger of Bell Atlantic and NYNEX—is at the forefront of the new communications, information, and entertainment industry. With 40.5 million telephone access lines and 6 million wireless customers worldwide, Bell Atlantic

companies are premier providers of advanced wireline voice and data services, market leaders in wireless services, and the world's largest publishers of directory information. Bell Atlantic companies are also among the world's largest investors in high-growth global communications markets, with operations and investments in 21 countries.

Additionally, Bell Atlantic provides Internet service and leads the market in fiber optics and specialized communications services, such as videoconferencing. "Our telecommunications technology allows companies to thrive right here in a relatively low-cost area with a highly skilled and educated workforce," says Director of Community Affairs Thomas Owens.

Although the name of Bell Atlantic may be new to the area, the merger represents the evolution of New York Telephone and NYNEX, and exemplifies more than 100 years of service in Central New York.

As New York State's largest private employer, Bell Atlantic employs 2,700 in Central New York, with 1,100 of those in Onondaga County. The highly trained and motivated workforce is committed to its number one priority, customer service, which is essential when the company handles millions of contacts each year. Even though Bell Atlantic is a large, global company, the local connection has never been more important—providing world-class service to the local market at competitive prices.The company considers its people to be a key competitive advantage, and maintains their expertise through continual training and educational opportunities.

Bell Atlantic utilizes the teamwork approach, incorporating employee volunteers, community partnerships, and corporate philanthropy. Maintaining a community presence is a priority evidenced by the various activities and programs sponsored by the company. The Bell Atlantic Foundation supports a variety of projects domestically and internationally, with an emphasis on new technology applications in education, health and human services, the arts and humanities, and civic development in the communities served by Bell Atlantic.

With fierce and growing competition in the telecommunications marketplace, Bell Atlantic is also looking for new opportunities for growth in the future, including entrance into long distance and continued development in the advanced telecommunications network. "It's a challenge operating in this new environment," says Owens, "and we're embracing it."

THE BELL ATLANTIC FOUNDATION SUPPORTS A VARIETY OF PROJECTS DOMESTICALLY AND INTERNATIONALLY, WITH AN EMPHASIS ON NEW TECHNOLOGY APPLICATIONS IN EDUCATION, HEALTH AND HUMAN SERVICES, THE ARTS AND HUMANITIES, AND CIVIC DEVELOPMENT IN THE COMMUNITIES SERVED BY BELL ATLANTIC.

◄ MIKE GREENLAR

David Broda, born and raised in Niagara Falls, New York, moved to the Syracuse area in 1970 and currently works for Syracuse University. The recipient of bachelor of arts degrees in photography and psychology, Broda specializes in photo conservation and facsimile reproduction. He has an enduring appreciation for honky-tonks, carnivals, and roadside attractions as permanent manifestations of the American way of life.

Michael Davis, a former rock-and-roll musician, is a self-taught photographer who won the New York Press Association's Photographer of the Year award in 1996. Employed by the *Syracuse New Times*, he specializes in photojournalism and street photography. He also plays jazz and blues on a Hammond B-3 organ.

C.M. Disalvo, who hails from Norwich, Connecticut, received a bachelor of science degree from the S.I. Newhouse School of Public Communications at Syracuse University. Self-employed at C.M. Disalvo Photography, she photographs families, children, and special events, as well as taking pictures for Auburn Memorial Hospital. She presently resides in Skaneateles, and has two daughters, Raven and Phoebe.

John Dowling, a self-employed photographer, received a bachelor of arts degree from Colby College and a master of science degree in photojournalism from the S.I. Newhouse School of Public Communications. Dowling specializes in photojournalism, corporate communications, advertising, sports, travel, fashion, and theater photography, and his clients include Black Star Publishing, the Coca-Cola Company, Subaru, Lockheed Martin, Bristol-Myers, and Syracuse University. Originally from Pelham, New York, he is a collector of 19th-century images, especially those created by George N. Barnard.

Mike Greenlar graduated from the Rochester Institute of Technology (RIT) with a bachelor of arts degree in journalism. Currently self-employed, Greenlar has seven years of newspaper experience, and his images have been published in *Time, Newsweek, Life, Forbes, Fortune*, and *Business Week*. He specializes in editorial photography of people and technology, as well as producing contemporary images of Native Americans. In addition to giving frequent lectures at RIT, he has taught photojournalism at the S.I. Newhouse School of Public Communications.

John G. Hodgson moved to the Syracuse area in 1975. He received a bachelor of science degree from RIT and a master of science degree from Syracuse University. Employed by SUNY Health Science Center, Hodgson specializes in medical photography.

Ray Hrynyk was born to Ukrainian parents in a refugee camp in postwar Germany. After moving to the Syracuse area in 1949, he graduated with honors from Syracuse University with a bachelor of arts degree in English. Using the pseudonym Spider Rybaak, Hrynyk has been a freelance outdoor writer/photographer, with an emphasis on Central New York, for more than 12 years. His features and photographs have appeared in more than 20 periodicals ranging from *American Legion Magazine* to *Soundings*. Covering subjects ranging from clothing and equipment reviews to vacation destinations, health products, and legislation, Hrynyk has received numerous awards from various newspapers and magazines. His images have been displayed at the New York State Fair for five of the past 10 years and in several exhibits at the Everson Museum of Art. A Vietnam veteran who served in Military Intelligence, Hrynyk remains active in veterans affairs.

David Lassman, a native of Syracuse, graduated from the S.I. Newhouse School of Public Communications with a bachelor of science degree in photography. He is currently employed by the Syracuse Newspapers.

Bud Lee studied at the Columbia University School of Fine Arts in New York and the National Academy of Fine Arts before moving to the Orlando area more than 20 years ago. A self-employed photojournalist, he was named *Life* magazine's News Photographer of the Year in 1967 and received the Military Photographer of the Year award in 1966. He also founded both the Florida Photographers Workshop and the Iowa Photographers Workshop. Lee's work can be seen in *Esquire, Life, Travel & Leisure, Rolling Stone*, the *Washington Post*, and the *New York Times*, as well as in Towery Publishing's *Treasures on Tampa Bay: Tampa, St. Petersburg, Clearwater; Orlando: The City Beautiful*; and *Jacksonville: Reflections of Excellence*.

Bob Mahoney, a self-employed location photographer, works primarily for editorial, corporate, and advertising clients. Originally from Schenectady, he moved to the Syracuse area in 1979 and graduated with a bachelor of science degree in photojournalism from the S.I. Newhouse School of Public Communications. Mahoney's images have been published in *Business Week, Forbes*,

Newsweek, Parade, Time, and *USA Today.* He spent a year documenting the lives of a 2,000-man marine expeditionary unit, traveling to Somalia, Europe, and North Carolina. The work was published, along with a narrative by David Wood, in the critically acclaimed book *A Sense of Values: American Marines in an Uncertain World.*

Michael J. Okoniewski, a self-employed photographer, is a native of Syracuse. Specializing in news, sports, and digital photography, he has had images published in the *New York Times, USA Today, Time, Newsweek,* and *Sports Illustrated.* His past assignments have included two U.S. tours with Pope John Paul II, the 1988 Seoul Olympiad, three bowl games with the Syracuse University football team, NCAA regional basketball tournaments, and several presidential campaigns.

Kenneth E. Peek graduated with a bachelor of science degree in professional photography from RIT. Originally from Scotia, New York, he moved to Syracuse in 1988 and works at SUNY Health Science Center. Specializing in architectural, travel, and location photography, Peek received an honorable mention in *Industrial Photography*'s 1994 magazine competition.

Jonathan Postal, born in New York City, lived and worked in London, Sydney, Milan, and New Orleans before settling in Memphis. Formerly the creative director of *Eye* magazine, he has had work featured in *Rolling Stone, Vanity Fair,* and numerous other publications. Today, Postal is a photo editor and staff photographer for Towery Publishing, and his images have appeared in many of Towery's books, including *Memphis: New Visions, New Horizons; Minneapolis-St. Paul: Linked to the Future; New Orleans: Rollin' on the River; Nashville: City of Note; The Image Is Rochester; Toronto Tapestry;* and *The Power of Pittsburgh.*

Steven Roberts has lived in Syracuse nearly all of his life. He works for ABC Photography, where he specializes in commercial, product, and aerial photography. Roberts' clients include Syracuse University, Midlakes Navigation, T.C. Timber, IKON, Solvay Paperboard, Sithe Energy, and Wegmans.

Robert H. Schulz Jr. is a native of Connecticut who moved to Syracuse in 1975. A member of the Syracuse Camera Club, he received a bachelor of science degree from the S.I. Newhouse School of Public Communications and studied at the Maine Photographic Workshops in Rockport. Schulz is an advertising copywriter with Eric Mower and Associates in Syracuse, and has been an avid photographer for 15 years. He takes pictures of everything from architecture to landscapes, but is especially interested in popular culture, candid street photography, strong graphics, and unusual light.

Ron Trinca is a New York native who earned a bachelor of science degree in professorial photography from RIT. The owner of his own studio, he specializes in commercial photography, specifically editorial, public relations, and advertising images. Trinca's clients include Bristol-Myers Squibb, the American Dairy Assocation, and LeMoyne College, and he is the recipient of the International Association of Business Communicator's Award of Merit in photography.

Emmanuel Vaucher, originally from Besançon, France, moved to the Syracuse area in 1994. Employed by Syracuse Language Systems, he specializes in taking pictures of fashion, landscapes, and people. Vaucher also enjoys traveling and working with his wife, Cerenna; he traveled across Europe in 1996 and across the United States in 1997.

Dan Vecchio, a native of Syracuse and a self-employed photographer, attended the Center for Photographic Studies for two years. Specializing in location and studio photography for corporate and industrial clients, Vecchio also enjoys photographing national parks across the United States.

Gerry Young attended Coffeyville College, RIT, and Syracuse University, and is currently employed by Ulysses Photographics. Specializing in all areas of commercial photography, he is the recipient of many awards given by the Professional Photographers Society of New York. Young covered the war in Vietnam for the U.S. Navy after graduating from Syracuse University's Navy Photojournalism program.

Other photographers and organizations that contributed to *Greater Syracuse: Center of an Empire* include Jonathan Adams, Randi Anglin, John Berry, Dick Blume, Stephen Cannerelli, Peter Chen, Harry Diorio, Suzanne Dunn, Mike Gabel, Matt Klicker, Li-Hua Lan, Nicholas Lisi, Sarah T. Morrison, Dennis Nett, the Onondaga Historical Association, Frank Ordonez, Anthony Potter, the *Syracuse Newspapers,* and Tom Watson.